THE EUROPEAN COMMUNITY, EASTERN EUROPE, AND RUSSIA

THE EUROPEAN COMMUNITY, EASTERN EUROPE, AND RUSSIA

Economic and Political Changes

NICHOLAS V. GIANARIS

PRAEGER

Westport, Connecticut
London

Library of Congress Cataloging-in-Publication Data

Gianaris, Nicholas V.
    The European Community, Eastern Europe, and Russia : economic and
political changes / Nicholas V. Gianaris.
        p.   cm.
    Includes bibliographical references and index.
    ISBN 0–275–94708–4 (alk. paper)
    1. European Economic Community countries—Economic conditions.
    2. European Economic Community countries—Politics and government.
    3. Europe, Eastern—Economic conditions—1989– 4. Europe, Eastern—
    Politics and government—1989– 5. Former Soviet republics—
    Economic conditions. 6. Former Soviet republics—Politics and
    government.   I. Title.
    HC241.2.G52   1994
    330.94—dc20   93–40198

British Library Cataloguing in Publication Data is available.

Library of Congress Catalog Card Number: 93–40198
ISBN: 0–275–94708–4

First published in 1994

Praeger Publishers, 88 Post Road West, Westport, CT 06881
An imprint of Greenwood Publishing Group, Inc.

Printed in the United States of America

∞™

The paper used in this book complies with the
Permanent Paper Standard issued by the National
Information Standards Organization (Z39.48–1984).

10 9 8 7 6 5 4 3 2 1

Copyright Acknowledgments

The author and publisher gratefully acknowledge permission to reprint the following
previously published material:

Selections reprinted by permission of Greenwood Publishing Group, Inc., Westport, CT,
from: *The European Community and the United States: Economic Relations* by Nicholas V.
Gianaris. Copyright © 1991 by Nicholas V. Gianaris; and *Contemporary Economic Systems: A
Regional and Country Approach* by Nicholas V. Gianaris. Copyright © 1993 by Nicholas V.
Gianaris.

Contents

Tables and Figures

TABLES

FIGURES

Preface

Europe is undergoing drastic economic and geopolitical changes that present problems of worldwide dimensions. Since the dawn of history, Europe has played a vital role in the formation and development of economic and sociocultural world events. Although centuries have passed and a unified Europe remains largely a dream, the near future can prove that yesterday's dreams may become the realities of tomorrow and all nations of the continent may merge and form a United States of Europe.

The potential effects of the integration of Western Europe on the rapid opening of Eastern Europe and Russia are expected to dramatically change global economic, political, and cultural relations. The removal of technical, monetary, and trade barriers within the European Community (EC) and the liberalization of the economies of the East European countries, including those of the Balkan Peninsula and Russia, create challenges and opportunities from the standpoint of trade, investment, and economic growth. However, as the EC moves toward closer economic and political integration, the question is whether the bloc will eliminate internal barriers only to create a larger barrier around the Community.

The vision of a community of unified and prosperous European democracies, ready to face the growing competition from the United States, Canada, and Mexico because of the North American Free Trade Agreement (NAFTA), and the Asian-Pacific Rim (Japan and other neighboring countries) can be realized through EC enlargement and eventual integration of all European nations.

The new trends toward privatization and democratization of property ownership in the previously centrally planned economies of Europe facilitate the process of EC enlargement. Similar measures of privatization of state enterprises, as well as employee participation and capital-labor comanagement, prevail in almost all EC countries. Such economic organizations help stimulate further EC expansion and integration.

This book weaves together a historical framework with comparative case studies of the region's nation-states. The result is an insightful analysis of how the interplay between politics and economics sets the stage for the dramatic events to come in the 1990s and perhaps the twenty-first century. From that standpoint, it is of great theoretical and practical use to students and scholars with a broad range of interests in the European continent.

The purpose of this book is to examine the structural changes and the main problems regarding economic and political integration, trade, joint ventures, and developmental trends between the EC and East European countries, including Russia. After a brief introduction in Chapter 1, a review of the historical and present trends of the EC countries toward formation and expansion, economic organization, and fiscal and monetary integration is presented in Chapters 2, 3, and 4, respectively. Chapters 5, 6, and 7 deal with Poland, the Czech and Slovak republics, and Hungary; whereas Chapter 8 deals with the rest of the Balkan countries. Finally, Chapters 9 and 10 deal with the relationship of Russia and the other former Soviet European republics (Armenia, Belarus, Georgia, Ukraine, and the Baltic countries) with the EC.

I want to acknowledge my indebtedness to Professors John Adams, S.J., Janis Barry-Figueroa, Ernest Block, Clive Daniel, George Kourvetaris, Laurence Krause, Victoria Litson, Ralph Meyer, Andreas Moschonas, Gus Papoulias, Adamandia Polis, Harry Psomiades, John Roche, Dominick Salvatore, Shapoor Vali, and Paul Vouras, as well as to financial and legal experts Bill Gianaris, Michael Gianaris, Dimitris Lavdas, Christ Poulos, and Christos G. Tzelios for their stimulating comments during the preparation of this book. Hisham Allagany, Patricia Kane, Juan Rodriguez, Telly C. Tzelios, and Julius Zamora provided valuable services in reviewing, typing, copying, and other technical support.

THE EUROPEAN COMMUNITY, EASTERN EUROPE, AND RUSSIA

1

Introduction

ECONOMIC AND GEOPOLITICAL TRENDS

Economic and Political Changes

The potential effects of the integration of Western Europe on the rapid opening of Eastern Europe and the former Union of Soviet Socialist Republics (USSR) are expected to dramatically change mutual trade and investment, as well as global political and cultural relations. The new trend toward privatization and democratization in the previously planned economies of Europe make joint ventures and acquisitions attractive and profitable, particularly in Hungary, the Czech and Slovak republics, Poland, as well as the former Soviet Union.

The removal of technical, monetary, and trade barriers within the European Community and the liberalization of the economies of East European countries and the former Soviet Union would be beneficial not only to Europe but to the world as a whole.

The East bloc countries, which have come out of long and painful central controls only recently, try to catch up economically and politically with the EC. The end of the cold war, the unification of Germany, and the drastic reforms in the former Soviet Union are important elements of peaceful co-existence, under which economic and political cooperation can flourish, not only among European nations but between them and other nations, particularly the United States and Japan. On the other hand, the structural economic reforms and the political openness in the East bloc countries may lead to further cooperation and the integration of the EC and East European countries, including Russia and the Balkan countries. The EC integration programs and the upheavals in Central and Eastern Europe present fertile pastures and attract many European and other companies for new markets, as well as direct and financial investments. National interests, in the context of a rapidly changing European system, are gradually subordinated to common regional systems and eventually to a global economy. The growing interdependence of trading nations requires a shift from isolated and hierarchical decision making to negotiations and common domestic and foreign economic policies.

Comparatively speaking, Poland was the first country to introduce drastic measure "shock therapy" for the transformation of its economy into the market system, followed by the Czech and Slovak republics as well as the former Soviet republics. On the other hand, Hungary began the introduction of reforms (the New Economic Mechanism) since 1968. The other ex-planned economies of Eastern Europe (Romania, Bulgaria, Albania) follow a slow pace of economic liberalization and openness, whereas the previous Yugoslav republics are under the process of economic and political adjustment as a result of severe ethnic and religious conflicts.[1]

Along with the democratization of Russia and other East bloc countries, there should be an establishment of proper institutions regarding property titles and mortgages for credit, as well as patent and copyright laws, to ensure an orderly transfer of ownership. Such efforts can be financed and supported by Western countries and world institutions, while international mutual funds can capitalize on Eastern Europe's dramatic changes and invest in productive ventures. As government subsidies are reduced and prices and unemployment rise, East European people need Western support because it is difficult to implement such drastic changes alone. It is important to remember that, in the long run, such a policy is expected to be beneficial to the Western economies as well.

In any case, the transformation from communism to capitalism remains the Gordian knot of the ex-Communist countries of Europe. Karl Marx and other socialists wrote how to transfer ownership from the private to the public sector, but there is no experience and not enough studies exist regarding the transformation from communism to capitalism.

Adjustment from a totalitarian to a democratic and competitive system is difficult. To a large extent, people do not understand the workings of capitalism and fear the free market system, because of its association with unemployment and inequalities. From that standpoint, economic policies suggested by economists become nightmares for the politicians. Laws introduced by politicians without related customs are worthless, as Roman writers suggested.

The reforms of economic management and political democracy increase expectations for more consumer goods and an improved standard of living. Such expectations are intensified through exposing the population to Western ways of life via tourism and rapidly spread communications. As a result, complaints about shortages of food and other products persist and rationing of meat and other consumer goods continues in a number of ex-planned economies. Long waiting lists for apartments, cars, and telephones as well as shoddy goods add to consumer frustration and despair.

The privatization process, including the transfer of state-owned firms to workers and employees, in East European countries and the former Soviet Union, is reinforcing the system of "people's capitalism." Selling state enterprises to individuals and making workers total or partial owners of the firms in which they work, with special discounts, seem to be effective alternatives to public- or private-sector monopolies. The saying that "in capitalism man exploits man, in communism it is the other way around" may not be relevant to an employee's capitalism.

People's capitalism accentuates widespread ownership of shares in farms and other enterprises mainly by low-income people. It shifts indirect ownership in public-sector firms to direct legal ownership by individuals. By privatizing public enterprises the government tries to maximize the number of shareholders. People's capitalism, which is primarily used for political support of privatization, may not be successful enough if the shares are resold by large segments of shareholders, especially low-income people. That is why the government provides incentives (bonuses) to people who retain their shares for a specified period.

Efforts of European Unity

Europe, which stands at a momentous crossroads, has a history that radically changed its face and that of the world. To understand current events, a review of related historical trends on the Continent is needed. The road to European unity goes far back into history.

From ancient times of the Greco-Roman period on to the Middle Ages, the industrial revolution, and later, efforts for a united Europe were promulgated on many occasions. Writers and rulers in ancient Greece and Rome supported or enforced, from time to time, unions of city-states for parts or the whole of Europe. The Greco-Roman dream of a united Europe, mainly through conquests, has permeated the Continent for centuries. It prevailed during the Roman period (31 B.C. to A.D. 476) and the Byzantine period (326–1453), especially at the time of Justinian's rule (A.D. 554). Similar efforts were made during the years of the Frankish Kingdom of Charlemagne, "King Father of Europe" (A.D. 800); Otto the Great in 962 and later (during the first German Reich); the Austro-Hungarian Hapsburg dynasty (mainly in the sixteenth century); and the period of Austrian Chancellor Metternich (toward the end of the eighteenth and the beginning of the nineteenth centuries). Also, forceful attempts to unify Europe were made during Napoleon Bonaparte's period (1799–1815); the new German Empire or the Second Reich (1871–1918) under Kaiser Wilhelm I and Otto von Bismarck; and recently by the alliance of Benito Mussolini of Italy and Adolf Hitler of

Germany. However, British Prime Minister Winston Churchill pointed out that it is proper to create a United States of Europe, as the Hapsburgs also suggested centuries ago.

From 1815 to 1854 five European powers (Britain, France, Prussia, Austria, and Russia) formed some kind of alliance (Concert) after the Napoleonic wars that reduced conflicts and kept peace for 40 years. Also, they established buffer zones, held regular conferences, and undertook joint actions—including military operations so that costly military buildup would be reduced and domestic economies would be strengthened.

From an economic point of view, the establishment of a German customs union (*Zollverein*, 1834) under Prussian leadership may be considered as the closest attempt of a union similar to the present European Community. It created a free-trade zone throughout much of Germany, removed commerce restrictions, and demonstrated the importance of cooperation and unity on economic and political matters.

For centuries, emperors, kings, feudal lords, theologians, artists, and many common people vainly yearned for unity among the divided and, in many cases, belligerent nations of Europe. Writers and philosophers, such as Victor Hugo and Voltaire and Goethe before him, as well as Edward Kine and Andreas Rigopoulos dreamed about a united Europe. Michelangelo and Rembrandt, with their famous paintings, contemplated a peaceful and prosperous united continent. Handel, Beethoven, Mozart, Wagner, and other composers advocated a harmonious and unified Europe, while Dante Alighieri, centuries before them (1300), supported the creation of a peaceful nation to engulf the whole of Europe.

Probably the lack of success in unifying Europe through so many centuries was due to the reliance of forcible conquests by the European rulers. However, the Renaissance movement, which had begun in fourteenth-century Italy, and had spread all over Europe during the late Middle Ages, incorporated a spirit of innovation and unity, a great reawakening of common interest in the literature, culture, and philosophy of ancient Greece and Rome.

The Christian religion, under its main denominations (Catholic, Orthodox, Protestant, Anglican), played a significant role in stimulating efforts toward European unity. However, in many cases, nationalistic, economic, and political forces proved to be more powerful in leading European nations into conflicts and destructive wars throughout history. And this occurred despite a number of appeals made by patriarchs, popes, and other theologians for unity and for a reawakening of the European religious soul as a root of unity.

Even before the Great Depression, French Foreign Minister Aristide Briand, a leading Eurocrat or "Euroenthusiast," proposed to the then League of Nations the creation of a United States of Europe. His effort to unify Europe by peaceful means was interrupted by World War II, a war that can be characterized as a European civil war, as was World War I as well. After the bombing raids were over and animosity and hatred were buried in the rubble, the centuries-old dream of the peaceful unity of Europe started slowly but surely to come to reality. The hope was to create a multinational democratic community with a free flow of goods, people, and information as well as a mutual free exchange of ideas and cultures.

The variety of European peoples with their different cultures and habits presents problems for a rapid movement of integration. Italians are considered to have a great respect for obscurity, while the French seem to be brittle and afraid of the future, with some degree of xenophobia and civilizing hypocrisy. On the other hand, the British are regarded as being preoccupied with a sense of economic and spiritual decline, while the Germans think about geopolitical and economic expansion.[2] Spain, Greece, and Portugal as less developed members of the European Community, and the East bloc countries that have come out of long and painful dictatorships only recently, try to catch up economically and politically with the rest of the community. In all these countries there is a strong spirit of a united Europe, a "Euromania," pushing for rapid economic and political development.

After World War I and particularly at the beginning of the Great Depression, new totalitarian fascist governments came into power all over Europe. The end of the 1930s depression came finally with World War II, from 1940 to 1945. Thereafter, mostly labor parties came to power in Western Europe. They introduced reforms regarding distribution of income, extension of welfare services by the state, and nationalizations—particularly in railroads, power, coal, and other heavy industries.

ECONOMIC AND DEFENSE COOPERATION

East European nations—mainly Poland, the Czech and Slovak republics, Hungary, Romania, and Bulgaria—were liberated from Nazi Germany by the Red Army in 1945 and came under the political and economic influence of the Soviet Union. From a military point of view, they, together with East Germany and Albania, became members of the Warsaw Pact (formed in 1955), a counterpart of the North Atlantic Treaty Organization (NATO, formed in 1949). Economically, these countries formed (in 1949) the Council for Mutual Economic Assistance (CMEA or Comecon), a similar but less effective organization than the Common Market of Western Europe or the European Community. Both the Warsaw Pact and Comecon were dominated up to 1990 by the Soviet Union. Yugoslavia.was loosely associated with both economic organizations and Albania, after 1961, was associated with neither. As for the other Balkan nations, Greece has been a full member of the European Community since 1981 and Turkey an associated member since 1964. Both the Warsaw Pact and Comecon were dissolved by 1991.

Although trade and investment among the CMEA member nations did not advance as much as that among the EC members, some cooperation on matters of production and long-term economic development were achieved. The low level of cooperation and advancement in foreign trade in Comecon was primarily due to duplication of industrial production. Trade among the members was primarily conducted on a bilateral basis. Each nation planned its own development and included a growing trade with other partners. There was not an integrated planning organ or a common economic policy for multinational allocation of resources or to take advantage of specialization and economies of large-scale production.

Western ideals of freedom, democracy, and laissez-faire economics inspired, to a large extent, the recent revolutionary changes in Eastern Europe and in the former Soviet Union in particular. As the Berlin Wall that confined such ideals collapsed, the ice of the cold war gradually melted and suspicions that prevailed for decades have evaporated. These changes are challenging established defense organizations, such as NATO, which has begun to be remodeled accordingly.

During the post-World War II period, Western and particularly American policies were built on fears of war between NATO and the former Warsaw Pact of the USSR and the question was how to overcome that long legacy of suspicion and mistrust. The support for rapid reforms to shift these precommunist countries into market economies, with privatization and "people's capitalism," by a consortium of the trilateral powers (EC, United States, Japan) would lead to mutual economic and geopolitical gains.

With the profound economic and political reforms toward free markets and pluralistic democratic systems in East European countries and the former USSR, the Warsaw Pact lost much of its importance. On the contrary, NATO, protecting the ideals of freedom and democracy, survived and acquired more importance.

The purpose of NATO in Western Europe, after embracing Germany as a junior partner, was to contain the Soviet Union from regional expansion and Germany from new militaristic adventurism. In other words, the main goal of the U.S.-centered alliance in Europe was to "keep the Americans in, the Russians out, and the Germans down." This is known as the strategy of "double containment." However, the new order created through mutually accepted dependence in the EC mitigated the revival of militarism and weakened security dilemmas in the region. In a democratic and federal Germany, anchored to an integrated European Community, militarism and supranationalism do not have much importance, particularly as a result of a gradual synchronization and solidarity with Eastern Europe and the former USSR. It seems that economic cooperation between Europe, North America, and Japan will be needed to provide socioeconomic stability and growth in that region and on a global scale.

On the other hand, the increasing preoccupation of the United States with Latin America and the Middle East results in fundamental changes in economic and security matters that were established after World War II. France,

Germany, and other EC member nations and eventually all of Europe are considering plans for their own defense strategy. This became more obvious with the removal from Europe of U.S. medium-range missiles, the expected reduction and the eventual removal of U.S. ground forces, as well as the weakening of America's atomic umbrella that protects NATO.

Other East European countries may join NATO in the near future; however, NATO needs drastic changes as well. Emphasis should be placed not so much on defense, as long as the Soviet and Warsaw Pact threat does not exist any more, but on economic, political, and cultural affairs of the member nations. Otherwise, initially NATO was established as a commonwealth of nations that shared the same democratic ideals. After the Korean War, it became a U.S.-led military bloc when West Germany became a member in April 1955.

Perhaps there might be no need for the existence of NATO, as long as there are no more adversaries, unless a new enemy is created to justify such an organization. Such may be the case with China or a united front of Islamic fundamentalists. However, there are fears that after the unification of Germany, an American-German axis may leave the other European nations, particularly Britain and France, out in the cold. In any case, it seems that for some time to come and until the complete emancipation of Europe, American engagement is essential to the stability of Europe. On the other hand, Western countries, mainly the European Community and the United States, can help the East form a constructive transition toward a pan-European security system and a rapid economic growth via investment ventures, managerial experts, and technological dissemination.

To help Eastern Europe and the former USSR look forward, the different nations and nationalities should moderate nationalist tempers and try to improve cooperation among themselves and with the EC, which should be their final destination. However, this requires proper training of the people concerned to shed their nationalist prejudices and accept democratic national equality and federalism. As Europe is entering a new age, cooperation agreements on matters of security such as those of Helsinki (August 1975) and Helsinki II (November 1990) promote détente and reforms in the rapidly changing old order of Europe.

The three centers of economic power—that is, the United States, the EC, and Japan—should combine economic resources to rebuild the new democracies of Eastern Europe. New capital investment, accompanied by modern technology and efficient management, and a reduction of the barriers to trade and investment would help elevate these economies from the vicious circle of low performance and lead them to stability and economic growth. It is in the interest of all countries, particularly those of Europe, to help avoid a collapse of the former Soviet republics, which could devastate the economies of Europe and negatively affect the world economy. It would seem that free market democratic systems, such as those of the United States, Japan, and the EC, offer a path to success for other countries to emulate. On the other hand, the failure of the former Soviet and East European economies proved that communism is the long, hard path from capitalism to capitalism.

From an economic standpoint, Germany and Japan have become the main competitors of the United States. Under the U.S. defense umbrella, both countries, which were the main U.S. rivals during World War II, managed to develop rapidly and challenge the American supremacy in international trade and finance.

THE LIMITS OF THE EC: THE QUESTION OF ENLARGEMENT

The old continent of Europe, which from the dawn of history played a vital role in sociocultural world events, is undergoing drastic economic and geopolitical changes. Although centuries have passed and Europe remains largely divided, the near future may prove that the European countries have realized the importance of their economic and political unification. Victor Hugo once commented that there would be a day when all European countries would merge into a higher society.

The vision of a community of prosperous and unified West European democracies, formed some four decades ago, has largely been realized. In addition to economic integration, an important issue considered by the European Community at present is the growing need for further political cooperation. Such cooperation may speed up and stabilize the long-run unification of Europe and prove that "politics can turn influence into affluence."

National interests, in the context of a rapidly changing European system, are gradually subordinated to a common regional and eventually global system in which narrow national goals must defer to the optimization of common goals.

For the improvement of their economies and their security position, all the countries of Central and Eastern Europe (CEE), as well as Russia and other countries of the Commonwealth of Independent States (CIS), want to join the EC. Trade and cooperation agreements (Europe Agreements) have first been negotiated with the Czech and Slovak republics, Hungary, and Poland. Similar negotiations are currently developing between the EC and Bulgaria and Romania, whereas the former Yugoslav republics (primarily Slovenia and Croatia) are expected to start cooperation agreements in the near future.

Moreover, the South European candidates—that is, Turkey, Cyprus, and Malta—want to be full members of the EC, as the Baltic countries (Lithuania, Estonia, Latvia), Russia, and other CIS countries do as well.

Recently, the EC accepted association status with Eastern and other European countries through European Agreements, which were signed by the

EC and Poland, the former Czechoslovakia, and Hungary in December 1991, and by the EC and Romania and Bulgaria in 1993. As a result, EC tariffs on imports from these countries are reduced from 5 percent in 1992 to zero in 1997, whereas their tariffs on imports from the EC will be kept for a period of ten years. Moreover, EC imports from Poland, the Czech and Slovak republics, and Hungary are growing by about 20 percent a year since the reforms of 1989. Czech exports to the EC increased drastically from $2.8 billion in 1989 to $7.3 billion in 1992.

The dismantling of West European trade and other barriers and the economic and political reforms of Eastern Europe are gradually becoming a reality. A unified market of Europe is expected to benefit business, workers, and consumers alike. In spite of some opposition, mainly from left-wing parties, politicians, economists, and the citizens in general support a unified Europe and talk about the creation of the United States of Europe, with prospects of advancing it to the level of the United States of America. Already, campaigns to alert citizens and businesses in the European countries have begun by almost all governments. They include conferences and seminars and even the creation of special ministries (in Belgium) and other institutions to deal with the implications of a "border-free Europe." It seems that what once was regarded as a dream, a utopian concept, is becoming a reality.

The European Community of 12 nations, with a population of 327 million and a total GDP more than $5 trillion, is almost equivalent in economic power to the United States, with a population of 254 million and a GDP of about $6 trillion. All EC nations should prepare for the race among themselves and together for the race with the United States and Japan. The gradual approach to a single market may be accompanied by a further political unification and in some years the European Parliament may become more influential and powerful than national parliaments.

EASTERN EUROPE AND THE BALKANS

After many wars and disturbances throughout history, East European countries—primarily Poland, the former Czechoslovaka, Hungary, Romania, and Bulgaria—came under the political and economic influence of the Soviet Union, during the post-World War II years.

For centuries, Poland faced disastrous wars with Germany, Sweden, Russia, and Turkey, which led to its economic deterioration. After World War II, the Soviet system of central planning, with collectivization of farms and nationalization of industries, was imposed. The pressure for reforms led to a number of riots since the 1950s, with the formation of the Solidarity union in 1980 and the movement for workers' control in industry. After the "shock therapy" of the economy and the election in 1990 of Lech Walesa, the Solidarity leader and a Nobel Prize winner, capitalism and the privazation of state enterprises gained importance.

The former Czechoslovakia, which lies between the agrarian regions of the Balkans and the industrialized areas of Europe, came into existence in 1918 as a result of the union of Czechs and Slovaks. Occupied by Nazi troops (1939–45) and liberated by the Soviet Army, Czechoslovakia came under Soviet influence and, like Poland and Hungary, it followed the system of central planning and state control of the economy. Some reforms implemented by Alexander Dubcek in 1968 (during the "Prague spring") were reversed by the intervention of Soviet troops to save the country from "capitalist wolves." A peaceful anticommunist revolution in 1989 enacted drastic reforms toward the market economy, denationalization, and foreign investment. As of 1993, the country is divided into the Czech Republic and the Slovak Republic (Slovakia).

As a result of wars and oppression, mainly by the Turks and the Hapsburgs and lately the Soviets, Hungary fell behind contemporary Europe. After World War II, the communist system was introduced. Although economic changes were reversed with the crush of the revolution of 1956 by Soviet and Warsaw Pact tanks, Hungary managed to implement a number of reforms, especially after the introduction of the New Economic Mechanism in 1968. More changes toward the free market and joint ventures were enacted after 1989.

Expansionary policies of big powers led the Balkans to ethnic, cultural, and religious differences difficult to reconcile. In ancient times the Illyrians, then the Hellenes (Greeks) under Alexander the Great, and later the Romans and the Byzantines occupied the area. Around the seventh century, the Slavs came and settled permanently. From 1389, when Ottoman Turks defeated the Serbian forces in Kosovo, and mostly until World War I, the area was controlled by the Turks.

Previous proposals and conferences for a Balkan economic and political cooperation and confederation have not succeeded. The Balkan countries produce competing primary products and a closer economic cooperation or integration is difficult. From a political point of view, conflicting interests of outside powers acted as drawbacks to their movement toward a confederation. As the saying goes, "when elephants quarrel, the grass is destroyed."

The poor Balkan countries (Yugoslavia, Romania, Bulgaria, Albania), which for centuries were under Turkish occupation and internal conflicts, introduced reforms similar to those of the other East European nations. Yugoslavia, which practiced the self-management system for the last four decades, has split into independent republics after severe ethnic conflicts.

The winds of freedom and democracy of Eastern Europe are blowing through the Balkan region as well. However, the Balkan area, which experienced four costly wars during the first half of this century, is troubled again by ethnic conflicts. The Greek minority of Albania, the Turkish minority in Bulgaria, and the Albanian minority in Yugoslavia are the main ethnic groups involved in serious disputes.

The Balkan countries are in a stage of dramatic political and economic changes and Western investments are needed to revitalize their economies, so they would be able to join the EC club. By helping them the West would be helped as well in the immediate future. Such an EC enlargement does not necessarily lead to a weak and chaotic Europe but to a prosperous Europe and more stable world.

As Chancellor Helmut Kohl of Germany said, "Poles and Hungarians, Czechs and Slovaks, and many other people and nations in Central, Eastern and South-Eastern Europe place their hopes in the Community. We cannot disappoint them."[3]

A BRIEF RETROSPECT OF RUSSIAN ECONOMIC DEVELOPMENT

Russia, the largest republic of the former USSR with a vast territory rich in oil and other resources, was inhabited primarily by Slavs, Scythians, Sarmatians, and other Asiatic peoples. Although Peter the Great and Catherine the Great achieved territorial and trade expansions and followed westernization policies, the country remained feudalistic and backward.

The Bolshevik Revolution and the "war for communism" (1917–21) introduced a communist system in which private property was abolished and factories were taken over by worker councils (Soviets). Because of low work incentives, mismanagement, and lack of coordination, production declined and a number of capitalist measures were reintroduced by V. I. Lenin (New Economic Policy, 1921–28).

Thereafter, a drastic program of collective farms (*kolkhozy*) and state farms (*sovkhozy*), as well as central planning, were initiated by Joseph Stalin and the Communist Party. Responding to forceful collectivization, the peasants resorted to destroying inventories and slaughtering livestock. But Stalin responded with more force and purged resisting peasants and others who were not carrying out his policy of quick industrialization, particularly during the 1930s.

The first five-year plan (FYP) of 1928–32 and the consequent long-term and annual plans, supervised by the State Planning Commission (Gosplan) and the central bank (Gosbank), emphasized industrialization at the neglect of consumer goods. Although material (bonuses) and nonmaterial incentives were given for plans' fulfillment, serious problems appeared regarding quality and quantity of production, as well as bureaucratic inertia. Moreover, false reporting, favors, and corruption on the part of managers and supervisors or party members were widespread, and severe punishments were enacted to reduce or eliminate them.

After the Bolshevik Revolution in 1917 and the establishment of the communist system, the former Soviet Union followed an economic policy of autarky. More or less, the same policy was imposed on the client states of

Eastern Europe after World War II. To a large extent, this was the result of fears that the communist system might be undermined and eventually destroyed by hostile capitalist countries.

The dramatic transformations of the Soviet system, after 1985 when Mikhail Gorbachev came to power, were expressed primarily by the terms economic restructuring (*perestroika*) and democratic openness (*glasnost*). Changes from the slow pace of reforms to more radical measures toward privatization and the market economic system occurred mainly after the failure of the military coup in August 1991, by hard-liners of the Communist Party, which was subsequently abolished by Gorbachev, Boris Yeltsin, and other architects of Soviet changes. As a result of the reforms toward Western capitalism, foreign investment and joint ventures, as well as financial support, are entering the former Soviet republics. Nevertheless, the conflicts and splits of these republics slow foreign investment and retard growth. A commonwealth of 11 republics was created in December 1991, when Gorbachev was removed from power, mainly by Yeltsin, who was elected president of Russia and continued the rapid privatization of the economy.

The recent revolutionary changes in Russia and the other former Soviet republics created new conditions for the EC and the European continent. The economic and political reforms were so dramatic that Western leaders booby-trapped themselves. Decades of ideological divisions and controls had not obliterated the notion of a common heritage and destiny of all Europe. This concept of a European whole and a free or a common European home was expressed at the December 1989 summit in Strasbourg, where EC members favored an associated status of the former East bloc countries, including Russia and other former Soviet republics. However, as Europe moves toward a self-reliant destiny it still needs the American presence for some time to come, because it lacks a constructive pan-European ideology and leadership.

In order to move closer to Western economies, Russia is establishing commodity and stock exchange markets, as well as mutual funds to facilitate new investment and joint ventures. The EC, together with the United States, Japan, and other nations provide aid to the former Soviet republics. Some $24 billion aid was approved, through the European Bank for Reconstruction and Development (established in Paris in May 1990), to help reform their economies in a fashion similar to the U.S. Marshall Plan for Western Europe in the post-World War II years.

REFORMS IN EX-PLANNED ECONOMIES

Russia and other countries of the former Eastern bloc are privatizing state enterprises through a mix of sales and direct giveaways. The success of privatization requires that high priority be given to the legal framework of property ownership and business operations, including laws defending private property and corporate enterprises, contracts, and commercial codes. However, when markets are free of controls, demand may not be sufficient to absorb all industrial production resulting from the excess capacity of the past. To avoid extensive unemployment, resources should be transferred elsewhere, primarily in services and new enterprises. Such a shift and adjustment of labor and capital, though, may take a long time, even decades.

The success of democracy in these countries would help the EC and the West in general to divert resources from military spending to civilian use and to integrate their economies with the rest of the world. From that standpoint, the West should help these newly established democracies to keep their reforms on track and their economies functioning. Building modern fiber-optic telephone networks, oil-drilling equipment, computers, and other high technology industries, instead of building bombs and missiles, would help the development of the ex-socialist countries, as well as the EC and other Western economies by creating new jobs to absorb the unemployed defense workers.

To support the process of democratization and economic reforms, an association agreement between the EC and Poland, analogous to those with Hungary and the Czech and Slovak republics, was signed on December 16, 1991, in Brussels (Europe Agreements).

Until recently, the former Soviet Union and the East European countries were seen as a threat to Western Europe, and their relations have been formulated within the context of U.S.-Soviet relations. However, the rapid changes in the East bloc countries for a free market system and decentralization in decision making point toward an economic interaction and an eventual partnership between them and the EC. As a result, the cold war polemics turned to mutual investment and development arguments.

In Russia and all East European countries, there are proposals to convert the collective farms into joint-stock companies. The shares may reflect the land brought into the collective and the number of years of work on the farm. There is a problem, though, regarding the sale of such shares, particularly to people outside the farms.

The government should stress a developmental rather than a regulatory policy with strict antitrust laws and bureaucratic inertia. Government and industry should work together, encouraging investment and technological improvement for higher growth and international competitiveness. In cooperation with enterprises, civil servants can use their expertise to introduce a competitive business framework and enhance innovations and factor productivity.

Japan's economic model of government support of private enterprises and the free market mechanism proved to be highly successful, particularly on international economic relations. On the contrary, the command economic system of the former planned economies, which eradicated the market mechanism of supply and demand and private enterprise initiatives, led to inefficiency and the complete collapse of the economy and its political system.

Changes that had been introduced in the recent past were considered too slow and too few to reduce bureaucracy, to give the people more voice in the management of the country, and to motivate productive incentives. It would seem that less controls on farming, industry, and small private business and more freedom to the marketplace would stimulate public initiative, improve quality, and increase production. Reducing rigidities in the system and avoiding apathy or neglect in the economy require material and nonmaterial incentives and more freedom in exchanges.

Gradually, it became clear that in the name of advancing the working class, the practicioners of the communist regimes reduced people into means of production. Through the establishment of the party elites, they turned talented working people into cogs of thudding machines without a clear purpose. As workers under these regimes say, "they pretend they pay us and we pretend we work." The result is inefficiency and low-quality products. This verifies an Aristotelian comment some 25 centuries ago, that common ownership leads to common neglect.

In order to reverse the recent fall in trade among themselves, Poland, Hungary, and the Czech and Slovak republics established the Vishehrad Group Free Trade Zone in November 1992. The group's aim is also to develop common policies toward EC membership.[4]

The ongoing reforms for the establishment of buoyant market economies in Eastern Europe brought about significant economic and political changes, but the optimism that prevailed initially began to wither away. The outlook for short-term economic growth is not encouraging. The marketization and democratization of these countries have not unleashed significant private initiative to mobilize sources of economic growth. As a result, gross domestic products (GDPs) declined and reformers continue to face a series of chicken-and-egg dilemmas, regarding priorities on antiinflationary policies and privatization of state enterprises. But the alternative to economic reforms is so bleak that risks are worth taking.

Many enterprises in Eastern Europe are now controlled jointly by their managers and workers. The managers are chosen or approved by the workers, who press for high wages and other benefits. They are interested in receiving high income now and not so much in the future of the enterprises in which they work. They might not be working when these enterprises become healthy and prosperous later, or they might not enjoy a fair share even if they remain with the same firm. Moreover, managers may appropriate enterprise property for themselves, as happened during the early stages of privatization when assets were sold or leased by managers to other firms owned by their friends or their foreign partners.

SUPPORT AND CRITICISM OF THE EC

It should not be disregarded, though, that there are overall objections to the economic unification of the European Community and eventually the whole of Europe, especially by the Left, as well as specific objections on agricultural policy, monetary unification, environmental considerations, and social interests.

Conservative and left-wing parties are the main opponents of the Common Agricultural Policy (CAP) and the establishment of the European Monetary System with a stronger alliance of the community's currencies and a common central bank. Also, the Green Party in Germany predicts environmental harm and deterioration of the weak, while labor unions are asking for protection and guarantees for the working classes. However, all see that there are no better alternatives and realize they must slowly change their attitudes or become gradually isolated. In the meantime, the community's economies are being tightly interwoven and other nations such as Norway, Sweden, Austria, Switzerland, and all the East bloc countries want closer ties with the EC and eventual membership.

To reinforce community cohesion, efforts are made toward the harmonization of the economic and social levels of the weaker and stronger member-states of the EC, by palliating economic asymmetries and social imbalances, reducing unemployment, improving training and education, and promoting health and social security. In addition to economic unification, and the possibility of political integration, their goal is to improve sociocultural conditions and to create a "community with a human face."

It seems that the EC influence is growing not only on economic but on sociopolitical matters as well. It has become more than the Europe of Charlemagne's conception. With its 12 member nations, it stretches from the Hebrides of Britain to Crete and it becomes more independent and powerful, instead of a mere collection of clients and allies of one group or another with different cultures.

The pressure of competition and the economic challenges from the United States and Japan, as well as the prospects of raising the rate of economic growth and reducing unemployment, made the idea of a single European market attractive to West and East European politicians and citizens. However, after the initial enthusiasm and excitement, skepticism appeared regarding the surrender of large chunks of national sovereignty and the difficult real problems expected. Such problems refer to the abolition of all frontiers and the consequent illegal immigration and crime, the inflationary expectation from a common currency and the creation of a European central bank, the leveling of tax rates, and the "social dimension" of workers' rights.

While big business firms favor the single market for their rapid expansion, labor unionists worry about the institutional rights they have achieved via difficult struggles throughout the years. Even politicians of different persuasions are cautious and express their skepticism as they realize that their countries are going through a long tunnel before they will come to the other side. Although there is no danger that the European integration project will be derailed, difficult testing lies ahead and tough decisions are expected to be made in the years to come. Nevertheless, Europeans remember their bitter history of wars. They know that "those who don't learn from history are doomed to repeat it." Looking back, they see that when Europe was divided, catastrophic wars and massive destructions occurred, while in periods of peace and cooperation economic advancement and sociocultural development occurred.

The elimination of national frontiers of the EC will favor business, particularly big corporations. Labor unions, however, complain that this will be accomplished over the rights of the workers. The idea of a single market with free circulation of goods, services, and people may not mean a better living for everyone. Some workers argue that the free domestic market of Western Europe may be considered a paradise for corporations and capitalists but a nightmare for the working class. Objections are raised mainly by French and German labor unions, which expect a movement of business firms to southern Europe where labor unions are not strong and eventually to Eastern Europe with cheap labor. British labor unions, on the other hand, seem to accept reality and now do not raise as much opposition as before.

Among the workers' guarantees demanded are the establishment of uniform policies regarding a 35-hour workweek and related industrial guidelines. Safety standards, health measures, workers' training, the right to collective bargaining, and workers' participation in corporation decision making are additional demands of the trade unions of the EC. Companies that choose to be "European," instead of remaining national, are expected, voluntarily, to introduce the employee participation in management that has prevailed for decades in Germany. This is a measure needed to compensate for the weakness of trade unionism, to preserve diversity, and to avoid conflicts that may stagnate Europe's economy.

Britain and the EC

Although British Prime Minister John Major proclaims that Britain's destiny is in Europe, he objects to the creation of a central European power in Brussels. He is against an excessive concentration of power in the 12-nation trade bloc because this would jeopardize the objectives of the EC and increase bureaucracy. A European superstate may lead to more detailed regulation from the center, suppression of nationhood, and less independence.

The British conservatives think that Europe's federalism, supported by Europeanists, is a utopia and the creation of a single market does not imply large transfers of national sovereignty of a political union. Their policies, though, have revived self-confidence and even arrogance in Britain, which was considered as the "sick man of Europe" a few years ago. They argue that Charles de Gaulle was right in arguing that people should be proud of their country and should identify with it.

The British conservatives argue that EC member-states should not surrender their history, traditions, and customs to a mixture of a European Parliament and the European Commission. Also, they do not like the vague jargon or the term "social partners," which means a dialogue between industry, trade unions, and the state. Moreover, they do not support the sitting of union representatives on corporate boards, as happens in Germany. But they want economic liberty and removal of constraints, not the imposition of new ones.

However, former Prime Minister Edward Heath, who took Britain into the EC in 1973, argues that the European Community is a single market and is concerned with a single central bank and a single currency. Heath and the British Labour Party believe that the EC proceeds slowly and surely to its destiny of unification, even without Britain.

France and the EC

In France, all political parties support the European integration, and they expect their country to be the first among equals both economically and politically. The drive for economic unity leads the socialist government of François Mitterrand to adjust its policies to those of the EC. Such policies include privatization of state-owned enterprises, reduction in public-sector expenditures and other austerity measures to curb inflation and eliminate budget deficits. This is a deviation from previous policies that France, Spain, Greece, and other EC countries followed in stimulating demand through generous wage increases, expansive monetary policy, and social spending policies that led to inflation, high trade deficits, and currency depreciation.

Many French politicians and executives of big business expect the European Community to be a single free market, similar to that of the United States. Then, German, Italian, Spanish, and other professional people would be able to open offices in Paris or Lyons, and French or other EC nations' lawyers and professionals in general would be able to operate in any other member nation. However, a nationalist backlash might be created among farmers, workers, and small businesspeople with chauvinistic tendencies who might react to the challenge of European unification.

Nevertheless, even Gaullists and others, who opposed unification in the past, gradually have abandoned their objections and are adjusting to the expansion of EC operations. They think that eventually Paris will be the capital of the EC and after the construction of the Calais tunnel, France will be a vital transportation and commercial center of Europe. On the other hand, the antiimmigrant National Front, the extreme right-wing party of Jean-Marie Le Pen with some 4.4 million voters, is against the EC market unification because its members are afraid of "labor invasion," while the Communist Party favors a larger European community from the Urals to the Atlantic.

Germany and the EC

The dramatic changes in Eastern Europe and particularly in former East Germany present a great challenge to the EC and U.S. policy makers and entrepreneurs. The outflow of large numbers of East Germans to West Germany indicated the strong desire of the Germans for reunification. Although Germany was united only from 1870 to 1945, the argument of the German traditionalists is that the envy of its European neighbors was responsible for the division of Germany before and after that period.

The German question is not affecting only East-West relations but also relations within the Western world. Both the EC and the United States are interested in creating a strong Germany that will be an important economic entity and will influence the trend toward a united Europe, an argument supported mainly by the Europeanists. The unification of the German Democratic Republic (GDR), or East Germany, with the Federal Republic of Germany (FRG), or West Germany, in 1990, may eventually unite the rest of Europe, because Europe's division is due in large part to the division of Germany, and vice versa. The fulfillment of German aspirations for unification came not from the West but from the Soviet disengagement, the massive emigration of East Germans, and the dismantling of the Berlin Wall.

Other European nations and the United States, based on historical experience and the fear of reviving nationalism, are skeptical about German unification. The slogan *ein Deutschland* reminds them of the catastrophic results of World War I and World War II. However, advanced technology in communications liquidated the old nationalistic concepts in Europe and prepared the ground for closer cooperation and even unification of neighboring countries.

Italy and the EC

Although the beginning of capitalism could be observed early (thirteenth century) in certain Mediterranean towns, particularly in Italian ports, it became widespread in Western Europe in the sixteenth century. The emancipation of the serfs from the landlords of the countryside of Italy transformed them into free laborers, competing for jobs to be provided by the capitalists of the towns.

The main characteristic of postwar Italy is the frequent change in government—there have been 52 postwar governments, averaging about one a year. But, surprisingly enough, the many changes have not had a great effect on Italy's economy or its relations with the rest of the European Community and other international institutions. Basically, the political system (with 13 parties) and the economic conditions are more or less stable. The changes are mostly in ministerial portfolios, with the Christian Democratic Party governing for some 40 years, and the Socialist Party governing for a few of the remaining years.

However, under the competitive pressures of the EC, the Italian people have grown tired of the old politicking and prefer stability in the government and the economy. That is why a feeling of political restructuring is in the air toward reducing the number of parties in a similar fashion as in the other EC countries and the United States. Chronic economic problems regarding employment, inflation, taxation, and high budget deficits require stable governments if Italy is to be able to stand toe-to-toe with the rest of Europe.

Spain and the EC

Spain, with a socialist government, realized that there is no better alternative than joining the rest of Western Europe and becoming a member of the EC. On January 1, 1986, Spain and Portugal became members of the EC. This resulted in a flood of European investment into Spain. Although there are fears of strong competition from the other more advanced members of the EC, Spanish people feel that their country became important and eventually it will become Europe's Florida or California. Along with other peoples of the EC, they are enthusiastic about the prospects of economic and eventual political unification of Europe.

Moreover, in a referendum in 1988, Spain and Portugal joined the Western European Union, a defense pact between EC members and NATO. And this was despite Prime Minister Gonzalez's opposition to Spain's entry into NATO before he came to power in 1982. Also, Spain, along with Britain, Italy, and Germany, participates in the Eurojet consortium for the development of aircraft and related armaments in the near future.

The Spanish economy, with about 5 percent growth annually, is the best-performing economy in Western Europe. Growing investment, mainly from other EC countries, and business confidence, after Spain's membership in the European Community, are primarily responsible for Spain's booming economy.

The Socialist government of Felipe Gonzalez faces mounting labor unrest. Workers want to share in the growing prosperity of the country, while the government tries to hold down inflation with limited pay raises for wages and pensions.

FOREIGN INVESTMENT IN EAST EUROPEAN COUNTRIES

To attract European and other foreign investments, East European governments have relaxed or abolished bureaucratic controls that remained from the collapsed communist system. New laws and regulations deal with private ownership, property rights, joint ventures, and other free market arrangements to create a favorable environment for investment expansion, economic stabilization, and growth, particularly in Poland, Hungary, and the Czech and Slovak republics.

Hungary and Poland are the most receptive and the easiest countries in Eastern Europe for foreign investors to enter. The Czech and Slovak republics, Hungary, and Russia require approval if joint ventures are formed with government entities; Bulgaria and Poland require approval for all foreign investment. Wholly owned foreign investment and full repatriation of profits are permitted by all East European countries, except Albania and Russia, which have specific restrictions.

Up to 1990, registered joint ventures in Eastern Europe were limited. The largest number of such joint ventures was in Hungary (628), followed by Poland (170), Bulgaria and the former Yugoslavia (41 each), the former Czechoslovakia (20), and Romania (5). EC and especially German companies have formed far more joint ventures in Eastern Europe than U.S. companies.

In order to avoid wealth concentration and monopolization in the production process by foreign or domestic investors, governments offer installment payment opportunities to promote privatization and diffusion of property ownership. Also, they divide large firms into small ones. Such measures try to attract small inventors to buy shares and to be acquainted with the spirit of capitalistic ownership, as well as to create a stable and democratic middle class. Nevertheless, the demand for shares of privatized public enterprises depends on their profitability. People are not investing their money in firms that have very low profitability or losses.

From a practical standpoint, intergovernmental cooperation to combat terrorism, drug trafficking, and international crime has been gradually promoted. Also, the EC suggested the establishment of a European audiovisual area, known as "Audiovisual Eureka," with a conclave of private- and public-sector broadcasters, writers, producers, film makers, directors, advertisers, and the like. In implementing the provisions of the Single European Act on the completion of the internal market, environmental problems are also to be considered. They include such issues as soil depletion, water resources, toxic wastes, acid rain and other forms of air pollution, depletion of the ozone layer, the "greenhouse effect," and nuclear contamination.

Franchise arrangements, like those pioneered by McDonald's restaurants and 7-Eleven stores, are novel ideas in postcommunist Eastern Europe; but they began to spread in a number of previously planned economies. Franchisers have to agree to buy a sizable percentage, perhaps three-fourths, of their merchandise from the prototype firms, the name and emblem of which they use, and also to be subject to regular inspections to make sure that they meet the standards set by these prototype firms.

The countries of Eastern Europe are in the difficult process of transforming their economies from the planning system to the market system. However, they need Western help, not in the form of welfare, but in the form of financial, technical, and managerial assistance, which would help revitalize their productive machinery, improve the distribution system, and organize their markets in a competitive fashion. Helping the former planned European economies to move forward again would help the Western economies as well.[5] By providing credit to these countries, Western nations open markets for their products, so that farmers can sell their grain, industries can supply products, and investors can enter into profitable ventures. This would help the European Community and the United States to save a great deal from wasteful farm supports and subsidies and to increase economic growth.

The movement toward the integration of Eastern Europe and the former USSR into a pan-European economy and the economic reforms on trade and investment in the region are expected to be the major preoccupations of international economics in the forthcoming years.

EC STABILITY AND GROWTH

The EC system is a hybrid of individualistic capitalism, with high incentives of production and profit making, and a social market system, with capital and labor comanagement or popular capitalism, which protects labor and supports a more equitable distribution of income and wealth. As such, it encourages investment and stimulates effective demand so that economic fluctuations can be mitigated.

Nevertheless, for Europe to succeed, a policy of closer integration and gradual enlargement is needed so that ethnic and border conflicts will be eliminated. The EC should support and eventually engulf the East European countries and even Russia to avoid massive immigration or waves of refugees in the EC capitals from these countries and to enlarge markets and investment opportunities. It seems that there is not a better alternative for a stable and prosperous Europe in the future, although it may appear as a utopian concept at present.

The EC, by virtue of its economic and sociopolitical strength and powerful influence, would be instrumental in accomplishing the unification of Europe and creating a common European home in the near future. Although Washington may be uncomfortable with the challenges in Europe and in Germany in particular, it can accommodate their growing independence and accept power as well as burden sharing.

The twenty-first century would belong to the House of Europe if the EC moves rapidly to economic integration and gradual absorption of Eastern and eventually the rest of Europe. Not only economies of scale would be improved from the enlargement of the market, but the infrastructure and the productive capacity of the continent would be enhanced. The educational level on both sides of Europe, West and East, is relatively high, especially for high science in Russia and other ex-communist countries. Natural resources are, to a large extent, available, whereas the distribution system is rapidly being developed. What is needed is primarily quick integration and extension of the EC to engulf the Central and East European nations.[6] From that standpoint, all nations of Europe should put aside old ethnic rivalries and border disputes and try to unite, so that they can face the expected aggressive competitions from other countries or groups of countries.

Our thesis is that, although in the short run EC enlargement may work against deepening, in the long run it would be beneficial for the EC to enlarge its territory and accept more neighboring countries until the integration of the whole Europe has been accomplished. Larger markets, new investment opportunities, and the expansion of European and other corporations, through mergers and acquisitions, require such enlargement. This is needed for an ever-growing international competition with American and Japanese corporations.

Expectations are that other European nations will joint the EC and form a pan-European union with common monetary and fiscal policies as developed in the EC conferences of Lisbon and Strasbourg in 1992.

It is important to examine the structural changes and the main problems regarding economic policies, joint ventures, trade, and developmental trends between the EC and the recently liberalized East bloc countries. Fieldwork was conducted primarily through periodic visits in the East European countries and Russia. These visits allowed this author the opportunity to observe, first hand, the drastic reforms regarding privatization, democratization, and economic changes, and to have discussions with leading economists and policy makers in the countries concerned.

The sweeping changes to be effected in trade, labor, and capital, as a result of the EC integration and East European reforms, will influence not only European, U.S., and Japanese economic and political conditions but also global relations and rearrangements with other countries, including the developing ones.

The following chapters, drawing on theory and empirical research, examine structural reforms and economic cooperation between the European Community and Eastern Europe, including the Balkan countries and Russia. The chapters provide an overview of the recent events and future trends in these countries where dramatic changes are occurring.

Part I

The European Community

2

Formation and Expansion

HISTORICAL TRENDS TOWARD UNIFICATION

Mythologically, in ancient Greece (which, according to Nietzsche, provided the nucleus of European civilization), Kadmos, son of Aginora, lost his sister Europa. His search to find her was in vain. Then he built a city, as model for people living together, named "Europe."

In paleolithic times, the Neanderthal race was common to the continent of Europe. It was replaced by the Cro-Magnon race in the late paleolithic period. The vast majority of Europeans were grouped by anthropologists in the Caucasian race, one of the great divisions of mankind that first appeared in Eastern Europe during the neolithic period of the Stone Age. Almost all of the varieties of speech used in Europe belong to the family of Indo-European languages, which includes the Balto-Slavic (Russian, Polish, Czechoslovakian, Serbian, Bulgarian), the Teutonic (English, German, Dutch, Scandinavian), the Italic (French, Catalan, Spanish, Portuguese, Italian, Romanian), the Hellenic (Greek), and the Celtic (Gaelic, Welsh, Breton) linguistic subfamilies.

According to archaeologists, the island of Crete was the place of European man's emergence from the Stone Age into the age of metals (bronze, iron). The Cretans (Minoans) were distinguished by their maritime and commercial activities along the Mediterranean shores (third millennium B.C.). The Hellenes or Greeks (mainly Achaeans or Mycenaens, Ionians, Dorians or Spartans, and later Athenians) were the first to leave a record of themselves and their neighbors.[1] They were descendants of a branch of the Indo-European race (living in the Alps and central Europe) to which Romans, Germans, Slavs, and other Europeans belong.

Although the concept of European union gained significant attention and started being implemented in the post-World War II years, previous attempts were made throughout history toward a European economic and political integration. On a small scale, federations or unions of city-states, which operated as independent economic and political units, can be observed in ancient Greece and Italy (in the fifth century B.C. and afterward).

The first economic and political unions or confederacies in history were the Achaean League and the Delian League developed in ancient Greece during the sixth to the third centuries B.C. They were established to formulate common economic and foreign policies on trade, coinage, and other matters.

During the period of the Roman Empire (31 B.C. to A.D. 476), agriculture was given high priority compared to other sectors. Small landholders and free laborers left the countryside and crowded into the towns, increasing the number of plebeians. The possession of large estates by the wealthy class and the nobles created the latifundia, which, together with the inefficiency of slave labor and the introduction of heavy taxation, accelerated the decline of the Roman Empire. The creation of a new commercial class, the patricians, and the new landowners necessitated a body of laws that later had a profound influence on legal and economic institutions.

The recognition of juristic or artificial persons (legal entities) by Roman laws was the most important development from the standpoint of invention and expansion of the corporate form of modern enterprises.

During the Middle Ages (A.D. 476 to about 1350) and the Renaissance period (1350–1500), trade among the European cities was limited. Agriculture, which was the main sector of the economy, declined and educational and technological advancement were at a standstill. It was thought that the Greco-Roman writers, particularly Aristotle, had provided complete scientific explanations for all subjects and no further improvement was possible.

Under mercantilism (1550–1776) emphasis was placed on foreign trade as a means of accumulating precious metals, as the most desirable form of national wealth, and the supremacy of the state over the individual. The state, being the locus of power, should support exports, create state monopolies, and establish colonies to increase national wealth. Commercial expansion by monopolies such as the Merchant Adventurers, the Eastland Company, the Muscovy Company, and the East India Company initially had as main objectives the search for the accumulation of precious metals, mainly gold and silver, which could be used to finance trade, pay large armies for foreign wars, or be retained as luxuries.

State and church financial facilities during the sixteenth and seventeenth centuries stimulated wealthy families, such as the Bardis, Medicis, and Fuggers, to undertake commercial and financial adventures and thus displace the medieval feudal lords. This new system of commercial capitalism was characterized by economic freedom, technical progress, and profit-seeking regardless of the social consequences and communal relationships.

The doctrine of mercantilism in England or cameralism in Germany and Colbertism in France (from Jean Colbert, the French finance minister) supported promotion of exports and protection of manufacturing and foreign trade by active government intervention. This intensified the policy of colonialism by the European nations, particularly England, Spain, France, Holland, and Portugal.

With the approaching end of colonialism, the European nations turned against each other. The result was terrible destruction and crashing economic setbacks in World Wars I and II. Subsequently, aging Europe, having learned a harsh lesson from previous belligerence and destructions, turned toward cooperation and eventual economic and political integration by forming the successful European Community, a dream that had been unrealized for centuries.

EVOLUTION OF THE EUROPEAN COMMUNITY

For several years, six European countries—France, West Germany, Italy, and the three Benelux nations (Belgium, Luxembourg, and the Netherlands)—tried to strengthen their economic and political bonds. Actually Belgium and Luxembourg had an economic union since 1921, which was joined by the Netherlands in 1944 in order to form the regional economic group known as the Benelux countries. Negotiations among these three nations had begun even from 1943 when they were under Nazi occupation.

After World War II, a ravaged Europe slowly set out on the path toward its crucial revival and eventual unification. The destruction of the war raised the question of how to avoid the pattern of European history of catastrophes followed by revivals followed by catastrophes, ad infinitum. The consensus was that Europe should not be doomed to oscillations between order and chaos. Instead, a new way of peace, stability, and prosperity should be found. A European supranationalism or a European family of nations was needed to submerge individual nationalism and historic enmities.

One of the first Europeanists was Jean Monnet, a stocky French peasant figure, who wanted to promote Europe's recovery in the post-World War II years and eventually its economic and political union. He pointed out that people taking risks and offering innovative ideas for European integration deserve the laurels. However, emphasis should be placed on institutions, such as the EC, because they can transmit things to successor generations. Monnet wanted not so much to be somebody, but to do something, especially to contribute to the union of the European peoples in liberty and diversity. He persuaded the United States, through President Franklin D. Roosevelt, to support the defense of Europe as "the arsenal of democracy." Also, he prepared the Schuman Plan, named for Robert Schuman, the French foreign minister (1950), for the creation of the European Coal and Steel Community (ECSC) in 1952, the forerunner of the EC.

The Schuman Plan was designed to effect Franco-German reconciliation and to make it impossible for the European nations to fight each other. Italy and the Benelux countries, together with France and West Germany, signed the treaty that established the ECSC. The idea was to provide a practical basis for gradual concrete economic and political achievements. Europe, after all, is essentially compact and indivisible. Viewed from an airplane, the jigsaw frontiers make little sense.

The European Economic Community (EEC) was established by the Treaty of Rome in 1957 with six members: Belgium, Luxembourg, the Netherlands, France, West Germany, and Italy, commonly known as the "Inner Six." It was formed to gradually reduce internal tariffs. Because the group was successful, the United Kingdom and Denmark, as well as Ireland, joined the EEC in 1973. Greece and Turkey became associate members in 1962 and 1964, respectively, and were allowed to export many of their products to the Community free from duty, while retaining tariffs during a transition period. Special arrangements and association agreements have been negotiated or signed with a number of countries in Africa, the Middle East, Asia, and Latin America, as well as Spain and Portugal. Greece became the tenth member of the EEC in 1981 and Spain and Portugal the eleventh and twelfth members in 1986.[2] Because of political and other noneconomic integration movements, the EEC is currently called the European Community. Table 2.1 shows some economic indicators of the EC.

For Spain and Portugal a ten-year transitional period (1986–95) was provided for agricultural products and a seven-year period for fish, for which tariffs would be gradually reduced by the EC. A similar five-year period was provided between the EC and Denmark, Ireland, and Britain. For industrial products the transitional period was three years for Spain and seven years for Portugal. No time interval was provided for the introduction of value added tax for Spain and only three years for Portugal, compared to five years for Greece (extended for another two years later). Also, a seven-year period was provided for the free movement of the Spanish and Portuguese workers in the EC, as was initially provided for Greece. Now, trade policy is basically dictated by Articles 110–116 of the Treaty of Rome.

There are four major institutions in the European Community for the formulation and implementation of economic and other related policies: the Commission, the Council, the European Parliament, and the Court of Justice. The Commission formulates and proposes related legislation and provides for the implementation of the Community's policies. There are 17 commission members (two each from Britain, France, Germany, Italy, and Spain and one from each of the other member-states) chosen for four-year terms by the 12 EC member-state governments. Jacques Delors, an energetic Frenchman, is the president of the Commission; Frans Andriessen, a former minister of the Netherlands, is the vice-president responsible for external relations and trade positions with the United States and other countries.

Table 2.1
Population (in millions), Per Capita GDP (in dollars), Growth of GDP, Inflation (average annual rates 1980–89, %), Unemployment (%), and General Government Expenditures over National Income (GG/Y) for the EC, 1990

Country	Population	Per Capita GDP	Growth of GDP	Inflation	Unemployment	GG/Y
Belgium	9.9	16,220	1.8	4.5	8.5	50.2
Britain	57.2	14,610	2.6	6.1	7.0	46.9
Denmark	5.1	20,450	2.2	6.0	7.7	68.4
France	56.4	17,820	2.1	6.5	9.4	56.7
Germany	62.1	18,354	1.9	2.7	5.5	50.3
Greece	10.0	5,350	1.6	18.2	7.8	41.4
Ireland	3.5	8,700	1.8	7.8	17.0	54.4
Italy	57.7	15,120	2.4	10.3	10.8	44.5
Luxembourg	0.4	16,220	1.9	4.5	1.8	42.6
Netherlands	14.9	15,920	1.7	1.9	8.7	59.5
Portugal	10.5	4,250	2.5	19.1	5.0	40.7
Spain	39.0	9,330	3.1	9.4	17.0	39.9
EC	326.7	13,328	2.2	6.4	8.2	49.6

Note: In some cases, earlier years' data were available. The growth of GDP, inflation, unemployment, and GG/Y for the EC is the average of Britain, France, Germany, and Italy.

Source: International Monetary Fund, *International Financial Statistics*; Organization for Economic Cooperation and Development, *National Accounts*; World Bank, *World Development Report*; all various issues; and ELEFTHEROTYPIA (newspaper), Athens, July 8, 1991, 24–25.

The rest of the commissioners have other assignments such as agricultural production and subsidy, financial affairs, budgetary problems, regional policies, transportation, cultural affairs, and environmental protection. The members of the Commission act not in the interest of their individual home-states but as representatives of the European Community as a whole.

The Council approves the legislation of the Community and is its decision-making institution. In contrast to the Commission, its members act as representatives of the particular member-state governments. For certain problems, the Council must consult with the Economic and Social Committee and the European Parliament. Under the revised procedures, a qualified majority is sufficient for the council's decisions, not unanimous approval as before. Individual member-states cannot exercise a veto anymore. This is a change that allows quick passage of EC proposals for further economic and political integration.

The European Parliament, elected by the voters of the individual member-states, has 518 members seated in nine political party groupings. These groups are not national but Community groups, such as the Socialist Group, the European People's Party, and so on. The Parliament advises the Commission and the Council on legislative matters and exercises democratic control over their actions through amendments and delays on related legislation.

The Court of Justice acts as the Supreme Court of the Community regarding the validity and the correct interpretation of its legislation. It is comprised of 13 judges and 6 advocates-general appointed for six years in agreement with the national governments. Through its decisions, the Court helped rapid integration by eliminating barriers to free trade and other restrictions within the Community. Together with other EC bodies, it has been a driving force behind the introduction of the Single European Act, effective in 1987, and the gradual unification of Western Europe.

Of the total 518 Europarliamentarians, Liberal or Free Democrats, the environmentalist Greens, and the Socialists were the main winners in the recent elections. The Conservatives and the Christian Democrats were the main losers. However, they both held strong positions with 100 and 48 seats, respectively, in 1989, compared to 181 seats for the Socialists, 41 for Communists, and 36 for the Green Party. In Britain, the Labour Party ended up with 45 seats in the European Parliament compared to 32 for the Conservative Party.

Depending on the population of each EC member-nation, the distribution of seats in the Europarliament was as follows in 1990: Britain, France, Germany, and Italy, 81 each; Spain, 60; the Netherlands, 25; Belgium, Greece, and Portugal, 24 each; Denmark, 16; Ireland, 15; and Luxembourg, 6. Although EC budget approval is usually a nightmare, for the first time in many years the Community's budget for 1989 of 46.2 billion ECUs (or $52.7 billion) was approved unanimously by the European Parliament and the Commission.

In accordance with the Community's Single Act, the EC reaffirms that it will not be a fortress region but a partner with outside nations, particularly the United States. Moreover, more progress on social aspects of the internal market is the intention of the EC Commission and the Community as a whole. Thus two key directives, which will significantly affect U.S. companies in Europe, are expected to provide for worker consultation and standard employment contracts. These directives will introduce new rules requiring firms to provide corporate information to workers and labor participation on matters of workplace health and safety, training, and even transnational mergers.

Regarding membership of other countries in the EC, Article 237 of the Treaty of Rome provided that any like-minded state could apply for membership, and the EC has been enlarged on a number of occasions since 1958.

Also, part of the treaty (Articles 131–136) provided that non-European countries could be brought into association with the Community. The usual EC practice of enlargement is the enactment of agreements with trade preferences for the candidate member-countries. However, member-governments in the Community have concluded long-term agreements with other countries, without contesting the EC's right to negotiate on matters of commercial policy.

Some serious questions concerning the future of the EC are: What is the relationship between enlargement and unification, or between widening versus deepening of the Community? Are there conflicting interests in the process of closer cooperation of the member-nations, regarding foreign policy, defense, and a single currency? What about trends toward expansion and incorporation of other European nations? The following sections attempt to answer such questions by reviewing the economic and geopolitical status of the countries and regional groups involved.

TRADE CREATION VERSUS TRADE DIVERSION

From a theoretical standpoint, the enlargement of the EC is expected to lead to trade creation. This is so because part of domestic production by some member-nations would be replaced by lower cost imports from other member-nations. This, in turn, leads to greater specialization based on the principle of comparative advantage and thereby to the increase in the welfare of the member-nations.

On the other hand, trade diversion, which reduces welfare, is not expected to occur to a significant extent, as long as lower cost imports from outside the Community may not be replaced by higher cost imports from EC member-nations. Likewise, the association and eventually integration of East European and other neighboring countries with the EC would lead to trade creation rather than to trade diversion, as long as domestic tariffs among members would fall and tariffs on imports from the rest of the world would not rise. Therefore, the greater the number of EC member-countries and the larger their size, the lower the cost of production and the more the welfare of the countries involved, particularly when they are closer geographically.

The effects of trade creation in a customs union such as the EC, when a part of domestic production of a member-country of the union is replaced by lower cost imports from another member-country, are shown in Figure 2.1. The vertical axis shows the price in dollars ($) and the horizontal axis shows the quantity (Q) of a commodity as related to demand (D) and supply (S) curves, whereas point E indicates the equilibrium of supply and demand. With tariffs, total consumption of the country before the formation of the customs union is shown by the line BB' or OM; domestic production is BF or OH and imports FB' or HM. The tariff revenue collected is the rectangle FGJB'. After the formation of the union, consumption is AA', domestic

Figure 2.1
Trade Creation

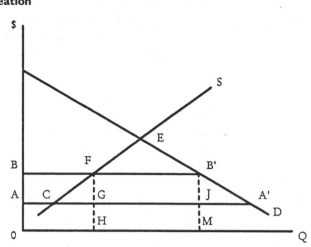

production AC and imports CA'. The revenue from tariffs disappears and the net gains of the country are equal to the sum of the two triangles CFG and A'B'J.

Figure 2.2 shows the effects of trade diversion when lower cost imports from outside a customs union, such as the EC, are replaced by higher cost imports from union members. Line AA' shows the position of the country under free world trade, with J'A' imports. A nondiscriminatory tariff shifts line AA' to CC' with FC' or KL imports. After reducing or eliminating tariffs among EC members, the imports of the country in question are JB' or IM. The welfare of the country is the summation of the two triangles FGJ and B'C'R, whereas the welfare loss from trade diversion is the rectangle GHNR. Thus, the net welfare loss is the difference between the rectangle GHNR minus the two triangles FGJ and B'C'R.

WEST AND CENTRAL EUROPEAN EC CANDIDATES

In 1960, that is, three years after the formation of the EEC, the European Free Trade Association (EFTA) was created in Stockholm. It included Austria, Britain, Denmark, Norway, Portugal, Sweden, and Switzerland. The EFTA (the "Outer Seven") as well as the EEC ("Inner Six") were formed to gradually reduce tariffs and encourage investment. However, the EFTA permitted the retention of individual external tariffs and, in the process of

Figure 2.2
Trade Diversion

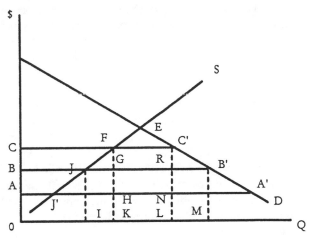

closer cooperation, it was not as successful as the EEC. As a result, Britain and Denmark, as well as Ireland, joined the EEC in 1973. On the other hand, Finland, Iceland, and Liechtenstein joined the EFTA. Moreover, there are some 66 African, Pacific, and Caribbean (APC) countries with which the EC maintains cooperative agreements and provides financial aid.

Under the pressure of businesses and the fear of being left outside the single European market, Austria, Finland, and Sweden have applied for full EC membership. Norway and Switzerland are expected to apply in the near future, although Norwegians had voted first (1972) against EC membership, mainly because of fear by fishermen that EC trawlers would wipe the sea clean of fish.[3]

Nevertheless, the severe loss of industrial competitiveness and the dissolution of the Warsaw Pact military alliance of the former Soviet Union and the East European nations intensified their desire for EC membership. It seems that all these countries will soon join the EC as their preferential trade relations are approaching the end. Through bilateral agreements with the EC, Sweden and other EFTA members already export their products duty free to the EC, and vice versa, without contributing to regional or agricultural programs and EC budget expenditures. Furthermore, the largest amount of their foreign trade is with the EC.

Encouraged by the drastic political and economic reforms in Eastern Europe and the former Soviet Union, Sweden and other EFTA countries agreed in December 1989 to crate a "European Economic Space" and abolish remaining tariffs and other restrictions. Also, industrial and other product standards would be harmonized and cooperation in environment, crime, and research and development would be increased. Moreover, democratization in Eastern Europe and the former Soviet republics removes the obstacle of neutrality and opens the way for EC membership. These efforts were further intensified as a result of the Conference on Security and Cooperation in Europe by 34 countries, including Sweden, in November 1990. On December 12, 1990, with an impressive vote of 198 to 105 and 26 abstentions, the Swedish Parliament decided to apply for EC membership and on July 1, 1991, it applied officially.

Fearing that it may lose its competitive edge and be isolated if it remains outside the EC, Switzerland announced plans to join the Community. After the referendum, on May 24, 1992, to join the World Bank and the International Monetary Fund with 56 percent in favor, Switzerland entered negotiations to participate in the EC. The seven-member Federal Council that governs the country decided to negotiate with the 12 EC nations for closer relations and eventual membership in the Community, with which Switzerland has two-thirds of its trade. Moreover, the end of the cold war and the common problems (drug abuse, immigration, economic fluctuations) it shares with the EC neighbors forced Switzerland to look afresh at its neutrality and to move toward integration with the EC. On the other hand, recent openness in its banking system, regarding secret foreign deposits, would give financial advantages in its economy and an increase in trade and investment transactions with other countries. Nevertheless, on December 6, 1992, Swiss voters rejected the move toward economic integration with the EC (50.3 percent against and 49.7 percent in favor). Also, 16 cantons of the country voted no and 7 cantons voted yes.

In November 1992 the European Community Commission recommended to the Community governments that Finland was ready to join the EC common monetary, foreign, and security policies. However, Finland, which applied for EC membership on March 18, 1992, was asked to drop its neutrality policy. The Commission asked for similar assurances from Austria and Sweden in order to join the common EC policies. With the disappearance of the shadow of the Soviet domination and the sharp decline of Finnish trade with Russia, Finland now moves gradually toward closer economic relations with the EC.

Liechtenstein, one of the seven members of EFTA, is a tiny state of 28,000 people between Austria and Switzerland. Many international corporations have their headquarters there to take advantage of favorable tax and secret banking laws. Although it follows, to a large extent, Switzerland's economic policy, it voted (December 1992) to join the EC. Iceland, another small EFTA member nation, is expected to apply for EC membership in the near future.

From economic and sociopolitical standpoints, the EFTA countries are largely at the same level with the advanced countries of the EC, as Table 2.2 shows. Per capita GNP in EFTA countries in 1990 varied from $19,060 for Austria to $32,680 for Switzerland, which was higher than the average of

Table 2.2
EFTA Countries Expected to Join the EC, 1990

Country	Population (millions)	Per Capita GDP (U.S. $)	Average Annual Inflat. 1980-90	Trade Balance (bil.$)
Sweden	8.6	23,660	7.4	3.5
Austria	7.7	19,060	3.6	-10.0
Switzerland	6.7	32,680	3.7	-6.4
Finland	5.0	26,040	6.8	0.8
Norway	4.2	23,120	5.5	7.6
Iceland	0.3	24,644	29.3	0.1

Note: In some cases earlier years' data were available.   The
        seventh member of EFTA is Liechtenstein.

Source: World Bank, World Development Report, 1992 (Washington,
DC: Oxford University Press, for the World Bank); International
Monetary Fund, International Financial Statistics (Washington,
DC: International Monetary Fund); and United Nations, Yearbook
of National Account Statistics (New York: United Nations), all
various issues.

the EC. This means that membership of the EFTA (in Greek meaning seven) countries to the EC would not present problems, as adjustment is expected to be easy. From that standpoint, mutual trade and investment would increase, as 33 million additional consumers would be added to the 345 million of the EC and enlarge the European markets.

Because of the expected closer relationship with the EC, mutual investment and joint ventures would increase, as entrepreneurs from EFTA and EC countries would move to each other's territory. Furthermore, the predicted larger markets would facilitate mergers and acquisitions between them and other countries, notably the United States and Japan.

For example, Volvo AB of Sweden and Renault Company, a French state-owned auto firm (partially privatized recently), each suggested they own 45 percent of truck operations of each other. A similar joint venture was agreed between Volvo and Enasa, an equivalent Spanish firm. Electrolux AB of Sweden agreed to acquire up to 20 percent shares of AEG Hausgerate AG, a unit of Daimler-Benz AG of Germany, for expansion in the production of washing machines, dishwashers, and other appliances. Nevertheless, such mergers and acquisitions may lead to the concentration of economic power and monopolistic capitalism, away from the "democratization of capital" and people's capitalism.

Norway's economy is gradually interwoven with the economies of the EC nations and, as a result, the country is a serious candidate for EC membership. Although in a past referendum 53 percent of the Norwegians voted against membership, the success of the EC is attracting them toward joining the club.

Table 2.3
Economic Indicators of Applicants and Potential Applicants for EC Membership, 1990

Countries	Population (millions)	Per Capita GNP, $	Average Annual Inflat. 1980-90	Trade Balance (bill.$)
Potential Applications				
Poland	38.2	1,690	54.3	3.6
Yugoslavia (former)	23.8	3,060	122.9	-2.7
Romania	23.2	1,640	1.8	-3.3
Czechoslovakia (former)	15.7	3,140	1.9	1.0
Hungary	10.3	2,780	9.0	0.5
Bulgaria	9.0	2,250	2.2	-0.5
Albania	3.3	1,290	n.a.	n.a.
Southern Applicants				
Turkey	56.1	1,630	13.2	-9.6
Cyprus	0.7	6,393	3.6	-1.5
Malta	0.3	6,365	1.2	-0.5

Note: In some cases earlier years' data were available. For Albania, Cyprus, and Malta GDP per capita. For trade balance, 1991.

Source: World Bank, World Development Report, 1992 (Washington, DC: Oxford University Press, for the World Bank); International Monetary Fund, International Financial Statistics (Washington, DC: International Monetary Fund); and United Nations, Yearbook of National Account Statistics (New York: United Nations), all various issues. For Albania, Athena, vol. 45, May 1991, 134.

SOUTHERN MEDITERRANEAN APPLICANTS

Stronger linkages and closer ties are also pursued between the EC and Cyprus, Malta, and Turkey, mainly through the Association/Cooperation Councils. These three southern Mediterranean countries have already applied for EC membership.

For Turkey, which has been an associate member of the EC for about three decades, membership may be further delayed because of reports of human rights violations, mainly against the Kurdish population; constant violations of the Greek sea and air space in the Aegean Sea; and the illegal occupation of about 40 percent of Cyprus since 1974. Moreover, the shift of the EC attention to Eastern Europe and Russia, as well as the low level of development in Turkey, act as drawbacks to early membership of that country to the EC. As Table 2.3 shows, the per capita GNP of Turkey was only $1,630 in 1990, compared to more than $6,000 for Cyprus and Malta (which signed an association agreement with the EC in 1970).

Cyprus, which negotiated an associated agreement with the EC in 1972, applied for membership in summer 1990. In the 1987 protocol the EC signed another agreement for the establishment of a customs union over a ten-year period. However, the Turkish invasion in 1974 and the unlawful occupation of 38 percent of the island thereafter complicated the relationship of the EC with Cyprus and more so with Turkey. The main problem is that the Turkish Cypriots, who constitute 18 percent of the population, do not accept less than 30 percent of the island's territory, including the region of Morfou, which generates about 40 percent of foreign earnings. Moreover, some 50,000 Turks were implanted from Eastern Turkey and took over the property that Greek Cypriots had been forced by Turkish troops to abandon. A peaceful settlement with the two communities can speed up EC membership. Cyprus, then, a tourist and offshore financial center, would improve greatly and all Cypriots, particularly the Turkish Cypriots with a per capita income less than half of that of the Greek Cypriots, would be better off.[4]

EAST EUROPEAN CANDIDATES

Countries Close to Membership

Poland, Hungary, and the Czech and Slovak republics (CSR) are interested in joining the EC as soon as the related institutional and economic reforms have been made. Similar aspirations prevail in Russia and other former communist states.

The EC is on the verge of a monumental situation that will open up the economies of Eastern Europe, as never before, to investment and trade in food, textiles, telecommunications, and other products and services. However, East European countries, with weak economies and institutions, will not be ready for full membership for some time to come. Moreover, they may fear colonization by their Western brethren, particularly Germany. Nevertheless, they continue to emphasize their connections with the EC and they have started to negotiate closer relations.

Since the collapse of communism, trade of the East European countries with the EC has increased sharply, accounting for more than half of their foreign trade. Recently, each country signed an interim association agreement aimed at its preparation for full membership in ten years. As a result, their products would have easier access to the EC, whereas few reciprocal obligations were imposed.

Although full membership of the East European countries to the EC is not expected soon, it will not take such a long transitional period as that of Turkey (since 1964), because there is not much difference in cultural, sociopolitical, religious, and economic conditions.

In the process of widening the Community, the EC Commission proposed elimination of tariffs over six years for imports from Poland, Hungary, and the Czech and Slovak republics. However, difficult problems and significant reactions, particularly from France, are expected from the opening of the EC markets to East European commodities such as textiles, coal, steel, and mainly agricultural and dairy products.

Regarding the split of the Czech and the Slovak republics, approved by the 300-seat Czechoslovakian parliament (183 votes in favor) on November 25, 1992, the EC, eager to minimize economic and political disruptions, warned them to form strong customs unions between themselves. Otherwise, each will have to negotiate a new association agreement, probably with less favorable terms.

A joining of Poland, Hungary, CSR, and other neighboring countries with the EC may lead to a further postponement of using a single currency in all member-nations in favor of another important cause—that is, the economic and political anchoring of these East European states. However, the aspirations of these and other former communist countries have been diminished somewhat because of the initial delays in the ratification or modification of the EC Treaty of Maastricht (1991) regarding the introduction of a common currency and the establishment of a European Central Bank before 1999. After all the EC members realign their currencies, it may be easier for the EC to reach out to Eastern Europe.

In almost all East European countries and Russia, free market reforms, privatization of state enterprises, and political democratization are rapidly enacted in order to make their systems similar to those of the EC. In the process of privatization, a part of ownership shares is usually given or sold at low prices to the employees working for these privatized state enterprises. Similar schemes of employee participation prevail in almost all EC countries, such as employee stock ownership plans (ESOPs) in Britain, codetermination or comanagement in Germany, and "popular capitalism" in France. Such similarities in economic organization help stimulate trends toward further EC expansion.

On the other hand, workers and individuals may have not enough money to buy state enterprises in auctions or otherwise. In some cases, enterprise executives, who were managers under the former communist system, and other domestic and foreign gangs create phony joint ventures to get export-import licenses and loans to buy vouchers or shares from individuals to control ownership. Some of them are engaged in illegal trade in precious metals, uranium for nuclear weapons, car thefts, and even prostitution and drug trafficking. Such operations, which can be observed in Russia, Poland and other East European countries, delay economic and political reforms and act as serious drawbacks to European integration.

The recent reforms in Eastern Europe brought a severe increase in exchange rates and a decline in per capita GDP, in terms of U.S. dollars. In Poland, for example, exchange rates increased drastically mainly after the "shock therapy" of January 1990 (from 503 zlotys per dollar in 1988 to 9,500 in 1990), whereas per capita GDP declined from $1,900 in 1985 to $1,700 in 1990.

As Table 2.3 shows, the per capita GNP of Poland, the former Czecho-slovakia, and Hungary is relatively low. However, that of the EC is far higher. From that standpoint, a number of years may be needed for these and other East European countries to be ready for EC membership. Nevertheless, a transitional period of associated membership may be used for economic and sociopolitical adjustment for full membership, as was used for other EC members in the past.

The Balkans and the EC

In order to induce de-Balkanization, stimulate social and economic devel-opment, and reduce the danger of a wider conflict in the Balkans, the Eu-ropean Community can move toward a closer cooperation agreement with the former Yugoslav republics and eventually the other Balkan countries (Albania, Bulgaria, Romania). The cost to the EC from tariff reduction and regional development and other assistance would be less than the ongoing cost of military involvement through the United Nations and NATO, and other nations including the United States and probably Russia.

An effective policy not only for the EC but for the United States and other countries may be to support an associated and even full membership of the former Yugoslav republics and other neighboring countries in the European Community. This would reduce ethnic and religious conflicts, rendering existing borders unimportant and giving hope for economic and sociopolitical improvement.

A closer EC cooperation with these republics would help increase invest-ment and trade, particularly with Germany, Austria (which is a serious can-didate for EC membership), and Greece (a full member of the EC since 1981). Thereafter, investment and trade with other countries, mainly the United States and Japan, would also increase. The main problem of the Balkan countries' entrance in the EC is their low per capita income ($5,464 average in 1990), compared to that of the EC ($13,328). However, Ireland, Greece, Spain, and Portugal were in a similar condition before their entrance in the EC, whereas Turkey with even lower per capital income ($1,350) has been associate member of the Community since 1964.

Furthermore, Greece, as a full member of the EC, can play a leading role in the EC-Balkan relations. Nevertheless, like other EC member nations, Greece, as well as Italy, faced a serious problem of Albanian refugees in March 1991 and later, and more refugees are expected from other neigh-boring republics, as long as the ethnic conflicts continue.

An EC enlargement to the Balkan countries would be advantageous not only to Greece, through more efficient transportation networks, but to all EC members, which would use the Balkan Peninsula as a natural bridge for mutual trade and investment with the Middle East. Already, negotiations are conducted between the EC and Romania, Bulgaria, and former Yugoslav republics for tariff reduction.

DEEPENING VERSUS ENLARGEMENT

Monetary and Political Union

The agreement of Maastricht, signed by the 12 EC member nations in December 1991, provided for the creation of a European monetary union (EMU), which aims at the establishment of a central bank (EuroFed), and a single currency by 1997 if a majority of members qualify, otherwise, by 1999 at the latest. Also, it calls for moves toward a political union and military cooperation. This agreement revitalized "Eurooptimism," regarding closer cooperation and EC deepening, which prevailed primarily before the mid–1980s. It favors a deeper Community with strict budgetary and monetary standards for inflationary controls and exchange rate stability.

A number of EC member nations ratified the Maastricht agreement. Ireland voted in favor (69 percent) on June 18, 1992, as did Greece (286 out of 300 parliament deputies) on July 31, 1992. Likewise, Italy and Spain ratified the treaty, as did France in a referendum, but with a small majority of the voters (51 percent).

In a referendum of May 18, 1993, Denmark approved the Maastricht Treaty by 56.3 percent to 43.2 percent. In a previous referendum (June 23, 1992), the treaty was rejected by 50.3 percent to 49.7 percent. However, the EC granted Denmark (and Britain) the right not to participate in the monetary union and other key provisions of the treaty.

By June 1993, all EC members had ratified the treaty, except Britain and Germany, which were expected to do so after the constitutional courts of both countries decided on the legal status regarding the social chapter, individual rights, and other issues. Nevertheless, both houses of the German Parliament approved the treaty in December 1992, as did Britain's House of Commons in July 1993. By October 1993, both courts decided favorably and the Maastricht Treaty is in force.

Some Germans and Britons oppose monetary and political union of the EC. Thus, prominent German economists put out a manifesto in which they expressed their disagreement for the replacement of the deutsche mark (DM) by the European Currency Unit (ECU). Moreover, many farmers, particularly in France, object to certain EC directives concerning standardization of products, as well as to the EC-U.S. agreement concerning reduction of farm-product subsidies. On the other hand, northern EC countries want to reduce their budget contributions regarding the support of the poorer southern member countries.

There are cases, though, in which EC members follow different policies than those dictated by the Maastricht Treaty. Germany, for example, increased substantially its interest rates in the summer of 1992, in order to avoid inflationary pressures stemming from its unification in October 1990. As a result, funds were drawn to the DM and severe pressures were put on the weak currencies of the other EC nations. This was particularly so for Britain and Italy, which left the European Monetary System (EMS, established in 1979). Moreover, Spain devalued its currency in September 1993 and was permitted by the EC to devalue it again, as was Portugal. On May 13, 1993, Spain devalued the peseta by 8 percent and Portugal the escudo by 6.5 percent. Other weak currencies, including the Danish krone, the Irish pound, and even the relatively stable French franc faced pressures of devaluation. Such disturbances proved that the convergence of fiscal and monetary policies and the EC deepening would be difficult at least in the short run.

On the other hand, Norway raised its key lending rate in two steps from 10 to 25 percent, whereas Sweden allowed its currency to float against the ECU. Although they are not members of the EC, both countries had pegged their currencies to the Exchange Rate Mechanism of the EC, until Sweden dropped out in November 1992.

All these problems and particularly pushing for an early monetary union may dig a deep ditch between the EC and other candidate member-countries, particularly those of Eastern Europe. Nevertheless, changes and compromises are expected to coordinate related policies and prepare the ground for further EC enlargement.

Sociopolitical Considerations

The dissolution of the Warsaw Pact and the gradual weakening of the American commitment to NATO increased the desire to broaden the EC eastward, from the standpoint of defense, as well. Thus, the 38-nation Conference on Security and Cooperation in Europe (CSCE) decided to establish a small secretariat in Prague, an office in Warsaw, and a center in Vienna (Chapter of Paris, November 1990), in order to prevent ethnic and other conflicts. However, mainly because of the required unanimity, CSCE has not been effective regarding the disintegration and the ethnic and religious conflicts in the former Yugoslavia, where echoes of World War I are currently heard. As the EC expands, difficult cooperation problems and pressures are expected from fragmenting tendencies by the absorption of the EFTA countries and the political and economic transformation of the East European countries.

Nevertheless, Britain favors EC expansion as an insurance against a supranational Community and as a way of palliating workers' rights and socialist tendencies. Also, Germany, a federal state, favors EC enlargement, in a federated form, for trade and investment expansion, although there is a serious problem of streams of immigrants expected to enter the country. Moreover, Germany may want to increase its political power by incorporating regions in the Czech and Slovak republics, as well as in Austria, Slovenia, Croatia, Ukraine, and the Baltics, with which it has historical and ethnic relations.

The question of EC enlargement versus deepening is related to the specter of new immigrants not only into Germany but in almost all other EC member-nations. In some cases, refugees and other immigrants have different cultural and religious backgrounds. For example, Muslims from Turkey and North Africa primarily enter Germany, France, Spain, and Britain. However, skin-heads and neo-Nazis in Germany, Jean-Marie Le Pen's National Front in France, and other conservative groups oppose such an immigration "inva-sion." With the expected end to border controls in 1995, the immigration problem may be intensified, unless coordinated measures are taken. Such developments may delay EC enlargement, at least in the short run.

Nevertheless, there are objections to the enlargement of the EC. France is reluctant to accept it because it would hold back an expected strong Europe to counterbalance a North American common market and the Asian-Pacific Rim. Britain, which is considered, mainly in France, as the "Trojan horse" of the United States to destroy the EC, seems to support enlargement for purposes of staving off a strong European federalism, which it mistrusts. Others fear that an EC enlargement with Austria and Eastern Europe would make Germany a powerful economy that would dominate Europe.

From a practical standpoint, institutional reforms are needed to accom-modate a growing EC for effective decision making and policy implemen-tation. The European Commission with more and more members would have a hard time agreeing on important decisions and monitoring application of its directives by individual members. The same thing can be said for ministerial meetings and a swelling European Parliament with all the trap-pings of legislative delays. Pessimists feel that enlargement may lead to in-flexibility and ever-growing crises.[5]

The resurgent economic nationalism and the difficulty meeting the limits on budget deficits by a number of member-countries (except France, Den-mark, and Ireland) may lead to a two-track approach regarding monetary union. Countries such as France and Germany with strong and relatively stable economies can proceed faster in monetary union, whereas countries with weaker economies such as Britain, Italy, Spain, and Greece can proceed slower. To facilitate the transition to a central bank and the monetary union, the EC established the European Monetary Institute in 1993. In any case, the exchange rate mechanism (ERM), already in operation, proved to be largely successful in currency realignment and exchange rate stability among the EC partners, thereby promoting intraregional trade and investment.

FUTURE PROSPECTS

As the European Community moves toward common fiscal and monetary policies and political union, serious questions remain: Can the gradual deepening of the EC be combined with a gradual broadening to engulf 18 or 24 or even more European countries? Is enlargement of the EC a recipe for its weakening, or is it a historical, economic, and political necessity?

For the EC to achieve its main goals—that is, "peace and the refusal to decline"—it should be enlarged to an ultimate membership of all the European nations. Although there are deeply rooted cultural and ethnic differences and many doubts and quarrels may appear in the process of enlargement, the momentum should remain irreversible. Going back to a divided and belligerent Europe would be horrible, as history has proven repeatedly.[6]

To meet the challenge of the coming economic-political battle with the United States and Japan and the preferential blocs they organize—that is, the North American Free Trade Agreement and the Asian-Pacific Rim—Europe has to move fast to heal differences and enlarge itself to an effective producer empire. By adding the advanced EFTA countries and the educated and low-wage peoples of Eastern Europe, it should not be obsessed with short-term obstacles but adopt advanced technology and cooperative policies that look forward to long-run goals into the twenty-first century.

Using short-run strategies for long-run goals, the EC should gradually engulf not only EFTA and East European countries, but also some of the republics of the Commonwealth of Independent States (the former Soviet Union). Because of the high degree of interdependence of these republics, it can be expected that they may form a new common market, based not on Moscow's dictated policies as in the past, but on voluntary agreements and democratic procedures. Such an "Eastern Economic Community," if established, could be a serious competitor to the EC.

Rapid reforms and adjustments in Poland, the Czech and Slovak republics, Romania, Bulgaria, Albania, and the former Yugoslav republics, as well as Cyprus, Malta, and Turkey toward EC membership would strengthen democratic institutions and increase trade and investment, particularly in hotels, telecommunications, printing, and financial and other services. It should be recognized, though, that it is difficult for the former communist economies of Europe to break the chains of centralized controls and change the policies of subsidized prices and guaranteed sales. Furthermore, many state enterprises are run by Workers' Councils, which present problems in the process of privatization and the spread of "peoples' capitalism," through the democratization of property ownership. Depending on future developments, the absorption of other European countries may transform the EC to a less cohesive Community. Already, there are arguments of a Community of different speeds and tiers.

Specifically, the East European countries, including those of the Balkan Peninsula and Russia, are in a stage of dramatic changes from a command and bureaucratic system to a market system. However, they need Western help, not in the form of welfare, but in the form of technical, managerial, and financial assistance, which would help revitalize their economies, so they would be able to join the EC club. By helping them to move forward, the West would be helped as well.

Finally, an EC enlargement does not necessarily lead to a weak and chaotic Europe, particularly when there is a gradual acceptance of new EC members, with certain adjustment required, as happened in the past. Assuming that the EC economic and political goals are accepted, other European countries may join the Community, which can reach even 50 members, an equal number of the American states, and form the "United States of Europe."

3

Economic Organization

PRIVATE VERSUS PUBLIC SECTOR

The limitations of the private and public sectors or the avoidance of extremes and the pursuit of the "mean" were advocated centuries ago by Solon, Aristotle, and other philosophers in ancient Greece. Thus, Solon introduced legislation to protect people from excesses of wealth and poverty. He thought that neither too much freedom nor oppression should prevail and that saturation feeds arrogance. He also restricted the maximum amounts to be spent on public entertainment and for the funerals of public officials. These concepts were reinforced by the Pythagorian doctrine of "limit" and the Aristotelian principle of "mean" or moderation. Although Aristotle supported private property and the private sector in general, criticizing Plato's communism and arguing that common ownership means common neglect, he suggested that some form of private possession with common use would bring about an effective democratic system where the two sisters equality of opportunity and liberty would prevail. In this system there would be a steady balance, an equilibrium in life with nothing in excess.[1]

A similar egalitarian social order with equality in the workplace, the polity, and the home was wished by Charles Fourier, C.-H. Saint-Simon, Thomas More, and Edward Bellamy. In some cooperatives owned by workers or communities and in small businesses operated by self-employed people, proposals for further democratic division of labor with rotation in positions and occupations, more learning in class and on the job, equal access to the means of production, and a constrained inequality are put forward. In France, Sweden, New Zealand, as well as other economies, there are indications of such socioeconomic trends.

Public enterprises are criticized as bureaucratic and inefficient. They are considered as political creatures that are influenced by pressure groups and politicians for more employment and low prices. As the critics say, the private sector is controlled by the government but the public sector is controlled by nobody. Poor management by political appointees and high costs from excessive union pressures, combined with low prices for social reasons, lead to frequent deficits and therefore to government subsidies of such public enterprises.

Max Weber stressed what Confucius and Plato initially pointed out centuries ago: the bureaucratization of society. With the development of civilization, the bureaucracy of the economic and political life increases. In democracies, voters elect politicians who pass laws and the bureaucrats administer them, without pursuing their own interest but that of the public.

C. Northcote Parkinson, though, expressed a different view and ridiculed government and industrial bureaucracy. He thought that bureaucrats serve their own objectives and that they are inefficient, damned, and demeaned employees. As the number of public-sector employees or bureaucrats grows, work expands to fill the time available for its completion. They produce services difficult to evaluate and receive payments not much related to their output. Bureaucrats are people working not only for the government, but also for nonprofit organizations, and even for staff departments of private corporations with expenditures not related to revenues (accountants, lawyers, and people working in public relations, advertising, research, and the like). In many cases, they are criticized that they work crossword puzzles in their offices, make calls to other bureaucrats, and hatch schemes of work expansion and increases in appropriations until their generous retirement. Although these characteristics may be exaggerated, bureaucracy's criticism is growing, while the Weberian optimistic view is gradually fading.

Because of all these problems, there is a privatization drive in a number of market economies, including Britain, France, Germany, Italy, Greece, and Portugal. Similar trends of privatization or decentralization can also be observed in former planned economies, such as the USSR, Hungary, Poland, and other East European countries.[2]

Critics of privatization point out that there are certain industries that are natural monopolies and should be controlled by the public sector for the protection of the consumers from excessive profiteering and exploitation. Monopolies and even oligopolies are largely not under the power of the competitive market for controls in prices and quality. Nevertheless, industries that are important to national security, such as aerospace and nuclear industries, should be controlled by the government. Another argument against privatization is that public enterprises are used to fight inflation by maintaining low prices and to reduce unemployment by employing extra labor for economic or political reasons. Moreover, there may be cases in which the government sells public enterprises to finance budget deficits or to favor speculators who resell stocks at far higher prices to make profits. This occurred in Britain and France where traders bought such stocks and sold them at higher prices in the open market, sometimes at double prices.

Some state-run enterprises are monopolies. Privatization of such enterprises may not change their nature from the standpoint of competition and market pricing. Thus, many enterprises sold to the private sector remain monopolies and as such they resort to price fixing, supply restrictions, and other anticompetitive and antisocial measures. They become sleeping monopolies with no interest in innovations and technological advancement. As economist Maurice Allais, the 1988 French Nobel Prize winner, argues, state-owned firms, many of which exist in the EC countries, may provide services that are socially efficient and economically viable through investment and determination of optimum prices. In that case, if there is a price change, no one can be made better off without making somebody else worse off, according to the principle of Pareto's optimality. From that standpoint, performance of state-owned enterprises may be equally or more socially efficient than private monopolies. In practical terms, this depends on the efficiency of the managers involved, regardless if they operate under public or private ownership.

From the EC countries, France has a high level of public ownership in a number of vital industries. It has 100 percent ownership in the post office and railways, as all other large EC countries do. Also, France, Germany, Italy, Greece, and the Netherlands have 100 percent public ownership in telecommunications, while Spain has 50 percent ownership. Almost all EC countries have large portions of public ownership in electricity, gas, coal, steel, and airlines. The United States has 100 percent public ownership in the post office and 25 percent in electricity and railways.

Rapid privatization in countries with large agricultural and commercial sectors, such as the southern EC and some East European and ex-Soviet countries, is harder than in countries with large industrial sectors. Division of labor and specialized skills in heavy industries and other manufacturing firms make quick adjustment to privatization not so difficult. However, it took Margaret Thatcher 12 years (1978–90) to privatize major state firms and some companies, such as British Telecom, which are not yet completely privatized. At the same time, some degree of protection and financial assistance is needed for some sensitive industries, such as electronics, until they have been prepared to face foreign competition.

Cooperation of managers and workers is needed to speed up the sales of state firms to the private sector. To achieve this, the government gives a substantial stake to the people working in these firms. To transfer total ownership to workers may lead to failure, as the system of the former Yugoslavia proved in many occasions. Probably a less than majority stake of the firms to their workers and employees may lead to good results, because it enhances productive incentives of the workers without the danger of reducing the efficiency of the firms. On the other hand, majority control of the firms by their workers may lead to short-run gains for the workers but to long-run pains for the firms and the economy as a whole. Depending on the labor- or capital-intensive nature of production of enterprises, proportional employee share in business operations, preserving work incentives, and enterprises expansion can be determined.

In the final analysis, giving state enterprises away is better than keeping them in government hands. By giving shares of such enterprises to citizens, inequities are reduced or eliminated and privatization is hastened. After all, the main goal of the economy is how to improve the living conditions of the human beings. Moreover, the citizens of each country are the natural owners of state firms.

Despite the severe pains, it pays to proceed with rapid privatization so that inconsistencies and conflicts can be avoided. It is not proper to turn back to government controls and inefficient state enterprises even if results are relatively good. Perfect results are desirable, but impossible, and we should not let perfect be the enemy of good. In any case, more time is needed to assess the outcome of the reforms.

Although we do not have much experience in applying such economic changes, some form of workers' capitalism or employee stock ownership plans could be used in the process of privatization. This economic system avoids extreme wealth accumulation and monopolization by individuals or the state and combines advantages from both capitalist and socialist systems.

Under this system, which has been implemented to some extent by the United States, Japan, and the European Community, work incentives and labor productivity improve, strikes and other disputes are less likely, since employee-owners share in decision making, and income distribution is more equitable.

CHANGES IN THE PUBLIC SECTOR

By nature, men and women are normally neither giants nor dwarfs. Likewise, in order to be efficient a state should not be too big, nor should it be too small, for it must be able to sustain itself. There seems to be a maximum size that should not be exceeded by any state or other authority. However, in some cases the state becomes very large and tends to be a giant or technical person. In this case, the relationship of the state and its members becomes loose and cumbersome and frequently governments collapse under their own weight as people try to regain their freedom.

When the government is far away from the local people, it becomes more inhuman, more demanding, and oppressive. More governing authorities are created between the people and the central government, more tax revenues are required to pay for growing public expenditure, and inefficiency and bureaucracy increase. In such cases, there is more confusion in applying state laws and regulations, more arbitrary and oppressive actions by in-between bureaucrats, and more corruption, which is difficult for the state to correct. On the other hand, people at a great distance from the central authority feel isolated and abandoned; their virtues are disregarded and their talents ignored. As politicians and policymakers become overwhelmed by the plethora of cases they must deal with, they let the bureaucrat clerks implement policy measures, thus increasing confusion and corruption. It is the task of political leaders to establish an equilibrium between the ideal and the real and to make the state mechanism less oppressive and more efficient.

For the last two centuries the countries that now comprise the EC, the United States, and other Western nations have experienced public-sector growth larger than that of the private sector. The gradual increase in public spending is due to the enlargement of government activities or functions in providing social services such as internal and external security, education and welfare, subsidies to agriculture, environmental protection, and other activities, and in producing goods and services with the characteristics of publicness and a growing social interest in their allocation.

About a century ago Adolph Wagner, a German political economist, promulgated the hypothesis that social progress in industrializing nations causes a proportionately higher growth of government, or the public sector, than growth of the overall economy.[3] Although Wagner's law of the expanding state activity explains important long-term trends, it was criticized as a self-determining theory of the state that omits the influence of wars, inflations, and other disturbances that push government expenditures to successively higher plateaus.

In addition to Adolph Wagner's predictions of a growing public sector as a result of economic development and the continued pressure for social progress, other economists expect growing public expenditures and outlays for sundries, yet falling proportions of family consumption spending, with greater income. Arthur Pigou thought that the public sector would grow with increasing national income and wealth, while Alan Peacock and Jack Wiseman presented empirical evidence supporting a regular growth of governmental activity mainly because of shifts of expenditures and revenues to new, higher levels in cases of wars and social disturbances with no return to the previous lower levels (this is the displacement effect).[4]

Economic growth in modern industrial societies leads to more specialization, impersonalization, and interdependencies in economic and social life that require a larger and more efficient public sector. Furthermore, industrialization and modern technology require large amounts of capital and long-run fixed investment in public utility projects (natural monopolies), which the private sector, interested primarily in short-run profits, may hesitate or may be unable to undertake.

Rapid technological changes and new social problems may force governments to intervene and seek proper solutions (this is the inspection effect).

Directly or indirectly, the displacement and/or the inspection effects frequently lead to the concentration of economic activities in the public sector at the expense of the private sector.

Market economies, like those of the United States and Western Europe, are characterized by the dominance of the private sector. They have, nonetheless, a sizable and growing public sector. In such mixed economies, the existence and growth of the public sector are justified primarily because of the growing monopolization of the market and the failure of the free market mechanism to perform well in the allocation and distribution of resources and products in certain sectors and industries of, primarily, the public domain.

Private/public ventures might be considered as another way of using the advantages of both sectors for effective enterprising. Utilizing private management techniques in public or collective ownership might prove to be beneficial in productive capital investment and employment creation.

However, it seems that certain governmental controls and policies tend to cripple growth rates by checking private investment and real growth. As a result of such policies, work incentives tend to decline and inflationary pressures to rise. Moreover, central and local governments tend to waste resources because their outlays are not subject to the disciplines of the market. From that point of view, public spending has been tapering off in recent years as it approaches its economic and political limits.

The privatization of state-owned enterprises acquired great importance in the recent past and it is a significant theme now. Private ownership seems to work better than common ownership because it stimulates work incentives and increases productivity. As Aristotle said, "it is clearly better that property should be private," and that "common ownership means common neglect."[5] Furthermore, John Stuart Mill, Rousseau, and Schumpeter believed that greater democratization of property ownership advances human intellect and increases efficiency.

The transfer of government-managed firms to the private sector in a large scale, as practiced in the EC and other countries, is a *nova terra* that needs further exploration and research. Such transfer of ownership may take place by giving low-price vouchers to citizens in order to buy shares of state enterprises, or by selling shares to the public or foreign investors, as practiced in many countries, including France and Greece, which are in the process of privatizing their large public sectors. Partial or total ownership may be given to the workers or employees of enterprises, a measure that is similar to employee stock ownership plans in the United States and the share economy of Japan.

Currently, there is a trend toward privatization and employee ownership, which may lead to the spread of property to more and more individuals and the eventual support of the theory of "people's capitalism." This economic system avoids extreme wealth accumulation and monopolization by individuals or the state. It generates a broader distribution of wealth, which helps the stability of the economy.

On the other hand, privatization and employee ownership may not be an elixir that always works toward better performance. Individual shareholders may lack training in appointing managers, be apathetic, or be influenced by political gimmicks on serious matters of enterprise decision making. That is why the stakes given to employees are normally less than the majority in each enterprise, whereas big investment companies or mutual funds keep majority controls.

The establishment of efficient institutions regarding property titles, mortgages for credit, patent and copyright laws for a successful transformation of enterprises from the public to the private sector are of great importance.

The EC system is a hybrid of individualistic capitalism, with high incentives of production and profit making, and a social market system, with capital and labor comanagement or popular capitalism, which protects labor and supports a more equitable distribution of income and wealth. As such, it encourages investment and stimulates effective demand so that economic fluctuations can be mitigated. The Council of Economic Ministers of the EC proposed and the related European Committee adopted in July 1991 the workers' participation in the annual results of enterprises in which they work, through their sharing in the capital stock. This measure covers both private and public enterprises.[6]

Privatization in Britain

After the Labour Party came to power in 1945, substantial economic changes were introduced. High rates of unemployment and widespread inequalities that prevailed in prewar British capitalism had to be corrected. Socialization of health, nationalization of a number of industries, and other reforms made Britain, one of the oldest capitalistic nations, a welfare state, similar to Sweden and other Scandinavian countries. Moreover, the independence of a number of colonies from the British hegemony deprived it of vital resources and markets and turned the country to unfavorable balance of payments and low rates of economic growth.

Immediately after World War II, a number of industries were nationalized in Britain by the Labour Party. Thus, the coal industry was nationalized in 1946 and put under the National Coal Board, which still operates a number of mines today. It is expected, though, that the industry would be transferred to the private sector if the Conservatives remain in power. More than 25 enterprises have been sold to the private sector since 1979 when Margaret Thatcher took office, providing some $50 billion for the British Treasury. Also, garbage collection services were contracted to private firms. A number of firms were sold totally or partially to their workers and employees, including the National Freight Consortium and British Telecom.

The British privatization program is closely related to a wider share ownership policy. Recently the proportion of adults owning shares increased from below 7 percent to 19 percent. About 52 percent of all individuals owning shares have shares in only one company. This is due primarily to the employee share ownership, which is present in a number of firms, mainly in privatized enterprises. One of these firms is British Telecom, with 98 percent of its employees being shareholders. However, the proportion of the total shares owned by employees is relatively small in many such enterprises, privatized or not, and the influence of employee-owners on decisions regarding wages and other matters is limited. From that point of view, the privatization program has impact on the width and not much on the depth of employee ownership in Britain.

To improve the efficiency of health services, the conservative Tory government announced the privatization of health care by applying free market methods to the state-financed health system. However, the new system, which resembles that of the United States, is criticized by many Britons that it upgrades treatment for the wealthy and downgrades that for the poor. To diffuse opposition, the Tories argue that the system extends patient choices by allowing them and their doctors to shop for good and cheap health care. It is a reformed system under which the National Health Service continues to offer services to all persons regardless of income but at the same time provides for better choices for those who are willing to pay for higher quality health care. Variations of such a system are considered by other EC member-nations.

France's Economic Organization

After the destruction caused by World War II, Jean Monnet proposed the creation of a Planning Commissariat for which he was appointed director in 1946. The main principles of French planning were to coordinate the economy through the cooperation of trade unionists, industrialists, and civil servants toward the modernization and growth of the economy. This form of decentralized democratic (*indicatif*) planning was to improve and not replace market operations. That is why the Commissariat Général au Plan remained small, with a staff of about 100 until it was merged into a new ministry in 1981.

The postwar five-year plans—from the first one of 1947–51 and up to the tenth one of 1989–93, as well as some interim or mini plans for specific unforeseeable reasons—have aimed primarily at formulating economic targets and using fiscal and monetary policies to achieve these targets. They show the directions in which the economy ought to go rather than providing specific targets for individual firms. In recent years, entrepreneurs gradually orient their production and distribution activities toward the EC rather than within a national framework, and French planners have experienced increased difficulties in projecting and communicating national economic targets. Overall because of the peculiar characteristics of France's "indicative planning," it is argued that it is mostly talk or that it more French than planning.

The economic policy of France is based on macrostability—through demand management, decentralized or indicative planning—and microeconomic coordination—through the free market mechanism. Individual firms form their investment production and distribution plans and try to correct inconsistencies between them and other related firms and sectors. To achieve a predefined rate of growth, a process of economic coordination is pursued through national planning. Usual and pragmatic fiscal and monetary policies, adjusted to the EC relative directives, are used during the implementation stages of the plans. The process of planning is one of cooperation among producers, workers, consumers, and the government in a way that planning would supplement and inform the market to perform better, thereby preserving the dynamism of competition.

In contrast to Dutch short-term stabilization plans, French medium-term or five-year plans aim at guiding resource allocation based on forecasts regarding final demand, labor supply, and investment requirements, assuming a certain technological level and a relatively constant incremental capital output ratio (ICOR). Although French planning is not a command-type of central planning, input-output tables are used, as they are in controlled or planned economies, but not with imperative force. The plans are self-fulfilling documents based on consultations. They are supported by tax alleviations, subsidies, and credit policies.

Nevertheless, forecasts of individual firms and the aggregated sectoral projections are largely unfulfilled in practice and, in many cases, they become wild guesses, mainly because of unforeseeable changes such as the student riots and the general strike of May 1968. However, this does not mean that planning does not have pedagogic and predictive values for business executives and public enterprises. Also, policy makers on fiscal and monetary matters may use plans' predictions, not only on domestic stabilization and growth policies, but also on issues of foreign trade and exchange rates, compatible with EC integration policies and long-term socioeconomic trends in the country.

Economic planning seemed to inspire the conservative and cautious French entrepreneurs, especially in the 1950s and 1960s, and made them less fatalistic and more aggressive executives. The appreciation of the entrepreneurial class, compared to the previous honorific professional classes of civil servants, lawyers, and the like, was largely the result of the American influence in the postwar years. Otherwise, planning in France was initially adopted from the U.S. Marshall Plan for the effective allocation of American aid for the rehabilitation of Europe.

In order to reduce wealth concentration, through private ownership, and distribute the power of decision making, through workers' consultation, the French government nationalized a number of private industries. The nationalization process, which started with railroads in the 1890s and was intensified after World War II, included such industries as coal, gas, telecommunications, electric power, insurance, some steel and auto companies, as well as banks and other chemical and textile firms. In the early 1980s, about one-third of the labor force worked for the government or for firms controlled by the public sector. A number of inefficient firms were supported with subsidies by the government to avoid unemployment, a policy that is known as "lemon socialism."

Before the coming of the socialists to power in 1981, workers' participation in enterprises was weak. Enterprise committees, which were created after World War II to introduce industrial democracy (*autogestion*), were not very effective in placing workers in managerial decision-making positions. Under the pressure of global competition, management acquired a dominant role over enterprise committees. Nevertheless, creative participation of workers and social groups in management stimulates incentives and increases productivity.

Germany's Social Market Economy

The economy of Germany can be characterized as a social market economy (*soziale Marktwirtschaft*). The Basic Law (*Grundgesetz*) of 1949, serving as the country's constitution, protects private property and establishes the main economic goals (Social Security, social equity, and social progress). Ideologically, the notion of social market economy has its roots in the Freiburg school of neoliberalism, as developed mainly by Walter Eucken and Alfred Mullet-Armack. However, it was put in practice primarily after Germany was split into the Federal Republic of Germany (Bundesrepublic Deutschland) or West Germany and the German Democratic Republic or East Germany. At the end of World War II, the Allied occupation forces (Britain, France, United States) put emphasis on the rehabilitation of the country and the recovery of its economy, using mainly the market system. East Germany came under the control of the Soviet Union, which introduced the planned economic system, which was abolished with the unification of Germany in October 1990.

In Germany and other EC nations, labor unions are stronger than in other countries. For example, about 40 percent of the local labor force in Germany belongs to unions, compared to less than 20 percent in the United States. The German Federation of Unions accounts for some four-fifths of all union membership. Wage-rate determination is made on an industry basis. Unions are entitled to strike, and management can close down or lock out firms in reaction to strikes. Politically motivated strikes are not permitted. For a strike to be legal, 75 percent of the workers should approve it in a secret ballot. In Germany, unions exercise their influence mainly through nominating representatives in work councils; but in other EC countries they are comparatively more influential and collective bargaining is more important, especially in Belgium and Italy and to a large extent in Britain, France, and the Netherlands, where employers press for comanagement for gaining labor peace.

To avoid labor shortages and keep wages down, Germany has allowed, from time to time, immigration of guest workers (*Gastarbeiter*). They are mainly from Turkey (637,000 in 1981), Yugoslavia (358,000), Italy (316,000), and Greece (132,000). There were 2.1 million guest workers in 1981 or about 8 percent of the labor force of Germany, compared to 100,000 in 1956 and 2.6 million in 1973.

There are now more than 5 million foreigners living in Germany in a total population of 80 million. However, many Germans are becoming impatient with the presence of foreign workers, primarily because of persistent unemployment and rising welfare costs. Also, there are problems of allowing foreigners with eight years' residence to vote in parliamentary and local elections. There are fears from the right wing that they may vote for leftist politicians, and rightist politicians present objections.

Nevertheless, for Europe to succeed, a policy of closer integration and gradual enlargement is needed so that ethnic and border conflicts be eliminated. The EC should support and eventually engulf the East European countries and even Russia to avoid massive immigration or waves of refugees in the EC capitals from these countries and to enlarge markets and investment opportunities. It seems that there is not a better alternative for a stable and prosperous Europe in the future, although it may appear as a utopian concept at present.

As European nations try to assert sovereign separatism, there is the danger of a fragmented Europe of tribal states. On the other hand, there is a fear that in such a fragmented Europe, Germany will be the dominant force. However, Germany seeks to reassure the other European countries, particularly France, that it wants not a German Europe, but a European Germany.

In the former East Germany, Treuhandanstalt (the organization for privatization) successfully privatized more than half of the 11,427 public enterprises in less than two years from the date of unification (October 1990). It is expected that the rest of these enterprises would be privatized in the near future. Although more than a million jobs were created with the program of privatization, more jobs were lost through bankruptcies and layoffs. The net result is 17 percent unemployment, compared to zero unemployment that prevailed in the ex-socialist East Germany. Moreover, tens of billions of DMs were and still are spent by the government for the support of the unemployed workers and their families, for improvement in wages, and cancellation of debts. Nevertheless, this is a painful process of adjustment until all or most of the public enterprises are transferred to the private sector, new revenues are collected from their sales, and additional jobs are created.

Workers in Germany are represented in the firms in which they work through the works councils. Such a representation, which goes back to 1891 when consultation of labor was required for shop rules, is known as code-termination (*Mitbestimmung*). In 1952 the Works Constitution Act introduced an equal representation of capital and labor in the supervisory boards (*Aufsichtrat*) for the iron, steel, and coal industries to avoid strikes and other disturbances. In other industries, labor had one-third representation and after 1976 one-half representation in firms with more than 2,000 workers.[7]

To avoid a stalemate in the selection of the chairman of the board of directors, the codetermination law requires that the chairman be a neutral person selected by the stockholders' representatives in case of a tie voting. To have representation in the shop level, where the supervisory board rarely is involved, the law requires that companies employing five or more employees have an enterprise council to deal with wages, firings, and other personnel matters.

In practice, codetermination gives employees a voice in enterprise decision making, particularly in layoffs, wage determination, and profit sharing on the factory level. Industrial-level wage contracts are reserved for the unions. Nevertheless, codetermination or comanagement of capital and labor does not seem to influence the transformation of the economic system toward a workers' capitalism as do ESOPs in the United States and other countries.

Italy's Structure

From the standpoint of regional integration, Italy is a classical example of dualism. Compared to the industrial north, the southern part of the country is backward, with a dominant primary sector, limited industrialization, rudimentary technology, low productivity, and low per capita income. Decentralization measures taken by the government from time to time have limited developmental effects. Regional development programs, financed partially or totally by special funds of the EC, are expected to reduce the gap between the more advanced north and less developed south and eventually stop the denudation of the poor southern region. Moreover, it is argued that developmental trickling-down or spread effects and EC support would reduce existing differences and inequalities. On the other hand, new investment from other EC countries and tourism would stimulate the economy of southern Italy and stop the backwash effects of the dualistic development process. Similar results are expected for other EC less-developed regions, primarily in France, Spain, Greece, and Portugal.

Under the pressures of labor unions, the Italian government restored wage indexing to progressive taxation to avoid the offsetting of wage increases by higher taxes. According to the unions, such an indexing would benefit factory and office workers, while shopowners, farmers, and self-employed professionals can avoid paying taxes and are not much influenced by wage indexing. Such measures, though, deviate from the austerity program, and, as the International Monetary Fund warned, the borrowing requirements are expected to be high. To reduce budget deficits, Italy's government approved the privatization of the national rail system (Ente Ferrovia dello Stato) by transforming it into a joint stock company capitalized at $37.8 billion. Similar reforms are also under consideration.

Other EC Countries

Spain, which tries to follow the EC policies, faces serious problems. A number of labor unions in a work force of 11 million resort from time to time to strikes. Usually the unions ask for increases in wages but the government offers no more than the rate of inflation. In the traditional process of negotiations between government, business, and labor, workers argue that profits are large (sometimes up to 200 percent) while raises in wages and salaries are held down to less than the rate of inflation.

To reduce inflation and increase growth, the Felipe Gonzalez government implemented a mixture of free-market and socialist policy by encouraging competition and foreign investment, slashing subsidies to moribund companies, and imposing an austerity program. Initially, following the successful Swedish policy, it devalued the peseta, tightened money supply, and encouraged exports. Nevertheless, personal income tax rates remained high (up to 56 percent) and government expenditures gradually rose to 45 percent of gross national product. A number of state-owned enterprises, left by Francisco Franco, the Spanish dictator for some 40 years, were privatized and companies could lay off workers more easily.

Portugal is also in the process of privatizing a large part of its public sector. Since 1989, about 60 enterprise groups, from banks and insurance companies to large industrial enterprises, including the refineries of Petrogal, have been transferred or are in the process of changing ownership from the public to the private sector. Workers and employees can buy shares of these enterprises on favorable terms, whereas private entrepreneurs and investors complain that they pay high prices to buy such shares and borrow large amounts of money from domestic and foreign banks to finance such purchases. It would seem that the Portuguese program of privatization is another example of "people's capitalism."

EC ESOPs

As mentioned, Britain and France have become resolved to the process of denationalization or privatization of state or semistate enterprises. Thus,

British Telecom (the state-owned telephone monopoly), Ferranti (the industrial electronics firm), British Aerospace (the aircraft and missiles firm), Britoil, British Sugar, Jaguar (the luxury car maker), British Petroleum, Cable and Wireless, and British Airways, which were totally or partially owned by the state, have been or are in the process of total or partial denationalization or have been taken to the market, with employee participations. The main reason is to encourage competition and increase efficiency. Thus, the stocks of the denationalized Telecom were divided between British institutions (47 percent), Telecom employees and the public (39 percent), and foreign investors (14 percent—United States, Canada, and Japan).

Moreover, the National Freight Company (producing trucks) was sold to employees in 1981. Since then it has become profitable and is expanding for the first time. On the other hand, two private shipyards, Tyne and Scott Lithgrow, agree with the workers' unions to cut wage costs and increase productivity so that they can eliminate the threat of closure.

To promote employee ownership and popular capitalism, Britain introduced recently a law that provides for the establishment of employee stock ownership plans. The lack of a legal status and the uncertainty over tax-exemption of ESOPs have discouraged British firms from ESOPing in the past. Now with tax relief assured, a number of companies transfer ownership share to their workers and employees. In a typical case, a trust or an ESOP borrows money and buys a company's equity. The company in subsequent years makes tax-free payments to the trust, which repays its debt and releases equivalent amounts of shares to the employees.

At times, labor unions buy and sell companies instead of letting others do that. Also, cross-Atlantic raiders are involved in ESOPs. Thus Sir James Goldsmith, the British raider who acquired the parent Crown Zellerbach Corporation a few years ago, will keep 10 percent of the equity and the rest (about 30 percent) will go to the other unions' financiers and debt holders. However, out of a number of leveraged ESOPs recently, only a few were initiated by unions.

Although there are only 15 ESOPs in Britain, compared to more than 10,000 in the United States, the tax relief and other advantages they enjoy would speed their spread to other companies as well. A conventional management buyout (MBO) would enjoy tax relief only if it includes an ESOP through distribution of shares to the workers. The split of ownership through ESOPs is supported by almost all political persuasions including the right-wing Adam Smith Institute and the left-wing Fabian Society in Britain. They are neither a capitalistic tool as wealth and power is split to many workers, nor a creeping collectivist tool as employees and workers become capital or wealth owners. The tax relief applies to those British ESOPs that distribute all shares to workers within seven years. However, the law discourages family-owned firms from establishing ESOPs as yet, because they must pay taxes on capital gains realized from sales of equity to an ESOP.[8]

Depending on the political philosophy of the British government in power, some companies were taken over by the state and later were transferred to the private sector to be taken over again by the state and so on. Thus, the steel industry was nationalized in 1949, denationalized in the 1950s, and renationalized in 1967. Similar companies, such as British Gas, the coal industry, and the public electric power corporation, as well as shipyards, airports, bus services, armament factories, hotels, ferries, public housing, garbage collection, and a host of other services are all being prepared for sale or leasing by the British government to the private sector or to their workers. Private and overseas investors, in addition to pension funds, and the employees of these companies are expected to be the major stockholders. However, the Labour Party has pledged to renationalize some privatized companies to protect the consumers and the workers.

Along these lines, France embraces "popular capitalism" and is in the process of selling off government-owned industry to employees and other private investors. The campaign of denationalizing some 65 public enterprises, a number of which had been nationalized by Charles de Gaulle, has been warmly received by employee-investors and other domestic and foreign financiers. They include such companies as Compagnie Générale d'Électricité, Paribas Banque, and other major commercial banks.

In Western Europe as a whole, a total of about 2,000 state enterprises, worth some $130 billion, are expected to be sold in a few years. The main reason for this denationalization is to encourage competition, increase efficiency, and remove governmental subsidies.

As in all market economies, the German economy is influenced by private- and public-sector activities. The social market economy (SME) of Germany is based primarily on the private sector, the free market mechanism, and labor-capital management or codetermination (*Mitbestimmung*). However, positive governmental activities are necessary to create a healthy environment for the market system, to break monopolies and cartels (through the Law Against Limitations on Competition, which is similar to U.S. antitrust legislation), and to provide Social Security and welfare.

Nevertheless, public and union-owned enterprises play an important role in certain sectors of the German economy such as transportation, communications, postal services, dwellings construction, and, to some extent, banking, and even mining and metallurgical operations. Union-owned enterprises, created to maximize social benefits, not profits, include Gruppe Neue Heimat (a large apartment construction company), Coop-Unternehmen (the second largest retail trade firm), and the Bank fur Gemein Wirtschaft (an interregional bank, providing credit facilities all over Germany).

Through large holding companies the federal government owns stocks in more than 3,000 firms. However, the waves of denationalization and decontrolization that prevail all over Europe, including the former USSR, engulfed Germany as well. Volkswagen and Veba are two companies in which privatization (*Privatisierung*) was carried out recently, through sales of shares to private groups, employees, and low-income persons on a preferential basis. This mixed economic system, combined with a relative harmonious labor-capital comanagement, and a high rate of saving and investment, is mainly responsible for the post-World War II German rapid growth or the so-called economic miracle (*Wirtschaftswunder*).

Employee ownership is spreading not only to large EC countries, where a number of state-owned or private enterprises are sold partially or totally to their employees and workers, but small ones as well. Thus in Portugal, Uniao Cervejeira, SA (which makes soft drinks), sold one-third of 3.2 million shares to its employees for 2,300 escudos or $15.3 each, about one-half to the public for 2,500 escudos or $16.7, and one-sixth to small savers and emigrant workers for 2,400 escudos or $16 each.

Related legislation for the establishment of ESOPs has also been enacted in Greece since 1988. It provides for the option of giving shares to employees and workers by the companies in which they work, instead of wage increases and other premiums. Because of the advantages of ESOPs expected, especially for weak and problematic public and private enterprises, all the political parties voted in favor of this legislation in the Greek Parliament.

In order to boost the single market's "social dimension," the European Commission considers certain ways of workers' participation in the process of decision making of the companies in which they work. One way is to follow the German model in which workers are represented on supervisory boards. Another way is that of France, with separate workers' councils. Or a new system to be agreed upon by management and the work force via collective bargaining may give the workers the option to participate or not. It seems that the Commission would base its decision regarding workers' participation on Articles 54 and 100A of the Treaty of Rome, which allow majority voting on such matters. To smooth out disagreements, particularly from Britain, the commissioners prefer to use the term "involvement" instead of "participation." Moreover, proposals are advanced that workers would merely share information on plant closures, alliances, and other strategic decisions but not consultation on day-to-day operations. Nevertheless, the European Parliament wants some form of workers' involvement in decision making.

A company under the European statute would be subject to the EC rules not only regarding workers' involvement but mergers, acquisitions, and joint ventures, as well as a single tax code. Companies incorporating under the EC rules could be able to write off losses in one member-nation against taxes in other member-nations. However, a number of the EC governments object to this privilege because they fear that their tax revenue might be reduced.

Harmonization of National Policies

Concerning the new trend of economic organization and market monopolization via mergers and acquisitions, there are questions of weakening national sovereignty and rising corporate colonialism in market economies. Although ideologies pass and nations remain, antitrust and takeover regulations in almost all nations become ineffective because of the growing capital concentration required by modern technology and international competition.

There are national differences in antimonopoly and takeover regulations that present more opportunities in certain countries, such as the United States, Britain, and the Netherlands, than in others, such as Germany, France, and Japan. For example, Germany has its traditional differences in takeovers through worker participation in management changes, and Japan through its cultural and family-type relations of companies and their employees.

On the other hand, banks in Germany may hold up to 20 percent of a company's shares; while in Italy the government controls some 26 percent of the entire stock market and the Agnelli, Benedetti, and Feruzzi families another 32 percent. Moreover, companies in the Netherlands can limit the voting power of shareholders or issue defense preference shares with a sizable discount in price; but in Belgium, with a more liberal legislation on takeovers and acquisitions, more than 50 percent of the market is owned by the French.

However, such limitations and differences in the EC and other European countries present problems for the integration of Europe and the formation of Europeanized companies, as well as for further economic cooperation with the United States, Japan, and other investor nations.

Nevertheless, the U.S. merger mania does not prevail in Europe. Mostly company stocks are held within families or related institutions, and mergers and acquisitions are primarily friendly. In Europe, joint ventures are preferable to takeovers.

In harmonization of the legal system of the member-countries, regarding corporate, antitrust, environmental, securities, labor, and other intra-Community relations, serious problems appear in the process of integration of the EC. Business and investment decisions are to be affected by such a harmonization not only among the member-nations but also between the EC and other associated and outside nations, including East European and former Soviet republics.[9]

The EC countries are recovering from the symptoms of nationalistic superiorities and the sickness of Eurosclerosis and are moving gradually toward closer cooperation and eventual unification. They are trying to revive the unifying aspirations that emerged from World War II. The success lesson of the United States may lead them to the formation of the United States of Europe. The community of the 12 European democracies is winning a fine victory over national egoism and prejudice without much cost. It is moving from a bitter past to a better future, and the United States is expected to play a vital role in this movement, as it did in the past.

At present, it is important for all Europeans, regardless of previous disputes and different economic and political systems, to intensify their efforts to unify and rebuild the "new Europe" for the sake of their peace and prosperity.

4

Fiscal, Monetary, and Trade Policies

FISCAL POLICY

This chapter deals with similarities and differences in fiscal and monetary policies. It examines governmental expenditures and taxation and their changes over time, as well as the relationship of money supply and credit to inflation, interest rates, and other related variables.

With a growing public sector in the EC economies, fiscal policy acquires great importance not only on matters of financing governmental expenditures but also on matters of countercyclical policy. General government expenditures include central or federal, state, and local government spending. The federalism of Germany establishes a division of powers between national and state governments, in contrast to other nonfederal countries such as Britain, France, Italy, Spain, Greece, and Portugal. Governmental spending involves payments for goods and services and other transfer and intergovernmental activities.

The EC public sectors have grown proportionately at a faster rate than the overall economy in the long run. For the EC countries (average of Britain, France, Germany, and Italy), general government expenditures increased from 36 percent of national income in 1950 to 50 percent in current years, as Figure 4.1 shows.

The expansion of the public sector, or the growing average propensity to spend, is the result of ever-increasing demand for government services, including those of regional and local units of government, which in turn leads to high elasticities of government expenditures with respect to national income. Such elasticities—that is, the percent change in government expenditures over the percent change in national income—were high (varying from

Figure 4.1
The Growing Public Sector of the EC

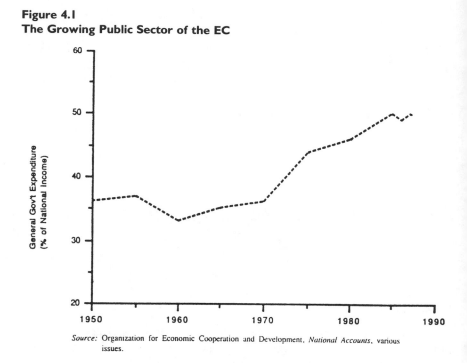

Source: Organization for Economic Cooperation and Development. *National Accounts*, various issues.

1.2 to 1.4), meaning that for each percentage increase in national income there was a higher than 1 percentage increase in general government expenditures for the EC, particularly after 1965.

Although there is a great gap in the per capita gross national product (GNP) among the EC countries, the differences in government outlays are not as large. Spain, Greece, and Portugal with relatively low per capita GNP have general government expenditure varying from 40 to 44 percent of national income, compared to 50 to 57 percent for Germany and France. The advanced EC countries with a larger public sector than the United States are taking measures of denationalization and relative reduction of government expenditures. As a result, the proportion of national income spent by the government may be the same or lower in the near future.

To achieve less intervention, less spending, and more competition, the EC reduced and even abolished governmental subsidies that were given to some industries in accordance with Article 92 of the EC. They are about 82 billion ECUs or $90 billion per year. Italy holds the first place in such subsidies followed by Germany, France, and Britain. However, subsidies are permitted for poor regions, for social policy, for programs of economic importance for the EC, and for cases in which free trade is not interrupted.

In 1992 the EC budget expenditures were 66.5 billion ECUs and are projected to be 87.5 billion ECUs in 1997. The credits for the Common Agricultural Policy were 53.1 percent of the total budget in 1992 and 45.3 percent projected for 1997; whereas for structural operations, including the newly created cohesion fund to help member countries enter the European Monetary Union, the percentages are 28 and 33.5, respectively.[1]

Favorable international economic conditions, particularly for agricultural prices, are expected to reduce the burden of member contributions to the Community's budget in the foreseeable future.

For the European Community, general government taxes, on the average, are higher (around 50 percent of national income) than those of the United States. In recent years, Britain cut its top marginal income tax from 83 to 60 percent, Italy from 72 to 62 percent, Portugal from 80 to 69 percent, Ireland from 77 to 65 percent, Sweden from 87 to 80 percent, and Greece from 63 to 50 percent. Further tax cuts are considered by some of these and other nations for work stimulation and higher productivity.

In general, the EC countries do not have high proportions of indirect taxes to national income (about 15 percent). Indirect (or consumption) taxes that are imposed initially on objects (*in rem* taxes) and include excises (mainly on fuel, beverages, tobacco, travel), sales taxes, value added taxes, stamps, and tariffs are levied against goods and services independently of the owner's ability to pay.

Indirect taxes, as percentages of total taxes, are higher in low-income EC countries such as Greece, Ireland, and Portugal than in the advanced EC countries. From that standpoint and as a result of the EC integration, a relative decrease in indirect taxes and structural changes in both direct and indirect taxes are expected to occur in the near future in the low-income countries. In EC countries with high indirect taxes, reduction or elimination of excise taxes and tariffs, according to the directives of the EC, would reduce tax revenue and exert pressure on domestic industries producing the same goods or close substitutes to imported goods. However, such a competitive process would reduce inefficiency, despite the expected detrimental effects on employment conditions.

The value added tax (VAT) is primarily a consumption tax and as such is included in indirect taxes. The VAT, which has been introduced by the EC member states, is a proportional tax on the value of all goods and services included in the firms' invoices, reduced by the amount of previous VAT liability. As the supporters of VAT argue, this tax is simple: it reduces consumption expenditures, decreases tax evasion, improves the flexibility of the tax structure, and stimulates investment and economic growth.

In the European Community the VATs have either replaced inefficient turnover or cascade taxes (e.g., in France, Germany, and the Netherlands), or have been required for EC membership in the Community. The VAT was introduced in France in 1954. At present, it raises about 50 percent of tax revenue in that country. In Germany, the VAT was proposed in 1918 and introduced in 1968. There it provides about 25 percent of government revenue. In Britain it provides 15 percent.

The revenues of the EC countries as a group come primarily from VATs (1 percent of the VAT collected by the member nations), customs duties, and special levies on agricultural imports (including sugar duties). Revenue from VATs is about 50 percent of the total revenue of the EC, as a unit separate from that of the individual member countries.

Most of the collected revenues are spent for the support of prices of agricultural products by a special EC fund known as FEOGA (Fond Européen d'Orientation et de Garantie Agricole); around 10 percent for the regional development of backward areas; and the rest for social policies, research, energy, and for aid to Third World countries (about 6 percent). Greece, Italy, Portugal, Spain, and to some extent France are the main recipients of subsidies for agricultural products and regional development.

The EC VAT rates vary from 6 percent for basic goods to 16 percent for most goods and services, and up to 38 percent for luxury goods. However, the sixth directive of the EC provides that enterprises with sales less than 10,000 European Currency Units are not liable to pay VATs. Moreover, there are special treatments for special small enterprises and those involved in agriculture, travel, and petroleum products. Also, exports and capital goods are normally exempted from taxation, so that investment and domestic production will be stimulated. There is discussion, though, to reduce and harmonize the VAT to 14–20 percent for most goods and to lower the rates to the range between 0 and 9 percent for "social sensitive" items. Most of the member-countries are willing to go on zero-rating taxes for food and children's clothing.

The support of social programs and the formation of welfare states, without a parallel increase in productivity, led to huge budgetary deficits and inflationary pressures in many EC countries. In addition, for decades governments of countries with market economies spent large amounts of money to subsidize moribund public enterprises in order to avoid high unemployment. However, this policy perpetuated inefficiency and low productivity. To reverse this trend, extensive privatization programs—that is, transfer of enterprises from the public to the private sector—were implemented.

Fiscal Measures in Germany

Unlike other EC countries, Germany has a federal system that allows state and local governments to have their own large budgets. France, Britain, Italy, and Spain, as well as other EC nations, have a centralized fiscal system with strong central government budget and weak state and local public finance. Furthermore, the Social Security System introduced first by Germany in the 1880s is independent of the central or federal government budget. Contributions by the employers and employees are collected by an independent institution, which is responsible for benefit payments. Normally, when its budget is in deficit, the central government budget would cover the difference.

Although there are some differences in taxation between Germany and other EC member-nations, there is a trend toward gradual adjustment to a common tax system in all these nations. At present, the most important tax is the VAT, which replaced turnover and other consumption taxes. In Germany the VAT was introduced in January 1968 and accounts for about one-fourth of the budget revenue of the federal government. According to the tax harmonization directive of the EC, all member-nations were to introduce the VAT by January 1, 1970. The general VAT rate is 11 percent at each stage of production with many agricultural products paying 5.5 percent, while some basic items are exempt from taxation. Luxury products pay higher VAT rates (up to 36 percent). Like the United States, Germany has a tripartite (federal, state, local) tax system with states absorbing about one-half and localities one-fourth of federal taxes. For the rest of Europe, this unique system does not apply.

Germany has a 10 percent tax on interest income, but many Germans do not declare it. This measure is driving domestic and foreign savers and investors to withholding-tax-free Luxembourg, to mark-dominated Eurobonds, or to relatively strong currencies including those of the United States, Britain, Canada, Australia, France, and Denmark with high interest rates and no tax withholding. It is expected that this measure will be introduced in all EC nations. However, there are pressures for modification or abolishment of this unpopular tax. For example, the exemption on interest income may be raised from DM 300 to 2,000 ($1,075).

The cost of the unification of Germany was expected to be absorbed by West Germany or its EC partners without strong spillovers on their economies. However, wages were higher than productivity, growth declined, fiscal transfers continued, and inflation increased during the early 1990s. All these forced interest rates to move from 6 to 10 percent, generating disturbances in the exchange rate mechanism currencies. As a result, investment from West to East declined and the convergence of the two German economies required far more time than initially projected.

The EC is circumscribed or preempted in many policy areas by Bonn or Germany's private sector. To avoid national monopolization and encourage democratic decision making, the EC members are to work together to resolve the complex global challenges of the coming decades.

France's Economic Policy

The adopted social policies in 1981–83 led France to inflationary pressures, trade deficits, and a decline in confidence for the franc. The reforms introduced since 1984 changed the course of the economy toward market-oriented incentives, decontrolling prices, and liberalizing capital markets. The idea of implementing socialist economic policies was largely abandoned, the fight against inflation continued, and an environment conducive to new investment was created. Nevertheless, Mitterrand said that he will end the program to sell government stakes in some 60 French companies, many of which were nationalized shortly after his first term started in 1981. Pragmatism, though, suggests that partial privatizations will occur in some firms, such as the Rhone-Poulenc chemical concern and the Pechiney metal company.

To encourage investment and stimulate economic growth, tax breaks to businesses are proposed. One of such measures is to reduce corporate income taxes on reinvestment earnings to 34 percent from the general level of 42 percent. Even the idea of reimposing a tax on large fortunes is challenged on the ground that large amounts of capital may leave France and reduce needed competitiveness in the more open European economy. Other measures expected to be introduced by the French government would aim at avoiding clashes between labor and management that could otherwise hobble the French economy.

Under competitive pressures from other EC countries, France's political ideology became less important as related to the economic issues of recent years.

Budget Deficits for Italy

Italy has complained that NATO neglects the Mediterranean member nations, particularly Italy, Greece, and Spain, and pays more attention to central and northern Europe concerning policy decisions and appointments of high-ranking officers. Although Italy accepted U.S. cruise missiles, permitted the transfer of 72 U.S. F-16 fighter planes ordered out of Spain, and has sent patrol ships to troubled areas, NATO follows an unbalanced policy in favor of north European members, while Italy along with other members in the southern region play a secondary role. However, Italy's defense spending (2–3 percent of GNP) is among NATO's lowest share compared to about 6–7 percent of the United States and Greece. Nevertheless, it is difficult for Italy to increase military expenditures because of high deficits. In spite of cutbacks in some cultural and health care programs, as well as in the national railroads, the budget deficits persist. However, efforts to balance the budget, through drastic reductions in expenditures or through increases in taxes, may lead the economy to recession with low or even negative rates of economic growth.

Instability in government affects economic stability as well, especially on matters of inflation and growth. Therefore, favorable developments abroad provide limited economic results, because fiscal and financial policies are primarily domestically generated. However, Italy's participation in EC policies, particularly in the European Monetary System, leads to the commitment of disinflationary policies. As a result, adjustments in fiscal and monetary policies initiate gradual efforts toward eliminating budget deficits and implementing prudent monetary policy. These policies are expected to decelerate inflation, reduce nominal interest rates, and improve investment confidence.

Italian ports on the Adriatic Sea and the Tyrrhenian Sea and several cities (Genoa, Livorno, Ravenna, Manfredonia) have to handle unacceptable levels of toxic waste and other forms of pollution. Protests and, at times, violent crowds have taken to the streets to express what they call "the rage of the poisoned." In a national referendum in 1987 the Italians voted against nuclear power plants. Across Italy and across Europe people demand environmental and health protection even at the sacrifice of lower industrial growth and material advancement.

Italy, among the worst EC nations on matters of public finance, has high annual budget deficits (about $85 billion a year or 10 percent of the GNP), compared to around 5 percent for the United States. In order to compete in the unified European market, Italy must reduce budget deficits and accumulated national debts. The first steps already have been taken in that direction by raising sales taxes, cutting income taxes, controlling tax evasion, and reducing spending. Also, a new capital-gains tax is considered but objections are raised as to its detrimental effects on investors' confidence. Moreover, a new value added tax of 4 percent on books, magazines, and newspapers, as well as the doubling of the 2 percent tax on bread, milk, and other necessities, were introduced.

In spite of the fact that Italy faced extensive political instability, with frequent government changes, during the post-World War II years, economic performance was satisfactory. Some Italian enterprises managed to expand domestically as well as internationally. Along with France and Germany, Italy had high rates of GNP growth in the post-World II years, especially in the 1950s and 1960s. This good economic performance was due primarily to the migration of workers from the poor agricultural sector to the modern industrial sector.

Spain's Performance

Spain performed relatively well during the last two decades. The overall rate of investment increased (from zero or negative in 1978–84 to about 15 percent currently) and inflation declined (from around 20 percent in 1978 to only 5 percent at present). However, unemployment remains high (19 percent), although reduced from its peak of 21.5 percent in 1985 and despite the more than 1.1 million jobs that were created during the last two years. This contradiction was due to the rapid increase of the number of women entering the labor force. Spanish policy makers argue that increases in wages lead to higher unemployment and inflation, while income and wealth redistribution and higher social welfare can be achieved through growth-oriented policies. This is what they call pragmatic or supply-side socialism.

Fueled by foreign investment and growing overall demand, Spain is under inflationary pressures. Inflation, which runs at 4–5 percent annually, is the measure for wage and pension raises. To hold inflation and to be a respected member of the EC, the socialist government of Felipe Gonzalez plans to allow business firms to hire young workers at low wages and to give wage raises in general no more than the rate of inflation. Such measures, along with the emphasis on monetary policy and other conservative measures, caused the two largest labor unions to object to these policies and ask the government "to get out of bed with businessmen and bankers." However, the nearly 20 percent unemployment, the highest in the EC, suggests that a favorable business climate is needed for the creation of more jobs.

MONETARY POLICY

On June 27, 1989, the 12 EC nations accepted in Madrid the first stage of the monetary union plan, which would end exchange controls and other restrictions in banking and insurance services. The first stage, starting on July 1, 1990, would be followed by two further stages that would involve the acceptance of a common currency and the establishment of a central European bank.

An intergovernmental conference would deal with the other two phases of the EC monetary union. Also, it would consider modifications of the initial charter of the EC (the Treaty of Rome of 1957) toward full economic union. In the process, Greece and Portugal are expected to join the European Monetary System, while France recently eliminated foreign exchange controls and restrictions on capital movements.

Monetary policy may be implemented through a short-term increase in money supply and reduction in interest rates. It is estimated that a reduction of interest rates by 1 percentage point increases real GNP by 0.5 to 1.5 percent in Europe and Japan and by approximately 0.5 to 1 percent in the United States after some two to three years. However, it must be recognized that monetary easing should be temporary, because extended growth, *ceteris paribus*, may lead to a rise in inflation.

High interest rates in one country attract capital inflow from other countries and affect exchange rate fluctuations. Typically, interest rates are raised to keep inflation checked. Recently Germany raised the discount rate, which is higher than that of the United States. This is the rate commercial banks pay for borrowing from central banks. Also, the short-term (Lombart) rate was raised in order to keep inflation at low levels.[2]

Although a similar increase in interest rates by the Bundesbank was criticized for contributing to the stock market crash in October 1987, the new increase is not related to the same variables of that time, the main one of which was the overinflated prices of stocks.

The drastic reforms in Eastern Europe and the economic union of West and East Germany attract capital investment and financial aid that put strains on the EC credit markets. Competition for funds raises interest rates in Europe and reduces bond prices. For example, interest rates on ten-year West German bonds (8.5 percent) rose above U.S. rates for the first time in more than ten years.

The development of the Eurodollar market, particularly after 1963, was the result of the efforts of the banks to escape national controls whenever their cost outweighed benefits. There are arguments that the Eurodollar market may be responsible for stimulating world inflation. Although the Eurodollar multiplier is not expected to be large, there is some influence upon inflation depending on the velocity or the speed of Eurodollar transactions. However, it is difficult to measure such a velocity and the related influence upon inflation, because, among other reasons, controls and supervisions of the market by central banks are limited or nonexistent. Moreover, domestic monetary policies become, to some extent, ineffective, especially in countries whose currencies are involved.

Of the EC member-nations, Greece and Portugal had high rates of inflation, followed by Italy, Spain, and Britain. The Netherlands, Germany, Belgium, and France had low rates of inflation in recent years and the other EC members were in between. At present, though, inflation (the Consumer Price Index) started raising again.

Although both fiscal and monetary policies are used to curb inflation by the governments considered, more emphasis is placed on monetarism and supply-side economics. Sometimes, though, reduction in government expenditures or tax increases are used to reduce inflation. This is particularly so in countries with large budget deficits. The idea is to reduce spending and aggregate demand, thereby suppressing inflation.[3]

Figures 4.2 and 4.3 show the movement of money supply and velocity of money for Germany and France, respectively. A similar constant or declining velocity of money can be observed for all EC members. This fact supports the policy of EC monetary integration, as long as money supply does not increase much for some EC members.

Expansionary economic policies in some EC members such as France, Italy, Spain, and Greece may find it difficult to adhere to strict antiinflationary policies of other members such as Germany. In 1979 the EC established the European Monetary System for currency stabilization and monetary policy coordination.[4] It also created the European Currency Unit, the value of which is based on a weighted average of the currencies of all members, with the German mark having more importance (30.1 percent weight in 1989), compared to the French franc (19 percent), the British pound (13), the Italian lira (10.15), the Dutch guider (9.4), the Belgian franc (7.6), the Spanish peseta (5.3), and other member currencies with lower weight. The ECU, which is adjusted every five years to the share of every member-nation to the GDP of the EC, is increasingly used as a real money with relatively stable exchange rates. In terms of dollars it is worth about $1.20.

Figure 4.2
Money Supply (M₁) and Velocity of Money (GDP/M₁) for Germany

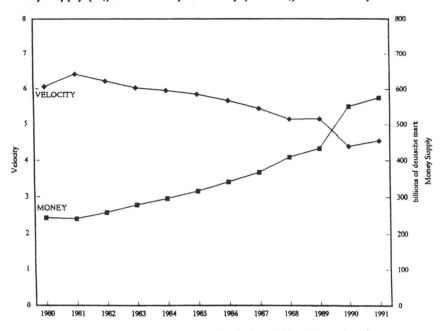

Source: International Monetary Fund, *International Financial Statistics*, various issues.

From time to time, different currencies are depreciated depending on the ratio of the consumer price index (P). Thus, if P for country A is 106 and for country B 103, then the depreciation of country A's currency would be 2.9 percent ($P_A/P_B = 106/103 = 1.029$).

The agreement of Maastricht, in the Netherlands (December 10, 1991), provides for political union and closer cooperation among the member-countries regarding budgetary deficits (no more than 3 percent of GNP), inflation (no more than 1.5 percent from the lowest average of three best-performing members), and exchange rate fluctuations (no more than 2.25 percent). Also, long-term interest rates should be no more than 2 percent above the average of the three best-performing members, whereas public-sector debt should not exceed 60 percent of GNP. Furthermore, matters concerning economic development and convergence of the standard of living of the people of the EC were considered in this Maastricht agreement, which was signed on February 7, 1992.

The Maastricht Treaty and other EC conferences aim at the completion of the Single Market, a stronger political cooperation and the strengthening of the links with Central, Southern, and Eastern Europe. Such treaties and conferences prepare the other European countries for EC enlargement and

Figure 4.3
Money Supply (M₁) and Velocity of Money (GDP/M₁) for France

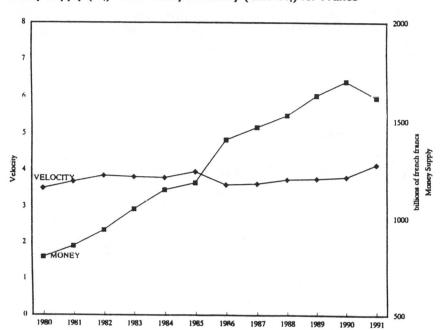

Source: International Monetary Fund, *International Financial Statistics*, various issues.

demonstrate that the Community cannot fossilize, but it must move forward. However, as the other European countries enter the EC Single Market, Europe is not supposed to erect a new economic iron curtain for other countries and continents.

The new five-year budgetary plan (1992–97) of the European Commission, which is known also as the Delors II package and is referred to as the Bill for Maastricht, provides, among other things, for the support of the poorer EC members (Greece, Ireland, Portugal, and Spain). This plan calls for an increase of spending by 31.5 percent during the period 1992–97, over the previous Delors I plan (1987–92), which called for the completion of the Single Market in early 1992. Germany is the Community's largest net contributor (with DM19 billion in 1991) in budget expenditures.

In addition to the initiatives of economic and monetary integration, the EC program fostered an agenda of social rights, tax harmonization, common industrial policy, and even political union. It seems that the successful example of the EC is followed by the North American Free Trade Agreement, which includes Canada, Mexico, and the United States, as well as by the Asian-Pacific Rim (Japan and other neighboring nations). In the question to whom the twenty-first century belongs, it seems that the EC has the momentum, although North America has the flexibility to challenge such a priority through technological improvement and aggressive innovations. On the other hand, Japan, with its closed corporate culture and tradition, seemed to have reached a plateau from which it would be difficult to move further up. The EC spends more for research and development and invests more for plant and equipment per employee than the United States.

FOREIGN TRADE AND INVESTMENT

Germany, the Locomotive of Europe

Germany has the highest amount of foreign trade in the Community, and the EC nations are the main importers of German products. Thus, France is the first country in buying German commodities (about 12 percent), followed by Britain, the Netherlands and Italy (around 10 percent each), Belgium and Luxembourg (8 percent each). The United States absorbs about 10 percent of German exports, Switzerland 6 percent, and Japan only 2 percent. With a record trade surplus of more than $80 billion a year ($81 billion in 1989), a rate of inflation around 2 percent, and a real economic growth of about 3 percent annually, the economy of Germany may be considered as the locomotive of the other EC economies.

However, large German trade surpluses present problems to other EC members, especially France, with trade deficits and pressures of currency realignment. Continuation of favorable trade conditions with other nations is expected to improve the rate of economic growth for the coming years. Nevertheless, the government plans to increase consumer taxes (on tobacco, liquor, gasoline, heating oil, natural gas, and insurance) to moderate the effects of tax cuts implemented in 1990 and reduce inflationary pressures.

Among other companies the government is subsidizing for a number of years is Messerchmitt-Bolkow-Blohm (MBB), the German partner in the European Airbus consortium, mainly in order to protect it against foreign competition. This policy, which includes exchange rate guarantees, has been criticized by the United States and other countries as unfair trade practices, but with limited results. The Europeans (including the French, British, and Spanish partner companies) argue that subsidies are needed because all transactions are in devalued dollars, which make sales difficult, and because the American competitive companies (Boeing and McDonnell Douglas) receive indirect subsidies through military contracts and monopolize the world market.

Similar criticism is made by American pharmaceutical companies, which control about 20 percent of the German market for pharmaceuticals, against the new policy of the German government to reduce national health insurance payments for a large number of drugs. About nine out of ten Germans are covered by the national health insurance system where employees and employers contribute equal amounts. Because drug prices are about 50 percent higher than in other EC countries (but less than in the United States), the government introduced controls on drug prices as Britain, France, and other EC nations have done for years. If a patient wants a more expensive drug than the cheaper one the government reimbursed, he or she would pay the difference. It is estimated that with a 40 percent price reduction, the government would save about $1 billion at the expense of the pharmaceutical industry. As a result, the profits of the industry would be reduced to about half and expenses for research and development would be declined significantly, allowing the United States and Japan to compete more effectively in inventions and innovations.

For Germany, which is a federal nation with a number of republics, adaptation to a federal Europe, which is expected to absorb large amounts of German exports, is easier. However, for other EC member-nations, such as France, Italy, and Spain, with no federal experience, things are more difficult. Moreover, Germany has the advantage of an advanced exporting industry and needs the markets of the other EC nations to sell steel, cars, electronics, and other industrial products.

Because of higher demand for steel in the EC there are signs of improvement in the steel market and in other exported German products. Germany accounts for about one-third of the EC steel production. This is one of the main reasons why Germany favors improvement of the EC, despite the sizable amount of subsidies and other expenses paid by Germany in support of the EC budget and to help poorer EC member nations. However, the steel and trucking industries may need restructuring and further protection for EC ecological, safety, and other regulations in order to survive competition.

Germany, a relatively small country with limited natural resources, proved to be the leading export country. According to the International Monetary Fund's statistics, Germany is the world leader in exports, with more than $500 billion per year, followed by the United States, Japan, and Italy. Other EC countries with a good record in exports are the Netherlands and Belgium/Luxembourg.

With a European Monetary System and a common currency, a united Germany would eventually become the financial center of an integrated Europe and may dominate global finance as well. Moreover, it will be a crucial link with the former USSR and other East European countries, sponsoring joint ventures and providing credit and technical training to them.

Therefore, it is more likely that U.S. firms will be leaning toward linkups with their German and European counterparts, where markets are more open than those of Japan and some other countries. Furthermore, with the Japanese pursuing an Asian-Pacific Basin common market and the prevailing bloc mentality, U.S. firms and policy makers should consider outward-looking policies, notably toward Germany and the East bloc. For that, a consultative partnership between the EC and the United States has been proposed to deal with institutional links and more trade and investment ventures.

A trans-European partnership extending from Berlin to Washington would include financial matters as well. This will be important as German stocks and bonds are expected to be more attractive, due to the benefits expected from the eventual EC financial unification and the opening of Eastern Europe. As a result, more American, Japanese, and other money will move to that region and U.S. markets are bound to suffer. Already, real returns on German bonds are higher than those on U.S. government bonds.

Relationship of Production, Investment, and Exports

A regression analysis for the EC (1970–90) shows that "exports" (EX) is an important variable in determining gross domestic product (GDP), GDP $= 144 + 3.4EX$, as is "investment" (INV), GDP $= 141 + 5.1INV$. In both cases, the correlation is very good (R $= .99$). This means that each additional unit of exports is related to 3.4 units of GDP and each unit of investment to 5.1 units of GDP, that is (*ceteris paribus*), the investment multiplier (5.1) is high. The related multiregression is: GDP $= -.07 + 3.4INV + 1.1EX$, (R $= .98$).

Competition Versus Protection

There seem to be two main trends in the Community concerning a more or less open market for other nonmember nations. France and Italy, where nationalistic and protectionist elements are strong, present pressures for less openness to trade with countries outside the Community. Article 115 of the EC treaty allows individual members to limit trade with non-EC countries, as the French and Italians have already done for their auto industries. However, EC countries with advanced industries competing effectively in international markets such as Germany and Britain reject protectionism and support an open EC market to the rest of the world in accordance with the rules of the General Agreement on Tariffs and Trade (GATT), and especially the Uruguay Round. In any case, many American and other foreign companies are locating operations in the EC in order to avoid possible protectionist measures in the future, such as those of Italy limiting Japanese auto imports. Already there is skepticism that national quotas may be used as EC quotas, and the trend toward establishing protectionist regional trade blocs may intensify to the detriment of free trade.

However, the EC may try to shield some of its enterprises from competition for a transitional period of adjustment, especially in the auto, textiles, and electronics industries. Some reciprocity measures may restrict trade in goods and services as well as direct and portfolio investment, by granting the same opportunities into the EC offered by other nations to EC companies operating in their countries. These measures are of great importance for foreign banks and other firms expecting to expand operations in the European countries.[5]

The costs of a fragmented European market in the past were high, while the benefits from a unified European market in the future are expected to be significant. Healthier competition, business and professional mobility, economies of scale, job creation, improved productivity, and better consumer choices are the European challenges.[6] The political and economic future of the EC and Eastern Europe would be of great importance to foreign trade, investment, and international finance. It is a historical challenge that will change the global economy forever. It will enhance Europe's role in the world and effect the redistribution of power in the twenty-first century.

The former communist nations of Eastern Europe lack the capital needed to modernize their mismanaged state industries and to proceed rapidly to privatization. Sizable sums of foreign capital can help such modernization and reorganization. Low wages, varying from $100 to $200 monthly, and a well-educated labor force would also help in a quick transformation and adjustment.

Concerning foreign trade, both exports and imports for Eastern Europe are expected to be far larger and diverse. Thus, it is predicted that imports from the West would be more than $260 billion, about fivefold of the present level. The European Community and mainly Germany would export annually about $133 billion, a fivefold increase, but the United States is expected to export about $50 billion per year—that is, a thirteenfold increase. However, in farm and dairy products the EC farmers would face strong competition but its consumers would harvest the benefits of lower costs from East European countries.

On the other hand, the production costs of exportables and other commodities are relatively high because workers and managers, in a number of enterprises, stopped working after the fulfillment of the planned quotas. As a researcher could observe, there was widespread lack of productive incentives on the part of workers and managers with fixed wages. A change in the remuneration system, based on labor productivity or piecework, could reduce laziness, stimulate productivity, reduce cost, and increase competitiveness.

The East European countries are in the process of replacing barter trade under Comecon with market-based international trade, through privatization, price liberalization, the creation of a financial intermediation system, and economic restructuring. However, during the time of adjustment, inflation, unemployment, fiscal deficits, and other disruptions seem to be inevitable.

On the other side, Western Europeans expect to take advantage of cheap labor and a growing East European market in trade and investment, especially if the economic reforms proposed are implemented.

Recently, the EC signed trade agreements with East bloc countries and is pursuing similar agreements in the future. It seems that expected economic changes and reforms in these countries would bring them closer to the EC economies and make stronger ties more attractive between the two groups.

The Question of Immigration

The dramatic changes in Eastern Europe increased the flow of immigrants in Western Europe, particularly in Germany. Also, many minorities are fleeing rising persecution in Eastern Europe and in some former Soviet republics. This is primarily the result of conflicts among resurfacing nationalist elements, which have been suppressed by communism and persistent poverty.

In Germany alone there are some 6.5 million legal immigrants, mainly from Eastern Europe and the Balkans. Some 450,000 foreigners arrived in 1991 and 660,000 in 1992. On May 26, 1993, German lawmakers approved (521 to 132) a constitutional change tightening Europe's most liberal asylum law. This was the result of conflicts between nationalistic and neo-Nazi groups and immigrants, mainly Turks and Gypsies. In France, the number is more than 3.6 million or 6 percent of the population (about 1 million North Africans), in Britain 3 percent, in the Netherlands 5, in Belgium 9, in Austria 5, and in Switzerland 17 percent.

It is expected that 2–5 million East European and former Soviet citizens will seek legal entry to Western Europe and 2–3 million ethnic Germans to enter the fatherland primarily from Poland, Ukraine, and Russia. There are 17 million immigrants already in Western Europe (5 percent of the population), 4 million of which are from North Africa and Turkey, while foreign-born children account for more than 10 percent. In France, for example, there are immigrants with three or four wives and 20 children each, collecting about $10,000 from the government without working.[7]

The wave of immigrants, who are fleeing poverty, repression, and ethnic conflicts, intensified racism and a movement toward fascism, particularly in Germany, France, and Italy. In Germany the number of young neo-Nazis has increased. In France recent elections gave sizable percentages to the racist National Front Party of Jean-Marie Le Pen, while Alessandra Mussolini, granddaughter of the Fascist dictator, was elected to the Italian Parliament.

The problem of refugees and immigrants in general may slow down and derail plans for political and currency unification of Europe. Also it may destabilize the economies of some East European countries, notably Hungary and Poland, which face problems of refugees, mainly from the former Yugoslav republics, Romania, and Ukraine, and even from Russia. In the coming years, the pressure of immigration will be greater primarily from Muslim countries where unemployment is more than 20 percent and per capita GNP ranges from $600 to $2,500. From that standpoint, strict quotas, similar to those in the United States, may be imposed by some European countries.

Although Europe has 373 people per square mile, compared to only 70 for the United States, the EC countries have low or zero birthrates, rapidly aging populations, and shrinking work forces. From that standpoint, an immigration policy is needed in the EC to select and train immigrants in order to support its social system and sustain high rates of economic growth.

THE ECONOMIC STRUGGLE OF THE NEW SUPERPOWERS

If the EC moves successfully to a closer integration of the European countries, it will be the number one economic and political superpower of the twenty-first century, replacing the United States and more so Japan. At present, the United States is considered being at the transition period of transferring the scepter of economic world power and leadership to Europe. It seems that there is a historical pattern of acme and decline in empires and superpowers from ancient Greece and Rome to Spain, Britain, and perhaps the United States. However, the duration of the present and future superpowers is far shorter than in the past largely because of the rapid advancements in information technologies and transportation.

With the proper agreements and policies, the EC and particularly Germany would be in a powerful position to dictate the rules of international trade and investment. The economic system of the EC is a combination of Anglo-Saxon individualistic capitalism and the social market economy related to the German and Japanese systems.

Although there appear, from time to time, some antithetical ethnic and religious tendencies, the pressure for economic development through foreign trade and investment, as well as the rapid improvement in communications, would lead to stronger economic-political integration and international cooperation. Narrow national interests are gradually subordinated to regional integration programs and the convergence of different national systems. It seems that the main function of the policy makers is to ride the tidal waves and lead societies to harmonious living conditions and long-term economic growth through regional and global agreements.

Nevertheless, regional integration gives advantages to merchants and investors operating inside the bloc but disadvantages to exporters outside the bloc, since barriers for insiders come down but they remain at current levels for outsiders. Therefore, such integration may lead to great achievements for the member countries but to a movement away from the doctrine of free world trade and its comparative advantages.

Economic integration and federalism seem to help avoid the pandemonium and the danger from excessive self-determination and strict ethnicity in international order. However, such integration and federalism should be the result of voluntary and democratic procedure and not oppression and dictatorial force, as happened in the former Soviet Union and Yugoslavia where ethnicities turned against each other.

The laissez-faire or free trade system, in which the consumer is the king, seems to be difficult in practice. In all countries, governments represent, to a large extent, domestic producers who try to maximize their markets. However, in order to export more they have to permit more imports, thereby making concessions to gain concessions and benefits from free trade policies of the respective governments. Nevertheless, producers organize into effective coalitions to protect themselves in cases of losses from foreign competition, fostering a drift toward protectionism.

Similar coalitions of interest groups, which push toward protection, can be observed in common markets or free trade agreements such as the EC and NAFTA. Thus, protection, through subsidies in agricultural products, the Airbus commercial industry, and other sectors, is a drift toward esoteric or regional protectionism and a deviation from the free trade principles of international economics. Such esoteric or inward-looking policies and a faceless bureaucracy, which is slowly developing in the EC, may be responsible for neglecting the chaotic problems in Eastern Europe and Russia, as well as the ethnic and religious conflicts in the former Yugoslavia.

Although the United States helped Europe and Japan after World War II to stabilize and develop their economies, they are criticized that they gradually grew into selfish protectionistic powers, using policies favoring intraregional and not open world trade, which at times turn against the U.S. economy and GATT policies.

The new wave of regional trading arrangements or the new regionalism is criticized that it may hinder the existing multilateral trading system. Such regional trading arrangements include the European Community, the North American Free Trade Agreement, and the *de facto* trading bloc in East Asia under the leadership of Japan (Asian-Pacific Rim). In addition, the Enterprise for the Americas Initiative (EAI) has been launched by the United States for a free trade area to include the whole hemisphere of the Americas. With the arrangements of NAFTA and EAI, the United States is gradually moving away from its commitment to multilateralism and its staunch support of GATT.

It seems that the world is moving toward a tripolar arrangement centered around the EC, the United States, and Japan. However, Japan has not moved fast because of its large stake in the U.S. market. If these blocs are complementary to multilateralism or internationalism, trade creation would be higher than trade diversion and total welfare of all countries would increase. If they are benign or turn inward to "fortress" blocs, trade diversion would be higher than trade creation and total welfare would decline.

The EC integration is used as a successful example for other groups of countries, primarily in Central and Latin America. Such groups include the MERCOSUR Pact (Brazil, Uruguay, Argentina, Paraguay), the Chile-Argentina Treaty, the Colombian-Venezuelan Customs Union, and the Andean Pact (Columbia, Peru, Bolivia, Ecuador, and Venezuela). Recently, all these groups have greatly reduced tariffs and increased trade among themselves. Also, they dropped tariffs and other restrictions for overseas trade. This led to trade creation and increase in welfare, not only for themselves but for outside countries as well (mainly the United States) for which exports in the area increased by more than 18 percent a year, compared to about a 5 percent rise for the rest of the world. Such a gradual and successful integration, which may lead to a Pan-American common market, shows the advantages of enlargement of integrated groups.

It seems that future years will be dominated by the struggle between regional economic pacts and international institutions. EC, NAFTA, and the Asian-Pacific Rim are expected to be the most important groups that are destined to influence global economic and political events in the near and remote future. However, the question is if these regional groups will complement or compete with such world institutions as GATT, the International Monetary Fund (IMF), the World Bank, and even the United Nations.

The recent past proved that regional alliances need not compete with these multinational or global institutions. Moreover, regional integration creates more trade than it diverts, as international specialization and comparative advantages are improved. Therefore, regionalism can be regarded as a step toward internationalism as long as internal walls are pulled down and external walls are not raised. Outsiders then are unlikely to lose much, as regional economic alliances are not threatening progress toward multilateral free trade. But insiders gain in welfare through trade liberalization. Thus, as a result of NAFTA, Mexico and the United States are estimated to gain $5 billion a year in welfare and an increase in trade by $25 billion ($17 billion increase in U.S. exports to Mexico and $8 billion increase of Mexican exports to the United States a year).

Part II

East European Countries

5

Poland

A BRIEF HISTORICAL REVIEW

Although nothing authentic is known about the early Slovanic tribes that laid the foundation of the Polish nation, some of these tribes united about A.D. 840 under King Piast. During the reign of Mieszko (962–992), a descendant of Piast, and that of his son Boleslav I (992–1025), Poland was expanded, especially after a successful war against the Holy Roman Emperor Henry II. At that time Christianity was established in the country. Thereafter, Poland faced divisions and invasions by the Danes, the Hungarians, the Russians, the Germans, and even the Mongols (1240–41). Under Ladislas I (1320–33), who inflicted decisive defeats on the Teutonic Knights, and his son Casimir III (1333–70), significant economic, judicial, and educational reforms were introduced and the prosperity of the country increased substantially.

During the Jagellon dynasty (1386–1572), which followed the Piast dynasty, successful wars were conducted against the Teutonic Knights, and Poland added more areas to its dominion and achieved a leading position in Europe.

For two centuries thereafter, disastrous wars with Sweden, Russia, and Turkey led to the economic and politic deterioration of the country. In 1683, however, Polish and German armies defeated a large Turkish army at the gates of Vienna, halting a serious Moslem threat to Christendom in Central and Western Europe.

In 1764 Russian troops invaded Poland and enthroned Stanislas II Augustus (a paramour of empress Catherine II). In 1772 a treaty of partition of Poland was signed, by which about one-fourth of the country was acquired by Russia, Austria, and Prussia, while the rest was politically restricted and officially termed as the Polish Commonwealth. After the Russians occupied the eastern and the Prussians the western parts of the country in 1793, another treaty of partition was signed, and by 1796 the whole country was partitioned among Russia, Prussia, and Austria. For 125 years Poland remained under the yoke of these three powers, except for a short period (1807–15) during which a tiny liberal state was created by Napoleon the Great of France as thousands of Poles served in his armies.

During World War I, Poles, conscripted into the armies of Russia and the Central Powers, fought each other. With the collapse of the Central Powers, the Republic of Poland was formally established in November 1918 and Joseph Pilsudski, a prominent politician, became the leader of the country. By the terms of the Treaty of Versailles (1919), Poland received substantial territorial grants, including a narrow belt along the Vistula River to the Baltic Sea (the Polish corridor). Also granted were significant economic rights in the Free City of Danzig, which Nazi Germany claimed later. This claim was used by Hitler as a reason for starting the war against Poland in September 1939.

In 1920 the Polish government requested from Russia restoration of the old boundaries. The Bolsheviks rejected that request and the Polish army, supported by France, advanced and captured most of Ukraine, including Kiev. In a counterattack the Russians advanced to the gates of Warsaw. With the Treaty of Riga on March 18, 1921, hostilities ended and Poland secured substantial territorial claims in the East.

For the two following decades, Poland, fearful of Germany and Russia, arranged alliances with France, Romania, Czechoslovakia, and other countries, as well as nonaggression pacts with Russia (1932) and Germany (1934). However, in March 1939 Nazi Germany demanded Danzig and important rights in the Polish corridor. Poland rejected these demands, Adolf Hitler denounced the German-Polish nonaggression pact, and on September 1, 1939, Germany invaded Poland and World War II began. In two weeks Nazi armies overran most of Poland, while the Anglo-French pledge of support to Poland did not materialize. On September 17, 1939, the Red Army invaded Poland and a partition treaty gave half of the country to Germany and half to Russia.[1]

Mainly because of the victory of the Polish army over Soviet forces in 1920, Joseph Stalin ordered the execution of 25,700 former Polish officers, landowners, clergymen, and others in the Katyn Forest (Russia) on March 5, 1940. The eastern part of Poland, which was under Russia, was occupied by Germany on June 1941 when Hitler invaded Russia.

POST-WORLD WAR II DEVELOPMENTS

The Polish people, as did other occupied people of Europe, suffered heavy casualties under the Nazi armies (5 million civilians and 600,000 soldiers)—

especially the Jewish section of the population, for which a policy of extermination was pursued. By March 1945 the German invaders were driven out of Poland by the Red Army that was aided by contingents of Polish troops and resistance groups.

In order to compensate Poland for seizing parts of its eastern territory for the Soviet Union, Stalin handed over to Poland the German regions of Silesia, Pomerania, and part of East Prussia. Although at the end of World War II the German population was expelled westward and was replaced by Poles from the eastern regions, which were under the Soviets, Germany may reclaim these territories in the future.

After the purging of "national Communists," who favored Yugoslav leader Tito's defiance of Stalin, the pro-Stalin communists became dominant. Even Wladyslaw Gomulka, secretary-general of the party, was jailed. A Soviet chief of the Polish army was installed and Poland became a satellite of the Soviet Union. In 1949, the Council for Mutual Economic Assistance (Comecon) was established as a counterpart of the European Recovery Program, a U.S.-sponsored plan for the rehabilitation of Europe that was created in 1948.

Collectivization of farms, nationalization of industries, and economic planning, similar to the Soviet model, were enacted. A six-year industrialization plan (1950–55), which gave emphasis to heavy industry at the neglect of the consumer sector, achieved good results regarding production of coal, steel, and other goods useful for capital formation and industrialization.[2] In 1956, and as a result of the Soviet reconciliation with Yugoslavia, the "national Communists" and Gomulka were exonerated. Gomulka, who was elected as the chief of the Polish Politburo, moved to dissolve inefficient collectives and to democratize the country. However, he declared that as long as NATO maintained troops in West Germany, Soviet troops would remain in Poland.

The measures of rapid industrialization led to workers' hardship and riots, especially in 1956. Similar riots in 1970 initiated some reforms based on Western markets and technology. This policy and the oil crisis of the 1970s forced Poland into heavy foreign debts without much economic improvement in the export sector.

The dismal conditions of the economy and severe shortages forced price increases and other austerity measures in 1980, which touched off workers' strikes at the Gdansk shipyard. Then the Solidarity Labor Union, created by Lech Walesa, negotiated with the Gierek government and achieved increases in wages, freedom of political prisoners and the press, reduction of the work week from six to five days, and other economic and political concessions. Many workers demanded a self-management system similar to that of Yugoslavia and free elections, but the government of General Wojciech Jaruzelski imposed martial law.

In the process of changing Poland's planned economy, a serious problem appeared in reshaping weapons factories into civilian manufacturing industries. With the collapse of communism and the cold war, military sales declined drastically and the need for adjustment to peacetime production became imperative. A successful case is that of the Pressta Metalworks enterprise in Bolechowo, which was reshaped from munitions industries to butane gas canisters, a portion of which is exported to Germany, Britain, and Israel.

With the landslide election of Solidarity leader Lech Walesa in December 1989 (the first free presidential election in many years), with a margin of 74 percent over Stanislav Tyminski (an emigre businessman from Peru and Canada), the processes of industrial adjustment, privatization, and other reforms were speeded up. A Nobel Prize winner, Walesa, who established the first free trade union (Solidarity) in Poland in August 1980, used innovative and democratic policies to enhance the principles of private ownership and free enterprise. The goal is to reverse the economic downturn, which was the result of severe austerity measures taken to reduce inflation and stabilize the nation's currency. Although people do not have to give bribes or use connections to obtain certain goods, declines in production and increases in unemployment, which were unconstitutional under communism, continue to exist.

ECONOMIC REFORMS: PRIVATIZATION AND EMPLOYEE PARTICIPATION

Limited economic reforms, similar to those of Hungary with more autonomy of enterprises, price flexibility, labor management, and less microeconomic planning were introduced in the early 1980s. The reforms of Mikhail Gorbachev in the Soviet Union encouraged further reforms in Poland. While the free elections in 1989 established a noncommunist government for the first time in many years, foreign debt continued to increase to more than $40 billion, despite the devaluation of the zloty by more than 40 percent since 1986.

From September 1989 Poland moved rapidly into a free market economy. Prices were left free to fluctuate according to supply and demand, subsidies were slashed, many industries were privatized, bankruptcies were permitted, the national currency (zloty) was stabilized and became convertible, interest rates were reduced, and foreign trade was liberalized. As a result, the state budgets have been balanced, food and other shortages were eliminated, inflation was reduced to around 4 percent, and trade balances became positive. Moreover, in order to attract foreign investment, profit transfers abroad were permitted, export and import restrictions were slashed, and other benefits to capital and technology transfers were provided.

Nevertheless, the quick jump of the Polish command and control economy into free markets led to some disappointing results. Unemployment, which was not allowed by the constitution under communism, has risen to more than 10 percent, production in state-run industries has dropped about 30 percent in a year, food prices have risen, on the average, by 15 times, and real earning power has declined by one-third. A doctor earned about $50 and a state pensioner $36 a month. Moreover, farmers, who count for about 22 percent of the work force, periodically, blocked roads and demanded government-guaranteed minimum prices for agricultural products, a policy practiced by the communists for decades. The rush to a free market economy created high expectations on the part of the consumers, which led to frustration and disappointment later, as Poland lacked the infrastructure and the hard work required to achieve high standards of living similar to those of the West. This may be one of the reasons why Solidarity split into different political groups.

Poland tried gradual, perestroika-type, reforms for a couple of years before 1990, but with not much success. It was the "shock therapy" of January 1990, which, although painful initially with hyperinflation and massive shortages, stabilized the economy later.[3] It seems that a gradual transformation from communism to capitalism proved to be ineffective, not only in Poland but primarily in the former Soviet Union. This was so mainly because it combined the worst elements of both systems by trying to create a market system but keeping predominantly state ownership.

Initially, the Polish program of privatization and democratization, and the drastic measures (shock therapy) taken for the transformation of the economy from the centrally planned to the free market system, although painful, was accepted with endurance and even enthusiasm. Lately, however, there are indications of change of policy toward the previous system, which may lead to high inflation because of government subsidies and income support for workers and pensioners.[4]

Moreover, the multiparty system with 26 parties, none of which has more than 13 percent of the popular vote, is the result of political reforms in 1989 and thereafter, which led to governmental weakness. Pressures by labor unions, pensioners, and other groups for higher income led to the printing of large amounts of money and the appearance of inflationary spirals.

The transformation of socialism to capitalism in Poland has not materialized without turbulence. A serious case of corruption was revealed recently involving PKO BP, the largest public saving institution of Poland, and Art-B, a private company that supervises scores of Polish firms. The scandal of some $30 million (1.5 trillion zlotys) involves other financial institutions as well and has led to the removal of Gregory Boztovits (the president of the National Bank of Poland), for being negligent in his supervisory duties, and the arrest of Boetsek Propof (the vice-president) for mismanagement of public funds, among other executives.

Despite the Roman Catholic doctrine and the papacy's suspicion of capitalism as the outcome of Protestant teachings, Poland's Catholicism and Pope John Paul II supported the capitalistic reforms and the spirit of private enterprise's profit making in Poland and other East European countries.

Nevertheless, economic reforms and privatization have been piecemeal. By

1993, only 54 out of 3,500 government enterprises have been sold to the private sector, 16 were listed on the new stock exchange of Warsaw, hundreds of primarily small firms were transferred to their employees and managers, whereas many state-owned large enterprises (dinosaurs) remained under government control. According to the Polish Development Bank, more than 1.5 million private businesses had been registered by July 1993, absorbing 56 percent of the work force, compared to 8,000 state-owned firms.

High inflation (running at 40 percent) and growing unemployment (more than 13 percent) forced many people into poverty. Many Poles are homeless and get their only meals at soup kitchens with the help of coupons by the Red Cross. They feel that the reforms made them "free and hungry," and that foreigners buy the Polish companies and lay the workers off. Such dismal conditions influenced the Parliament to defeat a bill introduced by Prime Minister Hanna Suchocka in March 1993, with a vote of 203 to 181 and 9 abstentions, which would have converted 600 state enterprises to private firms. On May 29, 1993, the coalition six-party government of Miss Suchocka collapsed when it lost by one vote (223 out of a total 445 votes of a 29-party Parliament) in protest of her tight budget. In the elections of September 19, 1993, the Polish Peasant Party headed by the former communist leader Waldermar Pawlak and the Democratic Left Alliance won 303 seats of the 460-member Parliament. On October 26, 1993, Pawlak became the sixth prime minister of Poland since the fall of communism.

Although Poland appeared to lead in transferring its economy to capitalism, the snail's pace of privatization of state-owned enterprises remains disappointing, mainly because people are poor and cannot afford to buy stocks. On the other hand, there are questions regarding the power of employees and workers in the process of privatization of the firms for which they work and the possible discounts in selling shares to them. Because workers and individuals do not have money, scrip or coupons are given to them to acquire stocks, as happens in the Czech and Slovak republics as well.

Nevertheless, a few large firms have been converted into shareholding companies, including Exbud, a building enterprise, Slaska, a cable company, Norblin Metal Rolling company, which makes copper wire and cable, and Prochnik, a textile manufacturer. Although these companies remain state-owned, they are run under commercial or market rules. Only profitable companies can be privatized easily, while the money-losing ones, which cannot be nursed back to healthy operation, are liquidated and their assets are sold in auctions.

Under a new Polish law, employees can elect one-third of the boards of directors. They are also entitled to buy up to 20 percent shares of their company at half the flotation price. However, managers of firms controlled by employees complain that they face limitations on making decisions for which responsibilities rest primarily on them. They think that it is better to be supervised by professional directors than employee councils.

In Poland, employee councils were established first in 1956 and were supported, to a large extent, by Solidarity economists in the 1980s. In 1990 the Polish Parliament permitted employee councils to fire managers and replace them with new ones. As a result, hundreds of managers were recently dismissed and many others are expected to be replaced soon.

Thus, the employee council of the Polkolor company, which produces television tubes outside Warsaw, replaced the general manager of the company with its own chairman. Polkolor, which uses American technology of the 1970s under license from RCA, has about 3,500 employees and is negotiating a partial transfer of ownership to Thomson, a large French electronics company. Another Polish company, in which the manager was elected by the employee council, is the Nowa Huta steel mill in Cracow, with some 28,000 employees.

Although employee councils and privatization have gained more importance since the fall of communism in Poland, state-run firms still account for a large percentage of industrial production. The main questions that remain in this transformation stage are what shape capitalism will take and how to deal with overstuffed enterprises. Workers want higher wages under capitalism but they also want to maintain their jobs that were guaranteed under state or communist control.

On the other hand, the new economic plan of the Solidarity-led government incorporated, among other reforms of transferring state ownership to private ownership, the setting up of ESOPs. In addition, the plan set up a stock market where the stocks of employees and other individuals and institutions can be exchanged. Other East bloc countries are expected to introduce similar measures in their economic reforms.

In its effort to create a competitive economy and an investment market, the Polish government sells state-run enterprises to private investors and the workers. More than 7,000 state firms or about 80 percent of the economy are expected to be transferred to the private sector. Already, a number of companies, dealing with various activities—from construction to textiles, glass works, and cable and audio equipment—are being privatized and many others are on the way to liquidation. Normally, up to 20 percent of the shares are reserved for the workers and employees of the companies involved at lower prices. Also, a limited portion of shares is being sold to foreigners and some are retained by the government. The shares are mostly held by national banks until they are transferred to the buyers or until stock markets are established to facilitate such exchanges. The Polish government collected $300 million from 18 state-owned firms it sold to foreign investors in 1991 and about $440 million in 1992.

Individual investors may apply for loans to buy stocks beyond the amount they can acquire with their coupons. This is particularly so for farmers who can buy stocks of local agricultural enterprises with borrowed funds on favorable terms. To discourage excessive foreign purchases, particularly by

Germany, government approval is required for foreigners acquiring more than 10 percent of any given enterprise.

In this Polish privatization plan, which is considered as the most ambitious blueprint of Eastern Europe for the transfer of factories and shops from the public to the private sector, employees and workers are offered generous advantages when they buy shares of the companies for which they work for incentive stimulation.[5] Beyond that amount and the equity reserved for coupons, the remaining amount of shares is offered to the general public over a number of years. There is criticism, though, that current communist managers may buy large amounts of shares and control the Polish industry, as only about 47 percent of the workers expressed interest in buying shares in their own firms. Moreover, lack of related financial institutions and proper capital markets may present difficulties for the success of the plan. From that standpoint, Western countries can help the transition process by creating mutual funds and providing financial and managerial assistance.

In the process of privatization, the Polish Parliament approved a plan that gives every citizen coupons that can be exchanged for shares in any of several thousands of state-owned enterprises that are slated for the private sector. About 90 percent of industry and commerce has been conducted by state-owned firms.

Poland was successful in selling small firms to the private sector or having local governments lease them to the workers, particularly regarding the wholesale and retail stores. However, it is more difficult to privatize large firms, whose shares have been put into several mutual funds and then distributed, mostly free, to adult citizens. On the other hand, currency convertibility helps the country to pull foreign resources into the economy, an indication of confidence for future investment and further development.[6]

A serious problem has appeared in state-owned firms as managers and workers, in coalition, are pressing the government for higher wages. Managers represent the workers rather than real owners and they do not bargain for the interests of the firms they manage, in a countervailing fashion, as is customary in market economies. This leads to inflationary pressures and macroeconomic instability.

The shareholders, who become the ultimate owners of state enterprises of their choice, cannot trade shares of the fund for a couple of years. The investment funds can close inefficient companies or expand productive ones, make new investments, borrow money, and issue new shares. They can restructure or merge state firms and even trade shares with each other. These funds are managed primarily by Western experts, although they are officially controlled by boards of Polish directors. Normally, about 30 percent of each firm's shares is kept by the government.

For a successful privatization of the Polish economy, the new Ministry of Ownership Transformation was established recently. Moreover, the Polish Employee Ownership Association helps such privatization and transfer of ownership to the workers of the related enterprises. It represents more than

100 healthy Polish firms with more than half a million workers. In these firms, employees and workers can buy 20 to 30 percent of shares on credit, in addition to 10 percent given free to them. Also, management can participate in enterprise ownership, mainly with performance incentives, as can other citizens through vouchers. Western investors are entitled to obtain controlling interest in such privatized firms through majority acquisition or management contracts. Employees have the option to buy the interests of foreign investors if such interests are sold and the money is available. This is considered as democratization of ownership in a free market economic system.

The free market idolatry and effectiveness depend on the dissemination of reasonable information regarding resources, products, and services. From that standpoint, the Polish-managed privatization program of each adult receiving equal shares in large mutual funds and transferring them into enterprise ownership seemed to be reasonable and practical. Such mutual funds are more specialized in enterprise evaluation and provide more reliable information than the direct auction system, through low-price vouchers provided by the governments of the Czech and Slovak republics, for example.

MONETARY POLICY

In Poland there was a relatively small annual increase in money supply from 1981 to 1988, but a drastic increase thereafter (from 6 billion zlotys in 1988 to more than 100 billion zlotys in 1991). Velocity of money (the ratio of GDP over money supply) increased from 2.5 in 1981 to 4.2 in 1986 and 6.2 in 1990. Given that real production growth remains low, the significant increases in money supply and money velocity fuel high rates of inflation. Figure 5.1 shows money supply and velocity trends.

During the last decade, the nominal interest rates were lower than inflation rates. The fact that inflationary rates are higher than the deposit rates leads to negative real interest rates. This policy discourages savings, which are badly needed to finance productive investment, and encourages wasteful consumption and foreign borrowing. The same thing can be observed with the growing exchange rates of zlotys per U.S. dollar. With the drastic reforms of 1989 and the shock therapy of January 1990, inflation rates increased dramatically (586 percent in 1990), as did negative real interest rates (558 percent), and exchange rates (9,500 zlotys per dollar). Thereafter, both inflation and negative real interest rates declined drastically.

FOREIGN TRADE

Growing Trade with the EC

Poland falls within the Great Plain of Europe; it is bordered by Russia in the East, the Czech and Slovak republics in the South, and Germany in the

Figure 5.1
Money Supply (M) and Velocity of Money (GDP/M) for Poland (in billions of zlotys)

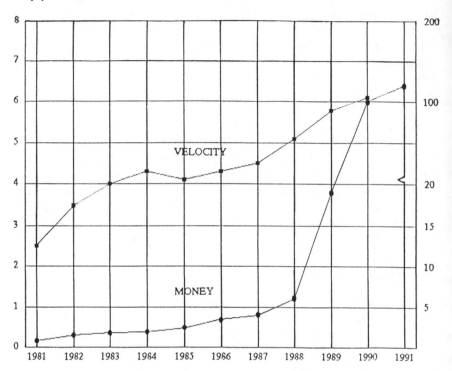

Source: International Monetary Fund, *International Financial Statistics*, various issues.

West. It is rich in mineral resources, primarily coal, iron, zinc, and copper ores, potassium salts, sulfur and related products. Also, more than half of its land is arable. In addition to agricultural and metal products, chemicals, fertilizers, cement, textiles, beet sugar, paper, machinery, glass, and textiles are the main manufacturing goods produced in the country. Coal, clothing, steel, and sugar are the main products exported, primarily to neighboring countries.

Poland, along with Hungary and the Czech and Slovak republics, called on the EC to lower trade barriers on imports of mainly agricultural products, steel, and textiles. Such measures would reduce the need for economic and technical aid and pave the way for their full membership to the EC. As their exports to the old Soviet bloc, primarily to Russia, continue to fall significantly, they have to find new markets in Western countries.[7] However, the EC keeps duties and other restrictions on their exported products, mainly on poultry and pork (up to 50 percent), and beef (up to 100 percent), whereas imports on mutton, apparel, and many other products are restricted.

According to United Nations and IMF statistics, every year, even after 1989 (the year of drastic reforms), Polish exports were higher than imports, resulting in surpluses. In 1990, for example, exports were $15.8 billion while imports were $12.2 billion, resulting in a foreign trade surplus of $3.6 or about 23 percent of the value of exports.[8]

Until recent years, the former Soviet Union absorbed the largest percentage of exports (around one-third), followed by the EC with about one-fourth. However, after 1980 the percentage of exports to the EC has gradually grown (from 19.5 percent in 1981 to 28.9 percent in 1988). More or less the same trends can be observed for Polish imports. They declined from 41 percent of total imports in 1981 to 23.3 percent in 1988 from the former Soviet Union, but they increased from 16.1 percent in 1981 to 28.6 in 1988 from the EC. Polish exports to North America are about 5 percent, and equal to imports, per year.

As expected, after the economic and political reforms of 1989 and later, trade with the other ex-Soviet bloc countries was reduced substantially and was dramatically increased with the EC, particularly Germany. Even before the reforms, Poland had about 18 percent of its total exports with West Germany (13 percent) and East Germany (5 percent) and about the same amount of imports. From that standpoint, the German arguments for closer relations and eventual membership of Poland to the EC are justified.

Although the current account balance, which also includes services, was negative up to 1990, it turned to a large surplus ($3.6 billion) in 1990. It seems that this is the result of austerity measures introduced in 1989 and later.

The main products exported by Poland are metal manufactures (about 44 percent), mining products (17 percent), chemicals (7 percent), textiles (6 percent), and agricultural products (5 to 6 percent). Because of the shift of trade from the former Soviet Union and other countries of Eastern Europe to Western countries, a restructuring of the economy is expected to emphasize specialization and exports of products for which demand in the West is relatively high. Given that wages are comparatively low in Poland, labor-intensive products and metal manufactures would be the main exportables, primarily to Western economies.

To help increase trade and investment, the U.S. Congress approved $852 million in assistance for Poland, whereas the IMF approved $2.48 billion in loans and the World Bank $1.67 billion. Furthermore, if austerity measures are taken, pertaining to wage restraints, reduction in government spending, and price adjustments to the supply and demand mechanism, then commercial EC and U.S. banks would extend loans to Poland and other East bloc countries. In such a case, the Polish zloty and other East bloc currencies may be convertible into EC, U.S., and other hard currencies.

Foreign Debt

Poland's foreign debt, which is over $50 billion (out of a total $153 billion for Eastern Europe and the former Soviet Union in 1990), and interest payments are periodically rescheduled or postponed by the Paris Club and other international creditors in order to help ease transition to a market economy. On the other hand, the governments of some creditor countries agreed on March 15, 1991, to forgive or write off about half the $33 billion debt to Poland. German, French, and Austrian banks are willing to further write off part of the Polish debt, but British and American banks object to that practice, because they like to avoid creating a bad precedent for other debtor countries. Nevertheless, in bilateral arrangements, the United States reduced the $3.8 billion official debt of Poland by 70 percent, while Germany forgave $5.5 billion out of $17 billion total debt. Also, France agreed to a significant debt relief.

Polish trade with Russia may be another source of debt as long as imports of Russian gas, oil, and other related products are worth more of Polish exports of pharmaceutical, coal, and food products to Russia. Although trade priorities are largely fixed with the EC, with the hope for eventual membership, the dependence on Russian gas became obvious in 1992 when shipments of natural gas were cut off by Russia, primarily because of limited production. Steel mills, fertilizer plants, automakers, glass and ceramic works, and even the Gdansk shipyards and the Galician metalworks factories were idle for some time.

FOREIGN INVESTMENT AND JOINT VENTURES

Poland was another leader, after Hungary, in introducing economic reforms toward the free market. Although the transfer of state industrial firms, primarily by giving equal shares to Polish citizens, has been slow, thousands of small state firms have already been transferred to the private sector. The democratically elected governments of Poland managed to free most prices, made the zloty convertible for most businesses, and enacted legislation favorable to foreign investment and trade. Also, they established a small stock exchange market for privatized enterprises, ironically at the former headquarters of the Communist Party.

New measures to encourage foreign investment include labor and pension laws, contract and bankruptcy rules, tax codes, tariff adjustments, and other regulations dealing with private property and free market operations. Nevertheless, foreign and especially American investment proved to be very difficult to enter the area. In spite of low wages and relatively high levels of education and technical skills, market uncertainties and political instability are primarily responsible for the slow flow of American and other foreign investment. That is why thousands of state enterprises remain unsold and joint ventures are limited. In addition, there are large debts of bankrupt state firms, including banks that extended loans to such firms.

European Investment

To normalize economic and cultural relations with Poland, Germany signed an agreement to formally establish the Oder and Neisse rivers border between the two countries as permanent. This German-Polish reconciliation was needed to calm fears of revival of German claims to lands that Poland acquired from Germany in 1945, in which sizable German minorities live.

Fiat SPA of Italy agreed to a $2 billion investment in the Polish car industry with Fabryka Samochodow Osobowych (FSO) and Fabryka Samochodow Malolitrazowych (FSM), both state-owned car makers. Initially, Fiat invested $650 million, an equal amount of investment provided by FSM, for the production of some 500,000 small cars (Micros) a year, 70,000 of which are expected to be exported to the West. Although Fiat's projects are modest, compared to those in the former USSR, with plans to produce 900,000 cars a year, they are significant for Poland because they provide management expertise, know-how, and jobs.

Unilever NV acquired a laundry detergent factory for $20 million and the largest margarine producer in Poland. It has spent more than $150 million in Eastern Europe, mainly to buy state-owned factories.

Jefferson Smurfit Group PLC, the Irish packaging company, is considering expansion in Poland and other East European countries, in the near future, for the production and distribution of soap packets, beer cartons, recycled newsprint, pizza boxes, and related products.

American Investment

In joint ventures with Polish banks and other firms, American companies invest in computers, cars, telecommunications, electronics, airlines, and other operations. First Commercial Bank, a middle-sized Polish bank, plans to develop a network of 40–50 stores throughout the country in the near future, with an initial cost of more than $2 billion to help finance such ventures.

Moreover, United Parcel Service agreed with its Polish counterpart to deliver packages in Warsaw and Cracow. However, there are only about 40 U.S. joint ventures in Poland, far fewer than in Germany.

Zaklady Celulozowa-Papierniecze SA, Poland's largest white-paper firm owned by the government, was acquired by the International Paper Company, which paid $150 million initially and plans to invest $175 million more over four years. Also, the Coca-Cola Company, the forerunner in foreign soft-drink sales, plans to open a bottling plant in Gdynia, investing about $200 million. Moreover, it plans to invest $1 billion in Eastern Europe, including $450 million in the eastern part of Germany.

CPC International Inc., which makes mayonnaise, Mazola corn oil, Mueller's pasta, and Skippy peanut butter, acquired an 80 percent stake in the Amino SA, a Polish state-owned food firm which manufactures desserts, soups, pasta, and other related products. The 20 percent balance was offered to the 700 employees of Amino.

American Telephone and Telegraph Company (AT&T) agreed with the state-owned Polish Telecommunications to expand the domestic telephone network and to connect it to the satellite system of AT&T. The new deal would provide fiber-optic technology, doubling the capacity of Poland's international exchange and making direct dialing easier for the development of business investment. Also, in November 1992 AT&T took over Telfa, worth $80 million.

IBM expects a drastic growth in sales of its products in Poland and other East European countries, where annual sales passed $300 million.

The Levi Strauss company decided to produce jeans in Poland to enjoy low labor costs and high demand. It pays wages of only $148 per month because of high unemployment in the area located about 100 kilometers from Warsaw, and charges $50 per pair of jeans. The factory is automated and labor costs count for only 15 percent of the total cost. Total production is more than 1.5 million units, the largest part of which is exported. However, there are bureaucratic problems in customs houses, in importing the required cloth from the United States as well as in distributing the jeans domestically. Local entrepreneurs must pay $200,000 to acquire Levi's right to manufacture such jeans.

The General Motors Corporation (GM), the largest American car maker, acquired 70 percent of the state-owned Factory of Passenger Cars (FSO is the Polish abbreviation). GM won control of this joint venture in competition with Automobiles Citroen, a unit of Peugeot SA of France. To encourage foreign investments, Poland offered GM, Fiat, and Volkswagen tax-free imports in 1992 for 10,000 cars each, as long as they invest more than $50 million. The import tax on cars is 35 percent.

The Polish Pro-Car is negotiating with Chrysler to buy the Omni and Horizon assembly lines and to transfer them from Detroit to Poland. These lines, which used to produce subcompact cars, stopped operations in the United States in February 1990 and are expected to start production of similar cars in Poland. Moreover, FSM signed a joint-venture agreement with TRW Inc. of Cleveland to assemble seat belts in Poland, mainly for domestic cars.

In its efforts to introduce a free market in telecommunications, the Polish government is gradually abolishing the state monopoly and opening the field to domestic and foreign, mainly American, competition. It is expected that the new system would increase the number of telephones to 30 per 100 people in a decade. At present, Poland has only 4 phones per 100 people, compared to about 50 for the United States, and 15 for the former Soviet Union.

In the field of insurance, the Warte Insurance and Reinsurance Company, based in Warsaw, formed a partnership with Travelers Insurance to provide coverage to American companies in Poland and eventually in other East European countries. The two partners will share the risk for property casualties.

Several joint ventures in Poland and Eastern Europe are negotiated by the U.S. Hornsby and Whisenand law firm. They include the representation of Johnson & Johnson Company to acquire a 55 percent share of the Lenin Shipyards in Gdansk, the birthplace of Solidarity, as well as deals to install cellular telephone systems in Poland and the rest of Eastern Europe.

Heim-Electric GmbH, an electronics firm in East Berlin, agreed to distribute gaming machines of the Bally Manufacturing Corporation of the United States to Poland and other East European countries, where more than 1,000 machines are expected to be sold per year.

Chase Enterprise, a U.S. communications company, agreed to enter into a joint venture with Poltelkob SA of Poland to establish a cable television firm, called Polska Telewizja Kablowa, in Warsaw and other cities. Total investment of Chase Enterprise, which has 70 percent ownership, is estimated at $900 million. The CNN news network and ESPN all-sports channel, among others, would be available to some 1.8 million Polish homes.

Citibank opened a branch in Warsaw in July 1991; while Digital Equipment Corporation formed an information technology unit, which started operations in October 1991.

Pepsico paid $25 million and acquired 40 percent of Wedel, a large state-owned candy company established in Warsaw in 1851. Furthermore, it plans to invest more than $50 million to build a new factory and modernize Wedel.

The Gerber Products Company completed a deal with Poland's Ministry of Privatization to buy 60 percent of Alima SA, the largest baby food and juices company of Central Europe. Employees and suppliers were offered the remaining 40 percent stake at half the price. Gerber payment for the joint venture was determined at $11.3 million, but it is expected that Gerber will invest $17 million more for the expansion of the factory, which is located in Rzeszow. This is the first manufacturing venture of Gerber outside the United States.

Curtis International opened a factory to assemble Japanese-made televisions and video recorders, which was built from scratch in Mlawa, north of Warsaw. The factory, which employs 250 people, was praised by everyone—from Catholic priests to communist *apparatchiks*—as an example of successful foreign venture. However, the company pressed the Polish government to raise tariffs for similar imported products for reasons of protection at the infant stage of operation.

Procter and Gamble invested $60 million to acquire 40 acres in Warsaw to develop a plant and install manufacturing lines for the production and distribution of diapers and related products.

Otis Elevator Company, a unit of United Technologies Corporation, acquired a 70 percent stake in a joint venture with PRDIE, a state-owned firm, to install and service elevators in Poland. The new firm, which is to be upgraded by Otis, is called Otis-Krakow.

LOT, the national airline of Poland, is dealing with Boeing Company for investment in Poland's aviation industry and for buying a fleet of medium-range planes, in addition to nine MD–80 jets bought from McDonnell Douglas for $350 million.

The Colgate-Palmolive Company established a factory near Warsaw to make toothpaste, Ajax household cleaners, Palmolive soap, and other Colgate products. Similar investment ventures have been approved by Colgate and the respective governments of Romania, Hungary, and Ukraine (near Kiev), and aim at business expansion into Eastern Europe and the former Soviet Union.

Other Foreign Investment

Northern Telecom Ltd. of Ontario (Canada), a unit of BCE Inc., created a joint venture with Elwro of Poland to produce and supply telephone switching equipment and other information technology.

The Mazda Motor Corporation of Japan, 24 percent of which is owned by the Ford Motor Company, increased its car exports and maintenance service stations in Poland and other central European and Balkan countries.

Correlation Analysis

A regression analysis for Poland (1980–90) shows that "exports" (EX) is a significant variable in determining net material product (NMP), NMP = 1.3 + 4.0 EX, as is "investment" (INV), NMP = 0.3 + 3.7 INV. In both cases, the correlation was very good (R = 0.99). Similar results were obtained for Hungary, as well. This means that each additional unit of exports is related to 4 units of NMP, and each unit of investment to 3.7 units of NMP.

6

Czech and Slovak Republics

A BRIEF HISTORICAL REVIEW

Before the coming of the Slavic people from the area between the Volga and Dnieper rivers at the end of the fifth century, the territory of the present-day Czech and Slovak republics was inhabited by Celtic tribes (Boii), who settled primarily in Bohemia after 400 B.C. It is not certain how and why they arrived and how they vanished. From the first century B.C. to about the fifth century A.D. Germanic people had inhabited the area. Ever since, three main Slavic tribes (Czechs, Moravians, and Slovaks) have lived in that area. From 1526 to 1918 the area was under the Hapsburg Empire.

In October 1918 and as a result of the defeat of the Austro-Hungarian Empire in World War I, the union of Czechs and Slovaks created a new nation-state named Czechoslovakia. Other sizable minorities are Germans and Magyars. The first president, elected by the National Assembly in 1918 was Tomás Masaryk who held office until 1935.[1]

After Adolf Hitler rose to power in 1933, Nazi agitation for the union of about 3 million Germans, living mainly in Sudetenland, with the Reich was intensified as it was for the union of Slovaks with Hungary (an ally of Germany). U.S. President Franklin Roosevelt appealed to Hitler, through Benito Mussolini, the Italian dictator, to resolve the crisis, and the Munich Pact of September 29, 1938, resulted in the partial dismemberment of Czechoslovakia.

With this Pact, signed by Germany, Italy, Britain, and France, Germany gained some 3.5 million inhabitants. On March 15, 1939, German troops occupied the rest of the country, except Carpatho-Ukraine that was annexed by Hungary. The Nazi occupation was marked by ruthless exploitation of resources and brutal oppression of the people. Underground resistance by the Czechs led to savage reprisals, such as the extermination of the male population of the town of Lidice in 1942, a familiar Nazi behavior in Kalavryta (Greece) and other towns occupied by the Germans.

As the Soviet and American armies moved toward Czechoslovakia, people revolted against the Nazi oppressors and helped defeat Germany in 1945. Thereafter, the country came under Soviet influence. The pre-World War II territories were restored to Czechoslovakia, with the exception of the Carpatho-Ukraine area, which was incorporated in the Soviet Union.

When the Communist Party became the dominant force in the country in 1949, nationalization of industries and trade and collectivization of the farms began. The main economic policies followed by Czechoslovakia, as was the case with other East European countries, were similar to those of the Soviet Union. In the process of sovietization of the economy, the government initially established state-owned cattle-raising and fruit-growing enterprises and later nearly all industry, including wholesale and foreign trade, had been nationalized as well.

ECONOMIC AND POLITICAL REFORMS

The economic reform movement that began in 1963 reached its highest point in 1968 when Alexander Dubcek replaced Antonin Novotny and the so-called Prague spring arrived. Centralized physical planning was, to a large extent, replaced by a market economy guided by economic regulations involving monetary, fiscal, and income policies. Workers were permitted to strike and elect their managers through their established councils, as in Yugoslavia. Enterprises were to decide on their inputs and outputs, while profits, after tax, could be allocated for bonuses or for developmental investment. However, Dubcek and his colleagues offended the Soviet leaders by introducing not only economic reforms, as the Hungarians did in 1968, but moving into political reforms as well. Then, implementing the Leonid Breshnev doctrine that socialist states must intervene to protect other socialist countries from revisionism, Warsaw Pact (mainly Soviet) troops and tanks invaded Prague on August 20, 1968, to save Czechoslovakia from the "capitalist wolves." Dubcek was replaced by Gustav Husak, a hard liner, who remained in power until 1987, when he was replaced by Milos Jakes. Under both rulers, no substantial reforms were conducted, production incentives declined, and productivity growth slowed down.

Czechoslovakia, following the example of Hungary and Poland, achieved a peaceful anticommunist revolution in December 1989, electing Vaclav Havel, a writer in opposition, as president. Havel proposed that Hungary, Poland, and Czechoslovakia could work in unison to return to a friendly community of stable Europe, after some four decades of Soviet domination. Thereafter, military organizations, such as NATO, should be dissolved and an all-European integration be pursued. A joint action to rejoin Europe would avoid rivalry among individual East European countries as they try to have more trade and joint ventures with the EC and other Western countries.

As a result of recent economic and political reforms, the Czechoslovak government ended subsidies on food and other farm products (worth about $1.1 billion) and prices rose substantially, especially of bread, meat, cheese and other dairy products. To counterbalance the effects of price increases on the consumers, the government distributed about $5.50 per month to each person and provided increase of assistance to mothers of young children. Further price increases occurred in home appliances and other products until free competition was restored.[2]

In the elections of June 6, 1992, Vladimir Meciar, the Slovak separatist, won 37 percent of the vote of the eastern republic. The leftists, actually communists, won 14 percent nationwide, but Vaclav Klaus, a right-wing powerful politician, and the Civic Democratic Alliance won the most seats in Parliament. Meciar pushed his separate program and, in coalition with the other parties, forced Havel to resign. The movement led to the disintegration in January 1993 of the 74-year-old federation. The new Czech Republic (with about 10 million people) and Slovak Republic (with around 5 million people) are likely to introduce separate currencies, two central banks, and an exchange rate between the two currencies.

Vaclav Havel, the previous president of Czechoslovakia, was elected president for a five-year term of the new Czech Republic on January 26, 1993. He was supported by Prime Minister Vaclav Klaus and received 109 votes in the 200-member Czech Parliament. On the other hand, the 150-seat Parliament of Slovakia elected Michael Kovac as the first president of the new republic on February 15, 1993. He was supported by Slovak Prime Minister Vladimir Meciar. The "velvet divorce" of the two Slavic republics was peaceful, in contrast to what happened in the Balkans and to some extent in the former Soviet Union. This can help them win favorable treatment from the EC and an inflow of foreign investment into their economies. Also, the division of public property, including the army and its weapons on a 2-to-1 ratio according to their populations, was peaceful. Moreover, the two republics agreed on a customs union regarding free movement of labor and commodities. Nevertheless, Slovakia, with a 600,000 Hungarian minority, is a relatively poor state and its economy depends largely on the Czech and other former European planned economies.

To raise income from the sale of electricity, Slovakia moved ahead with the construction of a vast hydroelectric dam by diverting the Danube River in Gabsikovo near Bratislava, the capital of the republic. However, Hungary and environmental groups from other nations oppose the construction of the dam because it will destroy wildlife, flood valuable land, disrupt river transport, and damage underground water. Similar criticism is directed against the four nuclear power plants of Slovakia and the possibility of radioactive material in case of accidents, as well as the extensive emissions of sulfur dioxide and nitrogen oxides, which contribute to acid rain and smog.

TRANSITION TO CAPITALISM: PRIVATIZATION PROGRAMS

The Czech and Slovak republics seem to be successful in the privatization of state-owned firms. Citizens 18 years or older can buy books of coupons that can be converted into shares of companies or mutual funds holding such shares. For 1,000 nonrefundable crowns (about $35), or around a week's average salary, Czechs and Slovaks can buy, mainly from the post office, a book of coupons consisting of 1,000 points, which can be used to buy stocks of enterprises of their choice.[3] Hundreds of thousands of people have bought stocks of many large firms, while thousands of small companies and shops have been sold directly at auction. Vital public utilities have remained in the hands of the government. The initial success of the privatization program has encouraged some foreign investors to participate in buying shares or to establish new firms.

The main difficulties of such privatization plans, similar to those enacted in Poland and the Baltic states (Lithuania, Latvia, Estonia), were and still are in evaluating assets of so many firms up for sale and the legal problems involved. In many cases, one-third of the firm would go up for bidding and the rest would be reserved for management, foreign investors, or the government. For the ordinary people with limited inside information, though, it is a kind of lottery, but with no large losses expected. In any case, shareholding gives people high motivation in the development process.

Czech Prime Minister Vaclav Klaus, an American-trained economist, introduced the voucher system to privatize government enterprises. With the help of mutual fund salesmen, the vouchers, worth a week's salary per book, were exchanged with stocks in privatized enterprises, which have been offered in waves at different times. Although Poland has moved faster in the process of privatization, mainly because most of its farmers always owned their land, as has Hungary because of extensive previous reforms, the successful voucher system of the Czech Republic was used also in Russia and other ex-Soviet republics. The domestic voucher holders are preferred to foreign buyers because capital is augmented by the government without selling the country to foreigners. With his pragmatic reform strategy, Klaus managed to privatize a number of government dinosaur companies and to balance the budget, as the Polish prime minister did as well, as they both try to work their way into the European Community.

To support Czech and Slovak interests in joining the EC and to attract foreign investment, a value added tax of 5 percent on food and some services and 23 percent for most other items was introduced in January 1993. The

VAT, which increased prices initially about 7 percent, was set mainly to replace the old turnover tax levied primarily on profits.

The privatization program of the former Czechoslovakia proved to be a successful example for other East European nations and the former Soviet Union. Millions of bids for shares of some 1,446 state enterprises take place in Prague every week. About one-third of these enterprises already have been transferred to the private sector and the rest are expected to be transferred in the near future.

The separation of Slovakia, as an independent republic, proved to be beneficial for the Czech privatization program. The prounion Slovak leaders are not in favor of quick privatization of mainly armaments industries, which are concentrated primarily in Slovakia.

The vouchers or coupons given to the adult population, which can be exchanged for shares in enterprises, are sold at a bargain $37 per booklet. Each booklet has a value of 1,000 points. For each 100 points the government offers three shares in state enterprises. If there are more stocks than bidders in a company, shares are given to those who bid, whereas lower prices are offered later for unsold shares. If there are more bidders than stocks, no shares are given and higher prices are raised later. Auctions are repeated until all stocks are distributed. The total value of the state enterprises to be privatized is estimated by the government at $9.3 billion. The process of this Thatcherite example of citizen shareholders and proper evaluation is expected to be improved with the development of the stock market.

Mutual funds, which were created recently, promised to buy back vouchers or shares at far higher prices, thereby generating great public interest for these financial instruments. To support small business and reinforce the private sector, the government cut personal taxes from a top rate of 97 percent to 47 percent and let capital gains go untaxed. As a result, a number of sectors, such as machinery, construction, banking, textiles, and glass are flourishing while foreign joint ventures, such as Skada-VW, Glavunion (a Czech-Belgium joint venture producing glasses), and related exports are rapidly expanding.

Nevertheless, the operations of some 400 mutual funds may lead to the concentration of wealth through the purchases of large amounts of enterprise shares and the weakening of the democratization of ownership. Already, these funds have about 55 percent of all vouchers issued. At times, they offer a tenfold return in a year. This procedure is speculative and works against the concept of "people's capitalism," which advocates the spread of property ownership to more and more people. This practice is largely followed by the free or low-priced vouchers or coupons, distributed to the public, to be exchanged with shares in state enterprises, not only in the former Czechoslovakia but in other East European countries and the former Soviet Union as well. Of the 11 million Czech and Slovak adults, some 8.6 million decided to take part in the voucher or shares process of this popular capitalism.

Some 200 foreign companies participate in serious bids to buy Czech enterprises, primarily in food processing, cement, and in the engineering and automotive parts sectors. They include ITT Automotive, Ford Motor Company, General Motors, TRW, Rockwell Automotive, Johnson Control, and Ferodo. Such foreign investors are looking mainly at the markets of the European Community. Nevertheless, some joint ventures, such as Dow Chemical and the Italian motorcycle firm Cagiva Varese, face difficulties in their bids for environmental and other reasons.

There is a serious problem for the Czech and Slovak republics as for other East European nations, regarding the bumpy transition to capitalism and the previously nationalized enterprises. Pre-World War II owners or heirs of such enterprises demand compensation for nationalization or transfer of ownership without any payment.

Thus, Thomas Bata, an heir of the Canadian Bata Shoe Company family, went to Prague to take back or to enter into a joint venture with Svit, the state-owned shoe and rubber factories operating in Zlin, a town close to Prague. The company was nationalized in 1945 after Jan Bata, an uncle of Thomas, was convicted of collaborating with the Nazis by making army boots for them during the 1930s when he was running the company. Although the government is skeptical about setting a precedent for other persons demanding similar compensations, it is eager to have back worldwide known industrial names, such as the Batas, to revitalize the industry and increase exports. Perhaps issuing stocks and giving the Batas a portion of shares may solve the problem to the satisfaction of both sides.

MONETARY POLICY

The supply of money was constant up to 1988, when it increased by about 15 percent; thereafter, it remained constant or declined. Such changes in money supply were primarily related to budget financing and covering other expenditures in the Czech and Slovak economies under reforms.

The velocity of money—that is, the ratio of gross domestic product over the money supply—was relatively constant and about 2.5 up to 1989. Thereafter, as a result of free market reforms, the average monetary unit (koruni) circulated faster and velocity increased. However, the changes in money supply and velocity were extensive enough to increase inflation and to depreciate the koruni after the reforms of 1989.

In both the Czech and Slovak republics, tax revenues are not sufficient to cover public-sector expenditures. Moreover, domestic borrowing by the government from the general public, by issuing bonds and other securities, is not normally used in these republics. An increase in money supply then is the main source of financing government deficits. Assuming other things the same, this measure leads to inflation.

As expected, prices were stable and inflationary rates very slow until 1989 for the former Czechoslovakia. Thereafter, prices increased substantially due mainly to the significant economic reforms introduced at that time. As a result, real interest rates were positive and exchange rates remained relatively constant until 1989. Thereafter, real interest rates became negative and exchange rates began to increase, because of the high increase in the consumer price index.

In June 1993 domestic and foreign investors, including some EC firms and more than 300 American businesses, began trading shares on a widespread basis in the newly created Prague Stock Exchange. Some 650 stocks of about 1,000 privatized companies were initially listed on the exchange. Although limited trading over the counter has been conducted for some months now, the participation of about 400 funds, including 13 large ones with control of 35 percent of all the shares in public hands, enhanced exchanges.[4]

FOREIGN TRADE

The territory of the Czech and Slovak republics lies in a strategic location between Eastern and Western Europe, as well as between the agrarian regions of the Balkans and the more industrialized areas of Europe. It comprises the previous provinces of Bohemia, Moravia, Silesia, and Slovakia.

The Czech and Slovak republics, along with Hungary and other East European countries, face a serious energy problem as Russia drastically cut oil supplies. In 1989, such supplies were reduced by 16 percent and in 1990 by 65 percent, because of difficulties in oil production. Czech oil imports from the former Soviet Union were about 16 million tons annually for previous years, at lower prices than those in the international markets. In exchange, low-quality machinery was exported to the former Soviet Union. To meet domestic oil demand, policy makers turned to other oil-producing nations, particularly Libya, Algeria, Syria, and Iran (through a pipe via the former Soviet Union).

Agricultural products, textiles, coal, and steel make up the largest part of Czech and Slovak exports, as they do for Poland and Hungary. However, in April 1993 the EC set quotas for steel, a ban on meat and dairy products, and tariff barriers for other cheap products from Eastern Europe. The Czech authorities retaliated with their own ban on imports of meat and milk products from the EC, as did the Polish and Hungarian authorities. Nevertheless, such short-run protective measures, enacted under the pressure of EC producer groups, would gradually wither away and the growing Czech and Slovak exports to the West of more than $600 million a month on the average would continue.

In contrast to what happened in Poland, the former Czechoslovakia had mostly positive balances of foreign trade during the previous decades, except in 1990 when there was a relatively large deficit, due primarily to the sizable decline in exports. Thus, exports in 1990 were $11.6 billion, compared to $14.2 billion in 1989 and $15.1 billion in 1988, while imports were $13.1 billion, $14.1 billion, and $14.8 billion, respectively. Also, the largely positive balance of services led to positive balances in the current accounts in all the previous years except 1990, in which there was a deficit of $1.2 billion.

Up to the year of reforms (1989), the main customers of Czechoslovak products were the former Soviet Union and other East European countries, where exports were about 44 percent and 32 percent of the total exports, respectively. Exports to the EC were about 10 percent of the total, and those to North America were less than 1 percent per year. However, a significant decline of exports to the ex-socialist countries of Europe and a drastic increase of exports to the EC can be observed after the economic and political reforms of 1989. More or less the same trends can be seen for imports. The main exported Czech and Slovak products are metal manufactures (about 60 percent of the total exports, annually), textiles (9 percent), and chemicals (around 8 percent).

Although they have close ties with the West, the Czechs and Slovaks retain high taxes on profits (more than 50 percent), a fact that discourages foreign and domestic investment in productive enterprises. On the other hand, currency convertibility is required to attract foreign firms to buy state-owned enterprises or to invest in new companies. This may take a number of years to be realized. In the meantime, the overvalued currency expands imports and cripples exports, thereby exaggerating the balance-of-payments problem of the country. However, more reliable financial and trade information is needed by potential buyers of state-run firms for effective decision making.

Although trade and other transactions with the former Soviet Union have largely been reduced, exports to the West have been up to more than $5 billion annually, compared to about $6 billion for Hungary and $9 billion for Poland. Machine tools, auto and truck parts, and textiles are among the most successful products exported to the West.

In October 1991 the United States lowered trade barriers to steel, textiles, and some other Czechoslovak products, so that more exports can be realized. At the same time, Vaclar Havel, then president of Czechoslovakia, signed an agreement that offers American investors guarantees on profit repatriation and freedom in currency exchanges. From that standpoint, American and other foreign investors are expected to play a major role in the privatization process of the overstaffed and outmoded state-owned enterprises.

The Czech Republic's exports account for about 75 percent of the federal exports to the European Community and show steady surplus and trade expansion. Also, the foreign debt is the lowest of Eastern Europe outside Romania. Entrepreneurial activities and exports were stimulated by decreasing interest rates since 1991 when controls were lifted. However, corporate tax rates are scheduled to increase from 40 to 50 percent. There are not specific regional incentives for investment in the poor areas of northern

Bohemia and Moravia. However, collection of value added taxes proved unsuccessful as local entrepreneurs are not bothered to calculate them.

As do other East European countries and Russia, the Czech and Slovak republics need American and other Western trade and investment in order to acquire modern technology, hard currencies, and management techniques. Such investments can be directed to export-promoting industries in such areas as steel, textiles, and farm products, where the country has a comparative advantage. Or they can be directed toward import substituting industries to help improve the foreign trade balance, save hard currency from the replacement of imported products, and reduce unemployment.

FOREIGN INVESTMENT AND JOINT VENTURES

As a result of the political and economic changes of the country toward a free market economy, foreign investment ventures have begun to be formed. Thus a European Community bank is projected to be established in Prague to offer financial and other services in the newly democratized East European countries. Moreover, the Czech and Slovak republics as well as Bulgaria applied and were accepted as members of the World Bank in 1990. About $1.6 billion in investments were made between 1989 and 1992, mainly from Germany, France, and the United States.

As other East European countries did after the dismantling of the Berlin Wall, the two republics also introduced a democratic system and allowed the establishment of Western-style car companies and joint ventures. As a result, a number of Western automakers moved into these republics and other neighboring countries to exploit the opportunities.

EC Investment

Volkswagen AG, the largest car firm in Western Europe, agreed to the formation of a joint venture with Skoda, the most advanced automobile firm in Eastern Europe. Similar movements are made by Adam Opel AG, a subsidiary of the General Motors Corporation in West Germany, Fiat, of Italy, Renault of France, and Suzuki of Japan, among others.[5]

The agreement between Volkswagen with Skoda provides for the creation of a third company, which would double production to 400,000 Favorit cars by the year 2000. Favorit, at present produced by Skoda, is a small family car considered as the best car in Eastern Europe. The cost to VW for the deal would be about $6 billion, some $750 million of which was paid initially for acquiring 25 percent of the new firm. Up to 1996 the acquisition would reach 70 percent of the firm, while the remaining 30 percent may be acquired during the process of privatization. This is the biggest capital investment in Eastern Europe and the largest cross-border industrial deal in history.[6]

With the coordination of the European Bank for Rehabilitation and Development, more Western companies are investing in the area. Thus, Mercedes-Benz AG, the well-known luxury auto company of Germany, created a joint venture with Avia, a Czech auto firm. Mercedes will invest more than $350 million and get a stake of 51 percent of the new company, which is expected to produce around 40,000 cars a year. Moreover, Mercedes is negotiating similar joint ventures with Liaz and Tatra enterprises for the production of trucks.

Siemens AG of Germany announced a joint venture with Skoda Plzen AS. In the new venture, called Skoda Energo, Siemens has a two-thirds stake, and the other one-third belongs to Skoda Plzen and Skoda Praha. Siemens, a dominant electronics company, paid $170 million and beat out the Westinghouse Electric Corporation and Asea Brown Boveri AB of Sweden. Also, Henkel, a German detergent maker, acquired related Czech properties.

Air France formed a joint venture with CSA, its Czech counterpart, in which 60 percent of the shares will remain with the government and 40 percent with Air France. The capital of the new firm will increase from $60 million to $150 million.

Unilever agreed to acquire the state-owned Povltavsk Tukov Zvody, which produces edible oils and fats, toilet soap, and skin cream. Cadbury-Schweppes PLC of Britain formed a partnership with Pepsico International to distribute Schweppes tonic water and other soft drinks in the Czech and Slovak republics and to other East European countries.

Renault, the French state-owned firm, loaned about $94 million (500 million francs) to Avia, the Prague-based vehicle manufacturing firm, to raise annual production to more than 20,000 light trucks.

Aircom Luftfahrthandels, the Austrian trading company, is negotiating to buy seven Soviet-built Tupovel 154 trijet airliners worth about $15 million each from the Czech Aerolinie to sell them to airlines in Asia or Africa.

American Investment

American investment in the Czech and Slovak republics is growing rapidly. Some U.S. companies with sizable investment and joint ventures include Philip Morris, Dow Chemical, Kmart, Ford, Cabot Corporation, Coca-Cola, Atlantic West, American Standard, and a host of other smaller firms.

In more detail, Philip Morris acquired a controlling stake in Tabak Kutna Hora, a cigarette maker that controls about 70 percent of the Czech market. This is the biggest joint venture ($312 million) since the reforms of 1989. A consortium including Atlantic Partners, a big American energy company, offered to buy Chabarovice, a Czech mining town near the German border, in which a $160 million investment is expected to modernize the place and exploit the rich deposits of brown coal. Dow Chemical Company plans to buy 90 percent of Chemicke Zavodi for $150 million, an offer Dow later lowered. Air Products and Chemicals Inc. purchased a controlling interest in Ferox, a Czech maker of cryogenic plants and other engineering products. Hewlett-Packard, a computer maker, established a sales and support subsidiary in the Czech republic.

Tatra Koprivnice, the oldest Czech truck company that stopped production because of heavy debts, agreed with Gerald Greenwald, a former vice-chairman of the Chrysler Corporation, and two other American executives to help salvage Tatra with their management expertise in return for a modest annual fee and a stake of 15 percent of Tatra.

Bell Atlantic Corporation and U.S. West, Inc. agreed to form a joint venture enterprise with the Czech Ministry of Posts and Telecommunications, in which 49 percent belongs to the above American companies, which committed $80 million, and 51 percent to this governmental agency. Anheuser-Busch, the American brewer of Budweiser beer, agreed to settle long-standing trademark differences with the original Czech producer of the same-name beer since the sixteenth century for expansion of sales all over Europe. At the same time, Pilsner Urquell brewery, a 158-year-old famous company, is in the process of transformation into a dynamic profit-making private firm of international importance.

Whirlpool International BV, the European subsidiary of the U.S.-based Whirlpool Corporation, and Tatramat AS agreed to produce washing machines and other appliances in Poprad. Whirlpool will own 43.8 percent of the venture, which will produce not only domestic appliances for the internal market but also for exports mainly to Poland and Hungary.[7]

The Minnesota Mining and Manufacturing Company (3M) established a subsidiary in Prague, in addition to 3M Hungary, which was established previously in Budapest.

Rockwell International Corporation agreed to assume majority ownership of a factory complex in Liberec, about 75 miles northeast of Prague, which produces window regulators and seat slides.

Kmart Corporation is negotiating the acquisition of 97 percent of Kotva, the largest department store in Prague. Kmart would buy 15 shops and create a supermarket chain.

McDonalds Corporation decided to open a restaurant in downtown Prague and many more are expected to open in the near future. The price of a hamburger is about 80 cents or 22 Czech crowns.

Conoco Inc. agreed with Bengina, a Czechoslovak oil enterprise, to lease and operate 13 gas stations in the country.

CPC International Inc. would acquire 77 percent of Zabreh, a mayonnaise and tartar-sauce producer. CPC, which produces Hellman's and Best Foods mayonnaise, Skippy peanut butter, and Mazola corn oil and margarine, has acquired businesses not only in the Czech and Slovak republics but in Hungary, Poland, and other East European countries as well.

TRW Inc. agreed to acquire Dacicke Strojirny SP, the Czech manufacturing firm that produces automobile engine valves.

Procter and Gamble (P&G) bought Rakona, the largest Czech detergent company for $20 million. P&G will pay at least another $24 million to upgrade and expand Rakona.

The Coca-Cola Company, through its partner, Coca-Cola Amatil Ltd., invested $28 million in the purchase and development of a soft-drink plant in Prague. The plant, which formerly belonged to Prague Confectioners and Sodaworks, will produce Coca-Cola, Sprite, Fanta, Kinley, Lift, and Cappy. This is part of about a $2 billion investment by Coca-Cola in Eastern Europe. Also, Pepsico established a number of restaurants in the Czech republic and other neighboring countries.

Westinghouse Electric Corporation announced that it would cooperate with Skoda, a Czech engineering firm, in nuclear power and technology.

In August 1992 the Czechoslovakia Investment Corporation was introduced on the London Stock Exchange. It is a $30 million close-up mutual fund, which helps the financing of investment in the Czech and Slovak republics.

Young and Rubicam, an American advertising firm with more than $6 billion worldwide billings, and AB Line Studios, a small private agency in Prague, created a new agency, Young and Rubicam Czechoslovakia, to expand business in Eastern Europe. Also, Saatchi and Saatchi Advertisement Worldwide and Ogilvy and Mather established offices not only in Prague but also in Budapest, Moscow, and other cities of Poland, the former East Germany, and the former Yugoslavia. Such movement eastward is motivated by big clients' desire to promote their products. Such clients include Kodak, Colgate, Xerox, Coca-Cola, Del Monte, and Nestlé. The success of Adidas athletic footwear in Budapest, where long lines of customers can be observed daily, supports the rapid spread of advertising companies. Adidas is a client of Young and Rubicam. It seems the Czechs prefer to attract investment from the United States and possibly from Japan, Britain, and France to counterbalance investment domination by Germany, about which they are skeptical for political reasons.

7

Hungary

A BRIEF HISTORICAL REVIEW

In ancient times (third century B.C.), the area of present-day Hungary was occupied by Celtic Eravisci warriors, retreating from defeat in Greece. In the first century B.C. the western part of the country was taken by the Roman Empire, which designated it the province of Pannonia. The Danube River was the border of the empire for the four next centuries. During the fifth to eighth centuries (the Age of Migration), Jazyges, Alans, Huns, Avars, Gothics, and other tribes alternatively invaded the area. Although Attila, the most dreadful Hun, operated in the area in the fifth century, the connection between the Huns and the Hungarians is rather coincidental.

The Hungarian people are considered as belonging to a branch of the Finno-Ugrian peoples who appeared in the area between the Ural Mountains and the River Volga about the first century B.C. Being a nomadic people known as Magyars and under the pressure of other tribes, they gradually moved westward. They crossed the Carpathian Mountains and, under Prince Arpad, occupied the territory around the Danube and Tisza rivers at the end of the ninth century. Later the Magyars extended their rule to Slovakia, Slovenia, and other surrounding areas.[1]

Charlemagne broke with the Avar Empire, while Magyar tribes settled in the region in the ninth century (896 and later). King Stephen I (1000–38), who attained sainthood, was a descendant of Arpad and the first king of Hungary. The Hungarians then adopted Christianity. During the Arpad dynasty until 1301, the feudal system prevailed in agriculture, while German, French, Greek, and Italian traders, along with Hungarian and other merchants, conducted trade in the area.

The invasion of the Mongols in 1241–42, under Batu Khan, destroyed many villages and towns, including Buda and Pest (later Budapest). This induced King Bela IV (1235–70) and later rulers up to the fifteenth century to build fortresses and other large buildings, remainders of which can be seen today.

János Hunyadi, the viceroy of Hungary, managed to rally the Hungarians and other Christian peoples to turn back the Turks in Belgrade (1456). During the reign of his son, known as Matthias Corvinus, from 1458 to 1490, a golden age of civic and intellectual development was achieved. King Matthias employed Italian artists to expand and beautify the Royal Palace, which is well preserved on Castle Hill, and other impressive buildings in Budapest, as the author observed recently.

From 1526 to 1686 Hungary came under the Turks, while the north and the west came under the control of the Hapsburg Empire. More than half (2,700) of the villages were destroyed by the marauding Turks, while people were forced into slavery. Also, heavy taxes were imposed by the Ottoman Turks, as they were in all occupied Balkan nations. After the Turks were finally routed by the armies of allied Christian powers, the Hapsburgs, who were also Holy Roman emperors, extended their rule all over Hungary, which became dependent on their policies for four centuries. As a result of the Turkish and Hapsburg oppression, Hungary fell economically and culturally behind contemporary Europe.

A reform movement in the 1840s grew into a struggle for independence, which was suppressed by the Hapsburgs with the assistance of Czar Nicholas I of Russia. In the following two decades the Viennese government kept tight economic and political control of Hungary. But Austria's defeat in the war with Prussia (1866) forced a compromise and the creation of the Austro-Hungarian dual monarchy (1867) that lasted for 50 years. In 1873 the three separate towns of Buda, Pest, and Óbuda were united and formed Budapest. Its present population is 2.2 million, about one-fifth of Hungary's population.

With World War I the Austro-Hungarian monarchy collapsed and a period of political turmoils and economic setbacks occurred during the interwar period. About two-thirds of the country was handed over to its neighbors. In June 1941 Hungary entered World War II on the side of Nazi Germany and a Hungarian force was sent to help Hitler fight the Soviet Union. Hitler's armies occupied Hungary from March 1944 until April 1945, when the Soviet army came and the system of communism, with a centrally planned economy, was established. Collectivization of agriculture and nationalization of industry began by the Socialist Workers' Party (Communist Party) in 1948.

POST-WORLD WAR II POLICIES

In the first five-year plan (1950–54) ambitious economic targets were forwarded under Premier Matzas Rakosi, a hard-line Stalinist. After Stalin's death in 1953, Rakosi was replaced by Imre Nagy, and more moderate policies, with emphasis on consumers' industries and less oppression, were followed. Nikita Khrushchev, who replaced Malenkov as a Soviet leader in February 1955, put Rakosi in power again. A peaceful demonstration in October 1956 and the escalated violence against the oppressive regime of Rakosi brought Soviet tanks into Budapest. Nagy was restored again by the Soviets. He introduced new economic reforms, including the establishment of enterprise workers' councils similar to those in Yugoslavia, disbanded the security police, and declared Hungary's neutrality. Hostilities were escalated with the Soviets, and Warsaw Pact tanks crushed the Hungarian revolution on November 4, 1956. Close to 3,000 people were killed, 20,000 left for the West, and Nagy and many of his associates were executed.

Thereafter, the Soviets installed Janos Kadar, who abolished the workers' councils but used cash incentives, not force, to attract farmers into cooperatives. Farm managers were not appointed by the party but by free peasant voting. Profitability and innovations were encouraged in industry and the market mechanism was slowly restored.

ECONOMIC CHANGES

After related discussions on reforms throughout Eastern Europe, the Kadar administration introduced more comprehensive economic reforms in 1968, known as the New Economic Mechanism (NEM). These reforms aimed at abandoning physical imperative planning and using financial means to achieve projected targets. Also, enterprises were free to purchase their inputs and to produce according to the orders of the consumers. However, regarding profitability and financial considerations, they were guided by the center. Further, economic reforms were initiated from 1979 onward.[2] These reforms were particularly successful in agriculture, services, construction, and other small-scale industries operated by the private sector. The new Hungarian reforms, though, did not challenge the Soviet political and international supremacy and avoided a new rolling of the tanks of the Warsaw Pact into Budapest, as happened in Prague in 1968. Under Karoly Grosz, the successor to Kadar, the role of central planning was further limited, more farms were decollectivized, and private firms flourished. Also, foreign exchanges and travel abroad were eased and joint ventures were encouraged, including the establishment of a business school with Hungarian and U.S. personnel (1988).

In addition to small private firms, free contracts of groups of individuals with enterprises were permitted for overtime work with extra pay, using their own equipment or that of the enterprises. Also, more autonomy and democracy were allowed in the appointment or election of management and representative councils.[3] A market for bonds was established, bankruptcy laws were introduced, the National Bank of Hungary became responsible only for money supply and interest rates, and new taxes on income and sales were imposed while those on enterprise profits were reduced.

In spite of the drastic economic and political reforms in Hungary and other East European countries, one can still observe severe controls on passports at airports and other border entrances, as well as on commodities at customs houses. Moreover, in restaurants and other shops, most of which are state-owned, some relaxation and laziness can be seen in services offered, while management is not eager to satisfy customers because they are responsible to government bureaucrats on whom their salaries and promotions depend.

To commemorate the first dismantling of the iron curtain along the Hungarian-Austrian border on August 18, 1989, the government decided to stage a Europe Day on that date every year. In this pan-European picnic people from neighboring and other countries participate. However, a suggested new regional cooperation plan spanning the Carpathian Mountains and the region of the Tisza River under an all-European security system, which was to replace the Warsaw Pact and perhaps NATO, was impractical and ill-conceived.

Moreover, the establishment of an institution to support small enterprises and to reduce state bureaucracy is in progress. Hungarian and other international economic experts, mainly from Germany, Sweden, the United States, and Canada, would supervise the institution that is expected to set up advisory bureaus for enterprises all over Hungary.

Privatization policy makers provide easy credit and other facilities to small investors in order to avoid the creation of domestic and foreign monopolies. This is what happened recently when 60 percent of the privatized property was acquired mainly by large foreign firms. In addition, the encouragement of small domestic investors to purchase stocks is expected to speed up privatization, because only 17 percent of the property of some 1,500 state enterprises has been privatized in Hungary.

Hungarian farmers who lost their land to collectivization some 40 years ago are entitled to coupons worth up to 5 million forints (about $65,000). They can use these coupons to buy land or shares of newly privatized state enterprises. However, they must farm the land for five years, so that speculation will be avoided.

Two mutual funds were established to channel investment in Hungary. The Austro-Hungary Fund, which opened with $27 million in assets in June 1990, is listed on the Amsterdam Stock Exchange and the Hungarian Investment Fund, with $100 million funds, is traded on the London Stock Exchange. The first fund has invested 40 percent in Hungary and 60 in Austria.

In the past three years, more than 60,000 private companies have been legally registered. Overall, the transition period to the market system was less painful, from the standpoint of decline in production and increase in inflation, in Hungary than in other East European countries.

Nevertheless, because of the severe austerity fiscal measures suggested by the International Monetary Fund and others, the standard of living is falling and the middle class is slipping into the ranks of the poor. With a deficit of $2 billion in a $12.2 billion budget, an inflation rate of 20 percent, 11.6 percent unemployment, 50,000 people homeless, and 70 to 90 percent of pensioners living below the poverty level ($85 per month), preserving social peace is difficult. To avoid social unrest, the government of Jozsef Antall and his Democratic Forum Party agreed to increase the minimum wage to about $115 a month and to modify the value added taxes, which are 6 percent on basics, such as bread and milk, and 25 percent on other items. Medicines and household electricity are exempted from value added taxes.

High rates of investment are required to achieve high rates of economic growth. The incremental capital output ratio (ICOR) in Hungary is 2.5. Assuming other things the same, for an annual rate of economic growth of 6 percent, about 15 percent of GDP investment is required, which is difficult to achieve in this transitional period.

MONETARY POLICY

The monetary policy of Hungary up to 1988 was reasonable with a relatively constant velocity of money and not much increase in money supply. That is why inflationary rates were kept below two digits. During the years of drastic reforms (1989, 1990), money supply increased significantly, as did the rates of inflation. Thereafter, a more stable monetary policy resulted in constant or declining money supply and constant velocity of money.

Because of relatively higher rates of inflation, compared to nominal interest rates, real interest rates were negative in Hungary during the last decade. However, Hungarian monetary policy makers managed to keep low rates of consumer price increase, and the negative real interest rates were not as high as in other East European countries. Likewise, variations in exchange rates were not large. They increased from 32.2 forints per dollar in 1980 to 47.3 forints in 1985 and 75.1 in 1991.

Hungary, which had a stock market from the 1860s until 1948, permits foreigners to buy shares up to 100 percent of public and private enterprises. The Budapest stock market is the only one in the planned economies where bonds are sold. Moreover, a new bankruptcy law was introduced recently in Hungary to take care of enterprise failures in a fashion similar to that of the West. However, foreign owners cannot shut down or transfer overseas their enterprises. A number of Western brokerage and investment firms also help raise funds for purchasing shares of Hungarian enterprises.

Hungary, which started reforms early, seems to be successful in selling state firms in auctions. Most of the money collected from such sales is used to retire previous debts.[4] Although there are more foreign investments in Hungary than in other East European countries, lack of accounting standards and uncertainties about future expectations are discouraging new business ventures. Moreover, there is some form of negativism on the part of population, regarding innovations, hard work ethics, and even the final success of the capitalist system. Being influenced by American TV series such as "Dallas," people think that they can easily become rich, regardless of the serious effort and hard work required. For decades, they received orders from the government about what to do and how to do things, and much time is needed to take initiatives on business enterprises and market risks.

Increasing prices (around 20 percent annually), growing debt (about $2,000 per person), and rising unemployment result in high income inequalities, poverty, homelessness, and parasitism. Although average wages are around $140 per month, a growing number of people are falling below the poverty level of about $85 per month.

FOREIGN TRADE

The trade balances of Hungary had mostly surpluses in the past. However, the balances of current accounts were largely negative, mainly because of the deficits in the services balances. Thus, in 1989 the trade balance was positive ($1,043 million), but the balance of current accounts was negative (− $588 million). In 1990, though, both balances were positive ($534 million for the trade balance and $379 for the current account balance). Merchandise exports were $9,151 million and merchandise imports were $8,617 in 1990.

Hungarian products were primarily exported to the former Soviet Union and the other East European countries (around 50 percent of the total exports). The EC absorbed about one-fifth of the Hungarian exports up to recent years. As expected, however, after the drastic free market reforms of 1989, exports to the previous socialist countries declined, but those to the EC member countries increased substantially.[5]

Among the first foreign companies that entered Hungary after the democratization of the late 1980s was the General Electric Company, which acquired a light bulb manufacturing firm. Also, the General Motors Corporation continues to buy automobile components in Hungary in order to increase its car sales in that country. However, trade and joint ventures have increased not only in Hungary but in other East European countries to take advantage of their untapped markets.

The unreliability of oil and gas supplies from the former Soviet Union forced Hungary to strengthen its links with the EC supply networks. In general, trade with the West is increasing. Currently, Germany is Hungary's biggest trading partner, ahead of Russia. Other important trading countries are Austria, the Czech and Slovak republics, Italy, and the United States (with which Hungary has about $200 million surplus a year).

Agricultural products, which count for about 30 percent of total exports, are competitive, as are fine chemicals and pharmaceuticals, medical instruments, and machine tools. Nevertheless, because of the more demanding

Western consumers, firms such as the important Ikarus bus company need modernization to be able to compete in unprotected markets. Likewise, the tourist industry needs further development to attract foreign visitors with hard currency. A good example is the Helia Hotel in Budapest, a joint venture with other Finnish groups, which offers hydrotherapy and other specialized medical treatments.

Recently the United States, which criticized the EC and France, in particular, of not reducing import barriers to meat and other products, refused to eliminate existing tariffs on Goya cheese imported from Hungary. The U.S. dairy industry is among the most protected, mainly because of strong lobbying by dairy farmers and their politicians.

FINANCIAL SUPPORT

The newly founded Central European Development Corporation (CEDC) announced a $10 million purchase of 50 percent interest of the General Banking and Trust Company, an important bank of Hungary. The investment functions of the CEDC, which was established by Americans, would concentrate on tourism, real estate, and communications, not only in Hungary but also in the Czech and Slovak republics and other neighboring nations.

There are about 60 American companies doing business in Hungary but many more from Germany and Austria. The fact that political and economic changes in Hungary started years ago makes the country more attractive to foreign investment and sophisticated management than other East bloc countries. Although the country has an external debt of $20 billion, recent cuts on food, housing, and other subsidies according to the prescriptions of the International Monetary Fund, are expected to stabilize the Hungarian economy and attract more investment ventures.

To help Hungary reform its economy, the World Bank and IMF provided loans—$80 million and $210 million in 1990, respectively. Likewise, the Export-Import Bank of Japan agreed to give loans up to $200 million to help Hungary restructure its economy. This is the first loan under a $1.95 billion aid package promised by Japan to Hungary and Poland in a tie-up with the World Bank's investment in East European nations.

The Central European Association, formed by U.S. and Canadian (mainly Andrew Sarlos of Hungarian origin) entrepreneurs, provides financial support for investment and transfer of technology into Hungary. More than $200 million have been provided currently for investment ventures, primarily in hotels, banks, and department stores in Budapest and elsewhere. However, the use of such investment funds is slow, mainly because of the slow process of privatization and related bureaucratic inertia.

The Central and Eastern European Center of Environmental Protection was established in 1990 in Budapest for data collection, consultation services, environmental education and its diffusion abroad, and managerial techniques to help resolve pollution problems. For the project, the United States contributed $5 million, the European Community $2 million, and Hungary 50 million forints and a further 80 million forints' worth of real estate.

Recently, the World Bank approved an information technology project of $140 million to support the modernization of the Hungarian financial system. The project would help automate the major banks, develop data processing facilities, and improve management information and communication networks. Similar projects are planned for other East European countries, notably Poland and the Czech and Slovak republics.

Overall, some 16 American companies have registered for insurance with the U.S. Overseas Private Investment Corporation covering $700 million investment in Hungary and 21 companies for $1.1 billion investment in Poland.

Other financial firms include Bear Stearns and Company, Price Waterhouse, and Peat Marwick, American consulting and accounting firms, and companies planning to finance stock market and investment operations in Hungary. With the recent agreement between Hungary and the EC, not only would trade in agricultural products rise, but more financial and investment ventures would occur.

An ambitious financial center of 11 stores, with 700,000-square-foot office complex, is under construction on the bank of the Danube River in Budapest to facilitate stock exchanges and other financial transactions in central Europe. The Budapest's Danube Financial Center, which was designed by Emery Roth and Sons (established in New York in 1902 by a Hungarian immigrant, Irmi Roth), is scheduled to open for business in 1994 with advanced computers and other modern equipment. Emery Roth was also involved in feasibility studies for ten Budapest hotels and is active in other similar projects.

Austria, Hungary, the Czech and Slovak republics, Slovenia, and Croatia have a common economic history and are expected to create stronger economic ties and perhaps an economic commonwealth in Central Europe or a new form of reintegration. From that standpoint, the Budapest's Danube Financial Center and similar institutions are expected to play a vital role in the development of the area, while new investment opportunities are created for Western and mainly EC businesses.

Hungary, however, with a large foreign debt (about $20 billion), needs financial support from the EC, the United States, and Japan to implement reforms and modernize its economy. The U.S. Congress recently approved $86 million assistance to Hungary (and $852 million to Poland), while additional assistance is expected from the International Monetary Fund as long as measures are taken to strengthen the economy. In the meantime, better relations with the West for Hungary would increase trade with both the EC and the United States so that Hungarian exports of textiles, steel, auto parts, machinery, wine, foods, and other products would increase.

Hungary was the first East bloc country to free itself from the ruble in trade settlements with the Soviet Union. Like the other countries under the influence of the Soviet system, Hungary has frequently had a surplus in rubles that could be spent for Russian goods that may not be wanted. Instead, the Soviets were asked to base trade on dollars that can be used by Hungary and other East European countries to buy sophisticated industrial and other products from the West. At the same time, efforts are made to make their own currencies convertible into hard Western currencies.

JOINT VENTURES AND OTHER INVESTMENT

Although Hungary had moved away from central planning and permitted the establishment of foreign investment and private enterprises, some government controls and bureaucratic inertia remain and act as drawbacks to free market reforms. This results in what is called "goulash communism." In addition, there is a cultural bias, which predates the 1940s, similar to that in France and other European countries, against capitalist enterprises and businesspeople and in favor of honorific professions such as lawyers, sociologists, civil clerks, and the like. To some extent, the pursuit of money is associated with cheating, unfairness, greed, and corruption. The notion that everything belongs to everybody and that everyone will be taken care of is still widespread in Hungary and other ex-communist countries.

In the rule-bound economy of Hungary, where a large number of enterprises belong to the state, joint ventures and foreign investment transactions have to go through a review of the State Property Agency so that sweetheart deals between current managers and foreign investors will be avoided. However, large deals can be more easily negotiated with the very top of the power structure. Some industrial products such as turbines are exchanged for local products such as cattle or eggs; whereas stock market exchanges, handled by the Joint Stock Company of State Ownership, which is under the government, are limited and private initiatives are restricted.

European Investment

According to the Hungarian Ministry of International Relations, there were 1,800 joint ventures in Hungary by June 1990 compared to only 280 at the end of 1989, and far more are expected as a result of the intensive economic and political reforms that have been introduced recently.

Attracted by the liberalization movement and the new legislation permitting 100 percent ownership, EC and other firms form joint ventures or invest in Hungary. They include the Tengelmann Group of West Germany, which together with Holland's Philips and Finland's Nokia, acquired an 18 percent stake in the Skala Co-op for $9.8 million, a large Hungarian retailer; and Telfos, a British engineering firm that acquired a 51 percent stake of the state-owned Ganz Railway Engineering. Moreover Novotrade, a software and computer firm, launched a share issue on a Western market for further investment in Hungary.

Bertetsmann AG, a West German publisher, became one of the owners of *Nepszabadsag*, Hungary's largest newspaper with about 400,000 circulation, by contributing $2.14 million (140 million forints). Other owner groups of the paper, which was the mouthpiece of the Hungarian Communist Party before the introduction of the multiparty system, include the editorial staff, which contributed 1.5 million forints, and Hungarian banks. Other foreign media companies began buying dozens of newspapers and magazines. However, the news agency MTI, television, and radio are still run by the state.

In order to stimulate foreign investment, the Hungarian government introduced tax incentives and guaranteed repatriation of profits in hard currency. As part of the reorientation of trade flows from the former East bloc to Western countries, Hungary is strengthening its links with the EC. This is the proper way to increase trade, introduce modern technology, and acquire needed hard currency, thereby increasing the possibilities of an early EC membership.

More than 2,000 joint-venture companies have been created by foreign investors and local partners during the last three years, compared to only 120 in previous years. More than 60 percent of them were from Germany and Austria, mainly in auto and information industries, whereas Switzerland is interested in the production of pharmaceuticals and food. The Hungarian national airline Moler, the state telecommunications company, and Videoton, an electronics group, are also in the process of sale.

In order to attract foreign investments, the government cut corporate profit taxes ranging from 60 percent to total exemption if profits are reinvested. Foreign shareholders need a license only if they take majority control.

Nevertheless, there is criticism even by members of the ruling Democratic Forum that the state is selling off its property too cheaply and that quick transfer of stakes to foreign partners exposes the negotiating managers to corruption risks. That is why the Hungarian Supreme Court overturned the deal of Quintus of Sweden, registered in the Netherlands, to buy 50 percent of the 50 hotels owned by the Hunger Hotels group for $80 million.

The French food company BSN and the Swiss Nestlé acquired a 43 percent stake of the Hungarian chocolate and biscuit company Cokoladovny. It is expected that they will acquire the majority of the shares of the new firm in a period of four years after increasing their investment to $75 million.

The majority stake (75 percent) of Allami Biztosito, the largest state-owned insurer of Hungary, was acquired by Aegon NV, the Dutch insurer. The Hungarian government retained 20 percent and the rest was acquired by Allami's employees.

Siemens AG of Germany agreed with IBM to introduce a telecommunications system in Hungary.

A trinational joint venture of an American-style management school was created in Hungary recently. An American professor (Daniel Fagel) is the dean of the school, which is the result of a joint venture of American, Italian, and Hungarian partners. The establishment of this institute was supported by Abel Aganbegyan, former advisor to Mikhail Gorbachev and chairman of the economics section of the Soviet Academy of Sciences, as a sign of active relations between East and West. The students of the school, around 300 per semester, including some Russians, pay tuition of about $12,000, or 600,000 forints. Two American professors, two Canadians, one Briton, and five Hungarians constitute the initial faculty.

In competition with McDonald's Corporation, Burger King, a subsidiary of the British food and leisure group Grand Metropolitan PLC, opened its world's largest restaurant in Budapest as a joint venture of a British-American investment group and the Hungarian state-owned Pannonia Hotels.

The Mirror Group of Britain acquired a 40 percent stake of *Esti Hirlap*, an evening daily newspaper in Budapest, whereas the paper's editorial board controls 20 percent and the other 40 percent is controlled by the Hungarian News Publishing Company. The Mirror Group, which was headed by the former Robert Maxwell in partnership with Merrill Lynch, had also acquired a 49 percent stake in *Magyar Hirlap*, which was controlled by the Hungarian government and the Communist Party, as was *Esti Hirlap*.

Whirlpool Hungarian Trading Ltd. was established in Hungary as a subsidiary of the European Whirlpool International BV, which in turn is a subsidiary of the U.S. Whirlpool Corporation, to sell and service appliances in Hungary.

The Heineken beer company of the Netherlands acquired a related beer company in Hungary.

American Investment

U.S. investment in Hungary is not extensive and sizable as yet. One of the U.S. ventures is an $80 million investment of Ford Motor Company in Szeekesfehvar, western Hungary, to produce cars that will be mostly exported. The Hungarian government offered tax and other benefits, while Ford agreed to reinvest its profits into the country and by 1996 to export about 200,000 cars annually, an amount equal to what is imported now. For the first two years Ford would export 5,000 cars to Hungary, which is now producing only buses and trucks.

Attracted by an inexpensive and relatively skilled Hungarian work force (average monthly wages are $150), GM and the state-owned Raba trucks company began the production of passenger cars, mainly for the domestic market. The Opel Astra car (worth $13,300) is the first produced in Hungary, because, under previous cooperation agreements with the former Comecon, only buses and trucks were to be produced in the country, while Poland, the former Czechoslovakia, East Germany, and Romania could have car plants.

GM owns two-thirds of the venture, Raba 21 percent, and the State Development Institute the rest of the shares.

The General Electric Company committed $150 million after acquiring control of Tungsram, a light-bulb enterprise in 1989. Nevertheless, GE, which has a 75 percent stake in Tungsram's plants in Hungary, recently registered heavy losses, slashed payrolls, and reduced the number of jobs from 18,200 to 10,200 in the last three years. Because of the continuing layoffs and the reduction in wages, which average about $280 per month, while inflation runs at 25 percent, labor union leaders threaten strikes and protests against these measures. To offset losses and pay off debts, which amount to around $250 million, the company plans to increase capital, but the Hungarian Credit Bank, which owns the majority of the remaining 25 percent stake is resisting the measure.[6]

The Guardian Company committed $120 million, in a joint venture with Hungarian Glass, for glass production. Moreover, Sara Lee committed $60 million, in partnership with Compack enterprise, for food processing. Also, a Schwinn Company of the United States has already invested in plants producing bicycles for the Polish economy and other neighboring markets, including those of Hungary.

Pepsico International, which has been in Hungary since 1969, announced that it decided to invest more than $115 million to buy 79 percent of the Capital Mineral Water and Refreshment Corporation and to improve manufacturing and distribution of beverages in Hungary. The remaining shares are owned by company workers and the city of Budapest. The main plants are at Tara, Soroksav, Margaret Island, and Kristalyviz.

On the other hand, Rubbermaid, Inc. announced a 50–50 joint venture with the Pannonplast Group of Budapest to produce rubber and plastic home products. The venture was enacted by Curver Rubbermaid Group of the Netherlands, a European affiliate of Rubbermaid, Inc.

Aluminum Company of America acquired a majority stake in a subsidiary of Hungarian Aluminum Industrial Corporation, which is a state-owned company of Hungary.

Moreover, Procter and Gamble formed two joint ventures in Hungary for the production and marketing of paper and personal care products, in addition to those in Poland.

U.S. West, Inc. agreed with Hungary to build a mobile cellular telephone system in Budapest, the first such network in the East bloc that would be expanded eventually to the entire country. This system will be faster and cheaper for the government than to rebuild the entire telephone infrastructure by tearing up the streets and installing miles of cable. U.S. West would own and operate 49 percent of the cellular network and Magyar Post, the Hungarian telephone and postal organization, the rest. Moreover, Citicorp's joint-venture bank in Budapest put together a management buyout of Apisz, the largest state-owned stationery supplier.

About 300 restaurants and food stores, including 15 Pizza Huts, 22 Kentucky Fried Chickens, some 40 Dunkin Donuts, and scores of other businesses have been or are planned to be established, primarily in Budapest, by George Hemingway, a California entrepreneur whose mother was from Hungary. Salomon Brothers in London raised $20 million to help expand Hemingway Holding AG, a company quoted on the Vienna Stock Exchange, which also made a franchise agreement with Pepsico to open a fried chicken chain and other stores in Hungary.[7]

In August 1991, Burger King, the American fast food chain, opened a large store in Budapest with the slogan "come to taste the new world." There is a problem, though, of price adjustment because of high inflation and small devaluations of the forint, which result in losses of joint ventures.

Columbian Chemicals Company, a subsidiary of Phelps Dodge Corporation, and Tiszai Vegyi Kombinat, a Hungarian petrochemical firm, formed a joint venture to establish a $55 million carbon production plant.

Hewlett Packard Company, a computer maker, formed a joint venture with Controll, a private Hungarian firm, for sales and support of computers.

Amway Corporation, with sales of cleaning and other products in 50 countries worth about $2.2 billion a year, expanded its operations to Hungary in 1991.

Other Foreign Investment

Suzuki Motor Corporation, the largest minicar producer in Japan and the third largest producer of motorcycles, invested $325 million in a joint venture with the Hungarian government to produce 60,000 passenger cars a year in Esztergon, a former Soviet military base, which the author of this book visited during his recent research trip to Hungary. The International Financial Corporation, an affiliate of the World Bank, provided $85 million credit to the Suzuki project, which is Japan's largest investment so far in the former Soviet bloc. In the Magyar Suzuki factory, which started in October 1992, 50 percent belongs to Suzuki and 40 percent to the Hungarian government, which provided ten-year tax breaks and other benefits in import duties. In return Suzuki promised to use 50 percent Hungarian-made components. However, workers were accustomed to generous vacations and other benefits under communism, which are expected to be reduced under the Japanese disciplinary system in which "team spirit" and hard work prevail.

The Nissan Motor Company and Magyar PGA SA, a unit of Pierre Guenant Automobile Motors SA, opened a sales company in Budapest, in which Magyar owns 74 percent. Moreover, Nissan has sales companies in the former Czechoslovakia, Poland, and the former Yugoslavia.

8

The Balkan Countries

INTRODUCTION

The countries of the Balkan Peninsula are located at the crossroads of Europe, Africa, and Asia and constitute a natural bridge between Europe and the Middle East. Although their economic systems are different, they tend to accept similar institutions and models of development. This causes a need for closer economic and cultural cooperation among them. However, it should be recognized that there are so many other social, political, and ethnic elements involved, mainly in the former Yugoslavia, that it would be improper to concentrate only on economic issues and disregard noneconomic factors.[1]

During the more than four centuries' occupation of the Balkans by the Ottoman Turks, many Christian subjects were converted to Islam; some of them to achieve high positions and receive benefits from their Turkish masters; some to protect their properties from heavy taxation and confiscations; and some to avoid prosecution and torture if they insisted against such forceful conversion to Islam. Also, some Turks were implanted to the Balkans from Konia. A similar policy of implanting Asian Turks in occupied northern Cyprus is followed currently.

Some Muslims in Albania, Bosnia, and other Balkan countries come from the janissaries, a large number of Christian children taken from their mothers by the Ottoman Turks, who trained and made them Turkish soldiers fighting against their unknown parents and brothers—one of the most horrible events in human history. According to Charles Adams, a historian, the Islamic tax policy is a reason for Islam's spread: "convert and pay no tax; keep your own religion and pay a head tax, or be put to death."[2]

In the Middle Ages, medieval Christian heretics of the Catholic religion, known as Bogomils (from the name of the Bulgarian priest meaning God-pleasing), and their ruler Hrvoje Vukcic-Hrvatinic invited the Turks to help repel the Hungarian ruler Sigmund. Thus, the Ottoman Turks managed to gain a foothold in Europe for five centuries. Moreover, Eastern Orthodox rulers of Byzantium used similar Ottoman alliances to advance their positions or to repel other invaders. In 1345, John Cantacugenus, a Byzantine official, invited the Ottoman Turks to support his bid for the throne, and in 1349 they were invited again to help save Salonika from the Serbs (under Stephen Dushan). But the invited Ottoman armies remained in the area and, further strengthened by additional troops, they gradually advanced all over the Balkan Peninsula and occupied it for about five centuries.

The Helenes (Greeks) or Morea (Peloponnesus) raised the banner of revolution against the Ottoman Turks (on March 21, 1821, in Aghia Lavra, Kalavryta) and achieved independence in 1828, with borders extending to Thessaly. Albania became independent in 1913 (Treaty of London), Romania in 1866, and Bulgaria, Serbia, and Montenegro in 1878 (Treaty of Berlin), whereas Bosnia and Herzegovina came under Austria (1878).

Proposals and movements for Balkan or Danubian confederations have been made on a number of occasions from the 1860s onward, primarily in the conferences of Athens (1930), Istanbul (1931), Bucharest (1932), and Salonica (1933), and again in Athens (1934) when the Balkan Entente was created. However, their importance was overshadowed by the expansionary policies of Italy and Germany.

Historically, the Balkan countries have been the powder keg of Europe. World War I began with the assassination of Archduke Franz Ferdinand in Sarajevo in 1914. Also, it is stipulated that Hitler's attack on Yugoslavia (operation "Retribution") and Greece on April 6, 1941, resulted in the postponement of the Russian attack (operation "Barbarossa") for six critical weeks that cost his defeat in the following winter outside Moscow.

After the drastic changes in Eastern Europe in 1989, ethnic rivalries, which were suppressed under communist rule in Albania, Bulgaria, Romania, and Yugoslavia since World War II, surfaced again. All these countries gradually and painfully are moving toward democracy and a market economy, while they pursue closer relations with Western Europe.

Recently, the break of the former Yugoslavia into independent republics presented problems to the EC and even a few deaths of the EC peace mission in the fighting among Serbs, Croats, and Muslims. A proper policy for the EC may be to accept them as associated members. The same policy may be followed for the other Balkan states, primarily Albania, Bulgaria, and Romania. Such a plan of enlarging the EC, by incorporating the Balkan Peninsula, can induce the peoples of the region to hard work, have high hopes for the future, and adopt rapid economic and political adjustments to EC policies and directives, including adaptation of democratic principles.

Table 8.1
Area (sq. km.), Population (millions), Work Force (millions), GNP (billion $),
Per Capita GNP (dollars), and Inflation (percentage) of the Balkan Countries,
1990

	Area	Population	Work force	GNP Per Capita	Inflation
Albania	28,750	3.3	1.5	1,200	n.a.
Bulgaria	110,910	9.0	4.3	1,840	7.8
Greece	131,940	10.3	3.9	6,340	17.7
Romania	237,500	23.0	10.7	1,390	6.2
Turkey	780,580	57.3	18.8	1,780	44.7
Yugoslavia	255,800	23.9	9.6	3,060	123.0

Source: _Athena_, vol. 45, May 1991, 134; and World Bank, _World Development Report_ (Washington, DC: Oxford University Press, for the World Bank, 1993).

Greece, on the other hand, like Odysseus in Homer's epic, returned to its European home after a long period of uncertainty and historical disturbances. As a full member of the European Community, Greece is expected to play a leading role in the improvement of EC relations with the other Balkan countries. Turkey has been an associate EC member since 1964.

The expectations of Poland, the Czech and Slovak republics, and Hungary to join the EC create favorable conditions for the inclusion of the Balkan states in the EC. Moreover, such an enlargement would be advantageous geographically, not only for Greece through more efficient transportation networks, but for all EC members that would use the Balkan Peninsula as a natural bridge for mutual trade and investment with the Middle East countries.

Rapid improvements in transportation and communications, the spread of multinational companies, and the 24-hour access to stock markets in a global economy liquidate nationalism and the notion of sovereignty. From that standpoint, the EC should consider further enlargement, incorporating East European and Balkan countries and introducing a democratic and free market system, without frontiers, all over Europe. Although there are growing pains from domestic economic, religious, and political feuds, the EC has to overcome borders and the emotion of virginity of sovereignty. Ethnic conflicts in the former Yugoslav republics show that movements to the opposite direction are far more painful economically, politically, and in terms of human lives. Market expansion and sociopolitical tranquility need to overcome borders and to introduce a new concept of transnational democracy. Table 8.1 shows the main indicators of the Balkan countries.

A DANUBE BASIN OR EUXENE COMMON MARKET?

The establishment of a Danube basin common market, including the old Hapsburg countries, as a buffer against a reunited strong Germany seems impractical in present-day Europe. Such a group that may include Austria, Hungary, the Czech and Slovak republics, Romania, and the former Yugoslavia may be useful to the security interests of the European Community and particularly to a rejuvenated Germany for some time to come. However, an economic association and eventual integration with the EC is more effective and beneficial to all European countries, instead of departmentalizing the old continent in different fortress groups.

A similar intrabloc common market for the Balkan countries (Albania, Bulgaria, Greece, Romania, Turkey, and the former Yugoslavia) is also impractical and not beneficial to the countries concerned. Intra-Balkan trade may impose costs upon the countries involved insofar as it means trade diversion. The beneficial effects of intrabloc trade on balance of payments, industrialization, and economic growth may not exceed the detrimental effects of the trade diversion of a Balkan common market. This may be so because the Balkan countries produce mainly competitive primary products, not so much complementary products, and a formation of a common market may make them poorer instead.

Recently, the neighboring countries of the Black Sea—primarily Turkey, Romania, Greece, Bulgaria, Armenia, and Georgia—agreed to create "the union of Euxene countries." Aristotle, in his writings about wonderful hearings named a similar formation at that time (fifth century B.C.) the common market of Euxene.[3] From an economic point of view, this infant union is not expected to have impressive results, mainly because these countries produce competitive products. However, from a sociopolitical standpoint such a union may prove to be beneficial for further cooperation, as a pioneering movement toward an eventual pan-European union, under the auspices of the EC. Already Greece is a full member and Turkey an associate member of the EC, while the other neighboring nations are also expected to become associate members in the near future. Again, a closer cooperation with the EC may be more beneficial, although painful for a transitional period of adjustment.

ALBANIA

A Brief Historical Review

The Albanians were late in showing signs of national consciousness, and the independence movement started primarily abroad. This was due mainly to the degree of autonomy they enjoyed under the Ottoman rule (1453–

1912). However, in 1881 they organized the Albanian League to unite the isolated regions of the country and to counter the interest of neighboring countries in territorial claims or domination, mainly because of Albania's strategic position on the Adriatic Sea. For this reason Albanians at times supported the Turks, and even joined the Young Turks movement.

Albania was born through the Treaty of London signed by the six great European powers in 1913. However, Greek troops occupied southern Albania or northern Epirus (where some 400,000 Greeks live), including Koristsa and Argyrokastron (1914–16). Montenegrins entered Scutari in the north, Serbians occupied Elbasan and Tirana (1915), and Italians occupied Valona and (later) Argyrokastron, and even Ioannina in Greece (1916). The French, who commanded the Salonika front, extended their position and occupied Koristsa. In 1920, Albania, supported by the British and by American President Woodrow Wilson, became a member of the League of Nations; in 1921 its boundaries were confirmed by the great powers, in spite of protests from Yugoslavia and Greece. By 1926, Yugoslavia, Britain, France, and Italy had signed the final agreement determining the present frontiers in Albania. In 1922, Ahmed Zogu became premier, and after a brief (1924–25) term he regained power and remained premier until 1939.

Zogu, following the example of the other Balkan countries, introduced land reforms and expropriated large estates from Moslem beys and the church and distributed them to the poor peasants. Except for some small handicrafts processing local materials, the country's economy was based primarily on agriculture, in which more than 80 percent of the population was engaged. Albania, with 85 percent of the population illiterate before World War II, was regarded as the most backward state of the Balkans and the whole of Europe.

After 1925, Italy penetrated Albania and concluded a number of military and economic agreements with Zogu, who in 1928 became King Zog. Through the Company for Economic Development of Albania, Italian engineers and financiers built roads, ports, agricultural projects, and other public works. They also drilled for oil and discovered two fields, one near Berat and one near Valona. Italian engineers later helped Albania increase oil production from 7,000 barrels in 1926 to 1,659,000 barrels in 1940. The crude oil and asphalt produced, together with other raw materials (hides, wool, livestock, olive oil, wine, spirits [raki], and lumber) were exported mainly to Italy. The Italian protectorate and the established controls continued until 1939, when King Zog was compelled to flee to Greece before the Italian invasion.

After the occupation of Albania in April 1939, Italy attacked Greece on October 28, 1940, using Albania as an army base for a projected gradual expansion into other Balkan areas. However, the Greeks resisted the invasion, pushing the Italians back to the Albanian mountains and ultimately occupying the major cities of Koristsa and Argyrokastron, and the naval base of Santi

Quaranta. However, Hitler's attack against Greece on April 6, 1941, helped the Italians to recapture the Albanian areas and to occupy Greece together with the Germans and Bulgarians.

After the war small Albania, under President Enver Hoxha (1945–85), followed the Soviet economic model. In 1961, however, the leadership changed its mind, and until 1975 came under the ideological influence of the People's Republic of China.

Economic Reforms

The winds of reform that blow throughout Eastern Europe affect Albania, although to a lesser extent. More investment emphasis is given to the less industrialized regions and less emphasis to the industrialized areas. Western enterprises with oil drilling equipment are invited to increase oil production. Albania, a tiny country of 3.3 million people, is self-sufficient in oil, producing an estimated 20 million barrels a year, small quantities of which are exported to Greece and Italy. It is also the world's third largest producer of chrome, behind South Africa and the former USSR, and second in the export of this strategically important product (more than 350,000 tons a year). Other major exports are olives, oranges, and dried fruits, primarily to Italy.

Seeing the tide of European changes, Ramiz Alia, the Albania leader after Hoxha, introduced limited reforms. They included price changes to reduce the gap between supply and demand, bonuses for key workers, and decentralization in decision making. Albania remains the poorest country of Europe and many people want to emigrate to other countries, particularly to Italy and Greece (more than 100,000 have already emigrated, mostly illegally).

In the free elections of March 22, 1992, the Democratic Party won 92 of Parliament's 140 seats. The communists, renamed socialists, who controlled the 3 million poor Albanians for almost half a century, won 38 seats. President Sali Berisha, a heart surgeon, and Prime Minister Alexander Meksi started moving rapidly toward privatization and free market reforms.

With the extension of nondiscriminatory treatment (most-favored-nation status) to Albania by the United States in August 1992, more foreign trade and investments are expected to flow into the country in the coming years. This would help Albania to implement free market democratic reforms and stabilize this volatile Balkan region. Although limited, foreign investments flow in. Thus, Chevron, one of the big U.S. petroleum companies, signed an agreement in August 1991 with DPNG, an Albanian petroleum firm, to search and produce coal and other petroleum products in Albania. Chevron acquired exclusive rights to exploit the products in an area of 1,800 square kilometers located some 50 kilometers southwest of Tirana, the capital of Albania. Also, some 70 Greek-Albanian joint ventures already operate in the country.

BULGARIA

A Brief Historical Review

Near the end of the seventh century, a Finno-Tatar race (later known as Bulgarians), together with other Slavs, moved from the Volga Valley to south of the Danube. Byzantium recognized them as permanent settlers at that time.

Because Bulgaria was close to Constantinople, the center of the Ottoman Empire, it was the first Balkan country to be occupied by, and the last to be liberated from, the Turks. There were some uprisings, such as that conducted by Michael the Brave in 1598, but they had limited or no success. Only after the establishment of the Autocephalous Exarchate Church in 1870 were serious efforts made to organize the people and achieve independence in 1878.

Before World War II, scarcity of natural resources, lack of capital, and unskilled labor and management were the causes of backwardness in industry and low productivity in other sectors. About half of the total capital in industry and transportation had been invested by foreigners.

During World War II, Bulgaria became an ally of the Axis Powers, as did Romania, while Greece and Yugoslavia joined the Allies. Turkey remained neutral. When Germany occupied Greece and Yugoslavia, the Bulgarian army was permitted to enter Yugoslav Macedonia as well as Greek western Thrace and eastern Macedonia. With respect to troop allocation to other fronts, Bulgaria, under King Boris, managed to stay aloof, mainly because of the traditionally large Russophile sentiment of the country.

During mid–1942 the Fatherland Front was organized by Georgi Dimitrov, a communist leader well known for his defiance of the Nazis during the Reichstag fire trial. The Front included Social Democrats, the left-wing Agrarian Party, and the Zveno group, which had connections in the army. The resistance against the Axis, however, was not as significant as in other occupied Balkan countries.

During the postwar years Bulgaria has closely followed the Soviet economic model of central planning and strict government controls. However, in order to obtain a better performance from the economy, the government introduced some market-oriented reforms in the early 1960s. According to directives emanating from the country's leaders, technical rationalization and computerization were to be used in order to attain more efficient performance. But these reforms did not accomplish much, mostly because of inflexibility in the centralized economy. It was difficult for the Communist Party to permit any loss of its authority because of an abstract and mechanical process that required the use of precise information in order to obtain reliable results.

Capital formation, as a percentage of national product, was higher in Bulgaria than in other Comecon countries during the 1980s, but there was less independence in production enterprises (subsidiaries and subdivisions). The gap between the growth rate of net national product and net economic welfare was greater than in Western market economies. President Todor Zhivkov and the planners responsible for policy making have tried to eliminate consumer frustration by keeping prices low, but inflation would have to rise if consumer lines were to be eliminated.

In the postwar years Bulgaria has experienced an unprecedented period of peace and progress, mainly because it has not had to confront any external threat and, unlike Romania, did not lose territory to its neighbors. Moreover, it does not suffer from internal disunity, as does Yugoslavia, or the political instability and the internal turmoil of Turkey.

Because of the common culture and linguistic and ethnic background with the Russians, a high degree of cooperation has been developed between Bulgaria and Russia. The glorification of the Russian army, which liberated the country from Turkey in 1878 and helped it establish the communist regime, cannot escape the visitor to present-day Bulgaria. On the other hand, because of Bulgaria's strategic location (close to the Dardanelles and Aegean coast), Russia has always kept a watchful eye upon the country.

Economic Reforms

As in other East bloc countries, the Bulgarian communist dictatorship of more than 40 years was overthrown, together with the long-tenured President Todor Zhivkov, on November 10, 1989. Thereafter, anticommunist demonstrators dismantled reminders of communist rule, including the mausoleum of Georgi Dimitrov (father of Bulgarian communism), burned the Communist Party headquarters, and eliminated other communist sacred symbols. Free elections on June 10, 1990, though, gave a reformed Communist (now called Socialist) Party 57 percent of parliamentary democracy. However, Bulgaria faces serious economic problems from reduced supplies of cheap Russian oil and gas, food shortages, and a heavy foreign debt of about $16 billion. Also, severe problems appear in the process of privatization of the economy, especially in land ownership.[4] The drastic reforms and the austerity measures introduced recently will suppress the living standard of the 9 million Bulgarians for some time to come.

Bulgaria has six Russian-built reactors, four of which are old and the most dangerous in the world. They need repairs to avoid accidents similar to that of Chernobyl in Ukraine in April 1986.

Although significant reforms were introduced, foreign investment remains limited, but further expectations are high. The Coca-Cola Export Corporation, a subsidiary of the Coca-Cola Company, together with Bulgaria's Central Cooperative Union and the Leventis Group subsidiary Clarina Holding SA, created the Coca-Cola Bottlers Sofia Ltd. This is the fifth joint venture of the Coca-Cola Company, making it the biggest foreign investor in Bulgaria. Also, there are some 500 Greek-Bulgarian joint ventures.

ROMANIA

A Brief Historical Review

Throughout history, Romania has perhaps been the nation in the Balkans most affected by foreign cultures. During the Byzantine era the Slavonic language and tradition were prevalent, while during the Ottoman period Greek culture was spread by the Phanariots and the monastic schools. Toward the end of the Ottoman occupation, revolutionaries and writers from Bucharest and Jassy spread the ideals of the French revolution and introduced the French language into the schools of Walachia and Moldavia. However, in reaction to the Greek revolution of 1821, the Turkish authorities replaced the Phanariot *hospodars* with Romanian boyars. On the other hand, a number of Romanian students, educated in Jesuit schools at Rome, started a systematic movement to replace the mainly Slavonic language with Latin, which was the tongue of their Dacian and Roman ancestors. During the postliberation years the influence of France and the rest of Western Europe was predominant.

The long tenure in office of Carol I (1866–1914) helped the economic development of the country. Some 2,000 miles of railroads were constructed. A large bridge at Cernavoda on the Danube connected Dobruja with the rest of Romania, and the Iron Gate was blasted to open the Danube to large ships. Moreover, the ever-increasing oil production around Ploesti (from 50,000 tons in 1890 to 1,885,000 in 1913) helped improve the financial and borrowing position of the country until 1917, when British engineers blew up the wells to avoid their falling into the hands of the Central Powers. By 1921, oil production was restored to prewar levels, and together with grain and lumber exports, provided enough foreign currency to pay for industrial imports.

During the interwar years Romania, like other Balkan countries, went through a turbulent period. Under pressure from the poor peasant masses and in order to stop the Bolshevik revolutionary spirit from crossing the Dniester River, King Ferdinand enacted a drastic land reform program between 1918 and 1921. Of 6 million hectares of land expropriated from absentee proprietors, foreigners, the crown, and large landowners, about two-thirds were distributed to some 1.4 million peasants; the rest was held for public use (forests, grazing, model farms, and roads). Although these reforms had political importance, mainly for the Liberal and National Peasant parties, economically they were insufficient to increase farm productivity. Moreover, under the pressure of the depression of the 1930s, many poor peasants sold their plots and became part of the growing rural proletariat class.

The death of King Ferdinand in 1927 and the succession of his son Carol II, a shrewd maneuverer, led Romania to further turbulence and instability. Although he had as a tutor Professor Nicholae Iorga, an internationally known historian, his unwise policies and his favoritism stimulated the fascist movement of the Iron Guards, and led to the dictatorship of 1938–40. Old nationalist feelings of the Romanians, surrounded by a sea of Slavs, and endemic anti-Semitism were growing. Apathy and a lack of cohesiveness, similar to that prevailing in Yugoslavia, brought on a national crisis in 1940 that resulted in the cession of Bessarabia and northern Bukovina to Russia (secret protocol of Hitler and Stalin of 1939), of northern Transylvania to Hungary, and of southern Dobruja to Bulgaria (Vienna Dictate of Hitler and Mussolini in 1940). Carol II and his mistress, Magda Lupescu, fled the country to avoid prosecution by avenging nationalists.

Changes in Economic Policy

Despite the efforts of the government and the political parties to carry out rapid industrialization, the Romanian economy remained largely agrarian. Close to 80 percent of the population lived in the rural sector by 1941, while only about 40 percent of the existing labor in this sector was needed. Ownership of small plots—about 58 percent of which were less than 3 hectares—was prevalent. Increases in land productivity and employment of surplus rural labor, rather than land distribution, seemed to be the most pressing problems. Land productivity (9.5 quintals per acre) was very low, less than one-third that of Denmark (29.4 quintals per acre). The average output was the lowest in Balkania, except for Greece. Lack of equipment, limited use of fertilizers, the practice of strip farming, and primitive methods of cultivation were the main reasons. In addition, the decline in agricultural prices by half, during the depression of the 1930s, intensified the dismal economic conditions of the population.[5]

Heavy indirect taxes on consumption and high tariffs on agricultural exports (up to 50 percent of their value) made things worse for the starving peasantry. On the other hand, high import duties and quotas to protect domestic industry did not greatly help to stimulate industrial growth. Other restrictive measures on foreign investment (not permitting more than 40 percent of foreign ownership and less than three-fourths native personnel) proved to hamper technological development. However, the rich mining and lumber resources of the country helped to establish a few raw-material-processing and metallurgical industries. Shortly before World War II petroleum was providing 46 percent, and lumber 12 percent of the export total. By that time Germany had imposed a semicolonial treaty on the country that called for specialization in the production of minerals and agricultural raw materials.

Under the dictatorship of General Ion Antonescu, Romania provided Germany with oil, munitions, and grain as well as some 30 army divisions for the Russian front. During the war the country suffered severe losses in Russia, especially during the winter of 1942–43 and the battle for Stalingrad. When the Soviet army crossed the Prut River and entered Romania in April 1944, the Russian dominance in the area became obvious.

After 1945 and under the Petru Groza regime, Romania was bound to the Soviet bloc and its interests were interwoven with those of the Comecon. However, after the death of Stalin in 1953 and under Gheorghe Gheorghiu-Dej, initiatives were taken toward some degree of interdependence and restoration of cultural relations with the West. Despite Soviet interventions in Hungary (1956), Czechoslovakia (1968), and Afghanistan (1980), Romanian leadership (under President Nicholae Ceausescu since 1965) managed to maintain a precarious position while attempting to develop its own identity. It pronounced, from time to time, its opposition to both NATO and the Warsaw Pact, and wished to retain its national independence. Although an ally of the Soviet Union, Romania was not as close an ally as Bulgaria, first because its population is primarily non-Slav and second because of the problem of Bessarabia. Moreover, Romanians felt and still feel that the Soviet Union and Comecon exploited their country's natural resources during the post-World War II years.

On December 22, 1989, Nicolae Ceausescu, the communist dictator since 1965, resigned, and was executed together with his wife Elena on December 25, 1989, by the army, which had revolted. This was the result of demonstrations and the massacre in Timisoara and Arad (Transylvania) of rioting people, mostly from the Hungarian minority and other anticommunist revolutions in other cities and in other East European countries. The Front for National Salvation, with Ion Iliescu as president, that took power on December 26, 1989, won the elections of May 20, 1990 (the first free elections since 1937) with 66 percent of the popular vote. Romania, in its efforts to turn the state-owned economy into a free market economy, faces severe problems, although it has a small foreign debt, compared to other East European countries. The process of selling state assets to the private sector, including foreign investors who can have full ownership of companies, continues with priorities in housing construction, food processing, tourism, and trade services. Also, free changes in prices are gradually introduced for almost all commodities and services, and economic hardship remains a serious problem for the 23 million Romanians.

Monetary and Investment Policies

The monetary policy of Romania was relatively stable up to the drastic economic and political changes at the end of 1989. Thereafter, the money supply increased significantly, whereas the velocity of money declined slightly, as Figure 8.1 shows.

Although there is currently relative stability in the country, the flow of

Figure 8.1
Money Supply (M) and Velocity of Money (GDP/M) for Romania

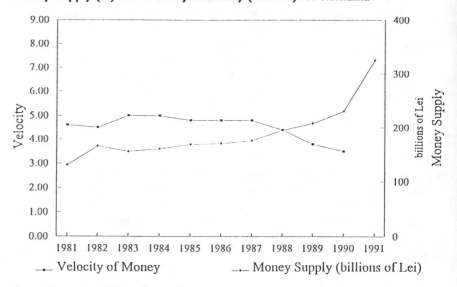

Source: International Monetary Fund, *International Financial Statistics*, various issues.

foreign investment is limited. However, future expectations are promising, particularly from the EC countries and the United States.

The Amoco Corporation and Rompetrol SA of Romania agreed to conduct exploration works for oil in the Carpathian Mountains. The new Amoco Romania Petroleum Company would spend $20 million initially for drilling operations on a 185,000-acre area.

Greek entrepreneurs have undertaken considerable investment initiatives in Romania. There are already 646 joint Greek-Romanian ventures in such sectors as aluminum, cigarette manufacturing, clothing, tourism, medicines, and pesticides. Moreover, a large part of the Romanian merchant fleet has been acquired by Greek shipowners. However, Germany holds the first place with 2,646 and Turkey the fourth place with 1,950 businesses.

FORMER YUGOSLAVIA

A Brief Historical Review

The economic history of Yugoslavia is related to the territorial complexity of the area, the expansionary trends of different neighboring powers, and the related resistance of the native people as well as their efforts to absorb and unite with each other. The valleys of the Danube, the Sava, and the

Morava have served as the main gateways of migrating people and other invading armies for centuries, while the Dinaric Alps and the other Balkan mountains served as a bastion against these movements.

Although little is known of the inhabitants of the region of the former Yugoslavia before the coming of the Slavs in the sixth Christian century, many archaeological remains attest that the area was peopled even at the early times of the Iron Age (Hollstat period).

Greek writers mentioned that the Illyrians had occupied the area west of the Vardar and north of the Epirus, driving the Thracians to the central and eastern regions of the Balkan peninsula. Moreover the infiltration of "Celtic" peoples from the north at the beginning of the fourth century B.C. had little and only temporary influence on the Illyrians.

Trade interruptions by pirates from the Illyrian coasts and the expansionary policies of the Roman Empire led to repeated Roman expeditions from the year 229 B.C. until A.D. 9, when Tiberius annexed the area named Illyricum, which at times incorporated areas from Vienna to Athens. The transportation network and the effective Roman administration stimulated commerce and mining operations, particularly in gold, silver, and copper, in the area. The eastern part of the Roman Empire from near Lake Scutari to the River Sava was separated administratively by Diocletian (A.D. 285). After 395, this eastern part became the Byzantine Empire, with its own Greek-speaking Orthodox world, contrasted to the Latin-speaking Catholic world of the western part of the Roman Empire.

With the collapse of the Roman Empire, Visigoths, Huns, Ostrogoths, and some other groups captured the whole coastal area of Dalmatia. This was reconquered by Justinian, the Byzantine emperor, by 535 but then captured and devastated by the Avars coming from the Danube plain during the second half of the sixth century.

At the same time and into the seventh century, the Slavs, dispersed by the Avar menace in eastern Europe, moved southward. By 650 they occupied Illyria and settled there permanently. They were mainly the Slovenes and the Croats, who came under Roman Catholic influence, and the Serbs in the south who were influenced by the Orthodox church of Constantinople.

When the Ottomans first came (1389 onward) into the Balkan Peninsula, they established military and administrative officials in strategic regions. Turkish chiefs (*beys*) received large tracts of land (*chifliks*); while Turkish peasants were transported from Asia Minor, mainly Konia, and were implanted in different areas.

During the five centuries of Turkish occupation, from 1389 when the Ottoman Turks defeated the Serbian forces of Prince Lazar in Kosovo until World War I, the Turks converted a large number of the Balkan subjects to Islam. The most effective measure of conversion was confiscation of property or heavy taxation on people not converted to Islam.

During the period 1792–1814, the economic conditions of the eastern provinces from Carniola to Dalmatia and Ragusa, under Napoleon's rule, were greatly improved. The administrative system of these "Illyrian Provinces," with Ljubljana as their capital, was reorganized. From 1815 to 1849 the area came under the Austrian Empire.

With the departure of the Turks, the Balkan countries, including then Yugoslavia, remained underdeveloped. About 80 percent of the population was engaged in agriculture and less than 10 percent in industry. While in other Balkan regions a great number of latifundia remained, in Serbia and other neighboring areas land was split among the peasants. Under such conditions, even the *Zadruga* (village cooperative) gave way to the individual farm unit.

The former Yugoslav state was born out of the collapse of the Central Powers in World War I. Its formation was the result of the Declaration of Corfu on July 20, 1917. This agreement, which was supported by Russia and the United States, provided for a constitutional and parliamentary monarchy under the Karageorgevich dynasty and the union of all Serbs, Croats, and Slovenes. On November 26, Montenegro joined Serbia and by December 1, 1918, the new kingdom of the Serbs, Croats, and Slovenes was proclaimed in Belgrade. The main defect of the new state, South Slav Kingdom, seemed to lie with the domination of the other ethnic groups by Serbia, a fact that condemned it to domestic disturbances and even the danger of full-scale civil war. In 1929 it was named Yugoslavia.

On April 6, 1941, Hitler's troops in Bulgaria entered Yugoslavia and Greece simultaneously. In a few days and after extensive air attacks on Belgrade, Yugoslavia was in the hands of the Axis, as was Greece. The Italians conquered Dalmatia, the Hungarians reached Osijek and Novi Sad, and the Bulgarians occupied a part of southern Yugoslavia and northern Greece. The Germans occupied northern Slovenia, while Croatia (except Dalmatia) and Montenegro were nominally designated independent. The puppet state of Croatia was left to the control of Ustashi fascists under Ante Pavelic, who turned against the Orthodox population of Bosnia and Serbia as well as against the Jews.[6]

Tito, the Croat metalworker Josip Broz who joined the Austrian army and later the Bolsheviks in Russia, managed to mobilize and unite large segments of the Yugoslav population against the occupation forces of Germany and Italy.

Dissolution of the Federation

After the break with Cominform (1948), Tito turned to the West for trade and aid. By 1958 about $2.5 billion in aid was given primarily by the United States, Britain, and France. Tito's longevity in power (1945–80) helped him to carry through not only his concepts of Yugoslav federalism and ethnic unity but also his innovative economic program of labor-managed enterprises.

Table 8.2
Economic Indicators of the Former Yugoslav Republics and Provinces, 1990

States	Population (in dollars)	Per Capita GNP (in dollars)	Monthly Salary (average in dollars)	Exports (percent of total)
Bosnia and Herzegovina	4.1	3,590	365	14
Croatia	4.8	7,110	512	21
Kosovo	1.6	1,520	254	1
Macedonia	1.9	3,330	300	4
Montenegro	0.6	3,970	371	2
Serbia	9.3	4,950	423	21
Slovenia	2.0	12,520	533	29
Voivodina	2.0	6,790	440	8

Source: "E Ekonomiki 'Vavel' tis Yugoslavias" Kathimerini,
          July 14, 1991, 72; and Chuck Sudetic, "Two Yugoslav
          Republics Move to Secede," New York Times, June 26,
          1991, A6; and "In a Jolt to Yugoslavia Unity, Slovenia
          Votes to Take Over Government Roles," New York Times,
          February 21, 1991, A3.

A difficult problem for the post-Tito system of rotation in government may have been the continuation of the status quo and the lack of reforms because of the short-run (one-year) authority of the rotating presidency among the six republics and the two provinces until the dissolution of the federation in 1991.

The growing resentment against the communist system in the former Yugoslavia added an ideological divide to the historical, cultural, and religious differences of the most prosperous republics of Croatia and Slovenia with Serbia. Out of the six republics (Serbia, Bosnia and Herzegovina, Croatia, Slovenia, Macedonia, Montenegro) and two provinces (Voivodina and Kosovo), Serbia was the most populous (with 9.3 million people) and exercised political and economic controls upon the others. The Catholic Croatians (4.8 million) and Slovenians (2.0 million), who were under Austria until 1918, did not want the hegemony of the Christian Orthodox Serbs, who threw off Turkish rule in the nineteenth century. Table 8.2 shows some economic indicators of the republics and provinces of the former Yugoslavia.

With the split of the former Yugoslavia into independent republics, ultranationalistic and religious differences, which were suppressed under the communist regime of Tito, came to the surface. With the hasty recognition of Slovenia, Croatia, and Bosnia-Herzegovina by Germany and other Western countries, the principle of self-determination was difficult to be reconciled with that of territorial determination. Thus, sizable minorities of Serbians were included under these republics without their consent. The internal boundaries of the former Yugoslav republics, as well as their names, were arbitrarily determined by Marshall Tito (a Croat) in 1945, mainly to weaken the Serbs by leaving about one-third of them outside Serbia. Such borders were never negotiated nor ratified by free elections. This became obvious with the independence vote of Bosnia-Herzegovina on February 29, 1992, in which the Serbs, about one-third of the population in this republic, objected and a severe civil war among Serbs, Croats, and Muslims broke out.[7]

The geographic region of Macedonia, liberated from the Turks, was divided in 1912–14: 51 percent retained by Greece, 38 percent parceled to Yugoslavia, and 10 percent to Bulgaria. For long-term expansionary reasons, Tito carved southern Yugoslavia as one of the six republics, during World War II, and named it "Macedonia." In 1991 the new republic named itself "Macedonia."

Greece objected to the use of such a name by Skopja on historical and geopolitical reasons and, together with other nations, has denied recognition of this republic until its name is changed, because Macedonia, the country of Aristotle and Alexander the Great, is the region where Greeks have been living for centuries.

Self-Management System

Since the reforms of 1965 and the 1970s, the country moved further toward the self-management system with the Basic Organizations of Associated Labor (BOALs) in each enterprise and self-supporting communes or local communities. Taxes were collected primarily by the republics and the communes but also by special funds, such as "public roads," "waterworks," and "joint ventures." Trade agreements were signed with the EC, particularly in the 1970s and 1980s.

Although the former Yugoslav republics became independent, the worker self-management system, which prevailed for four decades, seemed to remain largely in operation. However, as a reaction to the influence and the controls of one party (the former Communist, renamed Socialist, Party) and the undemocratic process of decision making, the pressures for changes and abolishment of the system increased. This was so, particularly for the advanced republics of Croatia and Slovenia, which began to adjust their economic system to that of the European Community, particularly that of Germany, as they expect an association status and eventually full membership to the Community.

Nevertheless, the European Community itself has adopted measures of workers' participation in enterprise decision making and, to some extent, employee ownership. Moreover, Germany has the system of codetermination or comanagement of capital and labor.

In any case, Serbia, the largest republic, and Montenegro, as well as the provinces of Voivodina and Kosovo and to some extent Bosnia and Herzegovina, maintain the system of self-management.

Relations with the EC

Since 1970, when an EC-Yugoslavia Joint Committee was established, a number of trade and investment agreements have been signed. Also, a joint declaration of economic cooperation in Belgrade was signed on December 2, 1976, that marked a turning point in EC-Yugoslavian relations.

A few days later, the European Investment Bank granted loans of $68.5 million (50 million ECUs or 1.25 billion dinars) for such projects of mutual interest as the extension of the high-tension electricity network and its connections with Greece, Italy, and other European countries, as well as the construction and widening of the trans-Yugoslavian motorway, which provides a direct link between the community on the one hand and Greece, Turkey, and the Middle East on the other.

The former Yugoslavia enjoys many benefits from the Community's generalized system of preferences. Some 310 agricultural products and all manufactures and semimanufactures are covered by this system, which provides complete freedom from customs duties. However, certain ceilings or quotas have been laid down for different industrial products.

From the viewpoint of foreign trade, the former Yugoslavia depends more and more on the EC. One-fourth of its exports go to and close to half of its imports come from the EC. Yugoslavia is in the twelfth position among the Community's customers and twenty-sixth among its suppliers. About half of the Yugoslav trade deficit is with the EC.

In the 1980s, Yugoslavia and the EC signed new agreements that permit gradual reduction of tariffs for Yugoslav exports of large quantities of wine, fruits, beef, textiles, metals, and other industrial products and extended investment loans.

Unfavorable weather conditions, mainly during the winter, and ethnic and other disturbances in Yugoslavia and other Balkan nations make transportation of passengers and products from the central and northern European countries to Greece and the Middle East, and vice versa, problematic. From that standpoint, other routes and transportation means, such as shipping from the western ports of Greece to Italy and other EC countries, play a vital role for the development of trade and tourism. Thus, the Greek ports of Patras and Igoumenitsa-Corfu facilitate a growing number of shipping routes to Brindisi, Agona, and other ports of Italy. Not only is the number of cargo ships growing, but new cruise-ferry boats are built to facilitate fast transportation of passengers. Patras then can become an important gateway to Europe. Also, improvement of the Egnatia highway (initially built during the period of the Roman Empire), connecting Igoumenitsa-Salonika-Volos, is expected to increase EC-Middle East trade and investment. Moreover, further widening of the Athens-Patras highway will improve internal and external transportation in the area.

Part III

Russia and Other Former Soviet Republics

9

Russia

A BRIEF HISTORICAL REVIEW

In ancient times, Russia was inhabited by nomadic tribes. In the north there were the Slavs. In the Crimean peninsula of the south, known as Scythia, there were Cimmerians, Scythians, Sarmatians, and other Asiatic peoples. Many settlements and trade posts were established in the Crimea and other Black Sea areas by Greek merchants, remains of which exist even today.

Migrations and successive invasions occurred mainly by the Goths of Scandinavia, who established the Ostrogothic Kingdom, the Huns of Mongolia (fourth century A.D.), the Avars (or Tatar people), the Magyars (a Hungarian people), and the Khazars (until the eleventh century). During that time, the Slavic tribes, known as Vends or Venedi, dwelled in the northeastern Carpathian Mountains. The western Slavic groups eventually evolved as Poles and Czechs, those of the south as the Serbs and Bulgars, and those of the east as the Russians.

In 988 Pagan Russia was converted to Christianity. Later a Scandinavian Viking people (the Rus) formed a dynasty, which reached its peak in 1054, controlling most of the area from the Baltic to the Byzantine Empire. Thereafter, the western part of the country was controlled by princes (Teutonic states) and the east by Genghis Khan's Golden Horde.

On the other hand, the occupation of Russia and the destruction of Kiev and other cities by the Mongols (1237–1452) cut ties with the West, forced people back to agriculture, and made them subservient to the autocratic Mongol rulers. As a result, the economic development of the country was held back. With the independence of the country (1452) the capital was moved from Kiev to Moscow. In 1547 Ivan the Terrible became czar at the age of 17.

Realizing that Russia remained backward compared to Western Europe, Peter the Great, who reigned from 1689 to 1725, initiated drastic reforms introducing technical training, sciences, and new technology. Also, he moved the Russian capital from Moscow to St. Petersburg (Leningrad), a new city closer to the Western world that he took from Sweden. To implement his program of westernization he resorted to autocratic repression. He even ordered the death by torture of his son (Alexis Petrovich, 1690–1718). In addition to the development of industry and trade, Peter achieved successive territorial expansions from the Baltic Sea to the Crimea and from Central Asia to Byelorussia.[1]

Westernization policies and expansion continued thereafter, especially under Catherine the Great (1762 and later). In 1812 Napoleon the Great of France invaded Russia, including Moscow, but he was defeated and turned back. Through successful wars against the Ottoman Turkish Empire, Russia achieved virtual control of the Dardanelles (1833). To block Russia from eventual mastery of Constantinople and the Straits of the Bosporos, France and Britain attacked and defeated Russia in the Crimean War (1853–56). In spite of the westernization policies and the nominal abolition of serfdom, Russia remained largely a feudalistic and backward country.

With the emancipation of the serfs (1861), about half of the land was assigned to the tilling peasants but the more productive land remained with the gentry. The peasants, who were obliged to pay redemptions, formed communes that assigned plots for cultivation in rotation, which Karl Marx appraised (1882) as an effective measure of common ownership. However, this communal system was not successful, mainly because of the low incentives of production in rotated plots scattered in different places.

To pay for redemption and taxes, the peasants increased production to the point that Russia became the first country to export grain toward the end of the nineteenth century. This enabled the country to import needed machinery and other material for the development of railways and other infrastructural facilities that helped increase the output of coal, oil, cloth, and other vital products.

THE BOLSHEVIK REVOLUTION, COMMUNISM, AND THE NEW ECONOMIC POLICY

Before the Bolshevik Revolution of 1917 there were serious but unsuccessful socialist movements in 1903 and especially in January 1905 when a massacre against the protesting workers occurred in St. Petersburg (Bloody Sunday). The Mensheviks advocated the overthrow of the czarist regime by democratic means, but the Bolsheviks believed in violent revolution and split from the Mensheviks in 1912. The reforms introduced by the established parliament (Duma) from 1906 to 1910 and later, including the release of the peasants from the communes and the cancellation of their debts, did not have major results. World War I, which started in Europe in 1914 and engulfed Russia, made things worse, as corruption continued and repression was intensified. In February 1917, riots took place in the capital, the czar was forced to abdicate his throne, and the moderate provisional government of Alexander Kerensky proceeded with slow and unsuccessful economic and other reforms until the Bolsheviks took power in the Russian capital on November 6–7 (October 24–25 in the then-prevailing Old Julian Calendar).

Although Marx predicted communism would be established first in advanced capitalist countries, it arrived in Russia instead, a backward country with limited industry and some 80 percent of its population illiterate, working in the rural sector under oppressive conditions. Under the leadership of Vladimir Lenin (1870–1924) and other revolutionaries, the Russian people (mainly peasants, soldiers, and workers) revolted against the oppressive socioeconomic system that prevailed under the czarist regimes. Under the slogan "Peace, Land and Bread," the Bolshevik revolutionaries overthrew the Labor Party provisional government of Alexander Kerensky and established worker councils (Soviets) to supervise the transformation of the economy to the new socialist system.

All the land of aristocrats, the church, and landlords was confiscated and distributed by local committees to the peasants for private use. The right to private property in the land was annulled forever without any indemnity. Selling of land and hiring outside labor were not permitted. Factories were taken over by the workers employed in them, who elected their own managers and equalized wages. Nationalization, however, involved heavy industry, communications, transportation, oil, grain trade, and banks.

The liberal printing of money to finance purchases from the peasants led to hyperinflation and a barter economy that some of Lenin's followers considered as a "naturalization" of the economy. This was expected to lead to the destruction of the bourgeois market economy and the establishment of the moneyless society with common ownership and selfless citizens that Marx envisioned in his last stage of ideal communism. However, severe shortages forced Communist Party activists and the police to go to the rural areas to collect, forcefully, badly needed food for the urban centers. As a result, many peasants reduced or concealed production and slaughtered their cattle, while a rationing system was introduced in the cities to void widespread starvation. Low incentives for work, mismanagement, and lack of coordination caused a severe decline in agricultural and industrial production and forced Lenin in 1921 to enact his New Economic Policy (NEP), which lasted until 1928.

To avoid the collapse of the Russian economy, significant changes were introduced. They included the denationalization of retail trade and small-scale industries; the replacement of forced requisitioning of farm products by a fixed tax in kind; permission for the employment of up to 20 persons by private entrepreneurs, who could also lease previous nationalized enterprises; and the determination of wages by the market. Also, many enterprises became independent (except for certain strategic industries), labor mobility and profit making were allowed, and collective bargaining was permitted. In a sense, this policy was considered as a strategic retreat from communism to capitalism, a step backward to stabilize the economy and prepare it for two steps forward, as Lenin said, toward full communism.

As a result of these measures of "capitalism under communism," work incentives were restored, peasants were producing more than they were consuming, and surplus of food and raw materials supported the development of industry. Production in 1925 was restored to the pre-World War I level. The performance of the private entrepreneurs and small farm owners or the class of "petty bourgeois" restored the economic growth of the country under the system of what may be called "market socialism."[2]

AGRICULTURAL PERFORMANCE

The debate on gradual or rapid industrialization or balanced versus unbalanced growth was terminated by Joseph Stalin through forceful collectivation of agriculture and the introduction of the central planning process.

Large cooperative farms have the advantage of implementing modern technology and thereby increasing productivity. The introduction of tractors and threshing and other machines make land cultivation easier and usually output per acre of land higher. Moreover, the creation of large collective tracts from scattered small family plots makes the use of modern equipment easier and land productivity higher; while the use of trained farm professionals as managers and specialists and the application of new research and development methods make collective farms more efficient than tiny family farms. However, production incentives in farm cooperatives are lower than in private plots, but they are higher than in state farms, because of the wage payments according to annual production or profit sharing that prevails in farm cooperatives.

Out of the three main types of agricultural institutions (*kolkhozy, sovkhozy,* and private plots), collective farms (*kolkhozy*) were jointly owned by their members, who shared in the harvests. State farms (*sovkhozy*) were owned by the state and run by the government, which paid employees and managers salaries and bonuses. Private plots, which were allotted to persons working in state farms or collectives (about two acres per person), could sell their products to free markets, as this author observed in his visits. Small plots were allotted to industrial workers in the cities.

Collective farms produced primarily sugar beets (about 90 percent of gross total output), cotton (65), grain (50), milk (40), meat (30), and potatoes (20). State farms produced mainly eggs (65), grain (48), meat (40), and potatoes (20). Private plots produced primarily potatoes (60), meat, milk, eggs (about 30 percent of each of gross total output), as well as other labor-intensive products such as vegetables, spices, and fruits.

The Soviet farms (except the private plots) were required to deliver their planned quotas to the government at very low procurement prices, especially during the Stalin period, and even later but at better prices. Cooperatives could sell additional output to the state at higher prices (up to 100 percent above procurement prices) or to consumers on the collective farm markets at prices determined by supply and demand.

The substantial subsidies paid by the government to the agricultural sector have not produced good results from the standpoint of production. The Soviet Union, which was the largest grain exporter years back, became the largest importer in spite of efforts of the Soviet leaders after Stalin, primarily Khrushchev, Brezhnev, and Gorbachev, to give high priority to agriculture.

The main reasons for low agricultural performance were organizational, technological, and climatic, particularly in Siberia and the northern region of the Soviet Union. Agricultural decisions ought to be made on time and by the farmers on the fields, not by central planners in remote cities. Moreover, farms were very large, incentives of cultivation were low, and prices did not respond to market changes. The establishment of the agroindustrial associations in 1982 have not improved conditions much.[3]

THE PLANNING PROCESS

Central Imperative Planning

The main feature of the Soviet economic system was the formation and implementation of central planning. The first five-year plan (FYP) of 1928–32 was introduced by Stalin and was followed by the second FYP of 1933–37 and consequent plans thereafter. In all the plans, emphasis was placed on producer goods (inputs for inputs) at the neglect of consumer agricultural goods.

A more practical five-year plan, the eighth in number, was implemented in 1965–70, while a long-run 20-year plan 1960–80 was adopted. The latter set production goals primarily, which proved difficult to achieve, as were the goals of a similar program, formulated in 1986, that aimed at a double output by the year 2000. To a large extent, these plans were ambitious and unrealistic and were modified by annual plans that were more practical.

The procedure of resource allocation and output apportioning was followed by the State Planning Commission (Gosplan), which formulated the plans and passed them down to ministries, regional units, and finally to individual state enterprises. After reviewing the plans, responsible officials suggested modifications and sent the plans to their superiors all the way back to Gosplan for adjustment and final revisions. After the approval by the Supreme Soviet (parliament), the plans had the force of law and were sent back to enterprise managers for implementation.

Incentives and Inefficiency

For a better coordination and fulfillment of the plans, there were material incentives (bonuses) and moral or nonmaterial ones including appraisals for serving fellow citizens and driving out selfishness; attractive vacations, usually on the shores of the Crimea; and receiving medals such as "Order of Lenin" or becoming "Heroes of Socialist Labor." Unsuccessful managers and workers, though, might lose bonuses, be demoted, or might be given undesirable vacations on the steppes of Siberia.

Although the system of bonuses increased managerial incentives in fulfilling the plans, serious problems appeared regarding quality and quantity of production, especially if it was based on output quotas. Normally, a manager who fulfilled the plan received extra payment of up to half of his or her basic salary, plus a certain percentage increase for overfulfillment. However, to get large bonus payments, managers overstated inputs needed in materials and labor in order to store and use them later for overfulfillment of output targets when there were shortages. Moreover, they asked for low output quotas, hid the real capacity of their firms, and underutilized resources for the plan's overfulfillment. Thus management and members of a truck-driving unit in Russia received bonuses for reporting that they had removed 2 million tons of snow, a quantity that could have fallen over many years.

ADMINISTRATIVE ORGANIZATION

After the death of Stalin and the end of his cruelty in 1953, economic reforms were introduced, mainly by Nikita Khrushchev until 1964. Also, the rate of economic growth was relatively high (5 to 7 percent a year), and the prestige of the country was high after the launching of Sputnik (the world's first satellite) in 1957. These events inspired Khrushchev to proclaim that the Soviet Union will "bury" the United States economically.

Khrushchev introduced decentralization reforms by transferring managerial authority from the center to the newly created Regional Economic Councils of the several republics to bring leadership closer to production, reduce bureaucracy, and avoid duplication. However, technological progress was not enough and the rate of industrial productivity was falling. Then new reforms were introduced in 1965 by Aleksei Kosygin, the successor to Khrushchev. A number of decision-making councils, including the Regional Economic Councils, were dissolved. These reforms, introduced mainly by Professor E. Liberman, enhanced the role of centralized planning management, but allowed the attainment of profits or surpluses to be used by enterprises for technological improvement and payment of bonuses for efficient labor performance.

Later, however, during the presidency of Leonid Brezhnev (1965 to the early 1980s), economic growth declined, in spite of the emphasis on agricultural investment. Also, income inequalities increased, with Brezhnev earning 40 times the salary of an office clerk. The economic decline continued during the twelfth five-year plan (1986–90) and thereafter.

During the 1970s, Soviet planners started moving away from collective farms toward a more industrialized agricultural system, which combined crop growing and harvesting with storage and processing and saved about 50 percent production costs, compared to nonspecialized collective and state farms.

Up to the political reforms of 1989, the locus of power rested with the Communist Party, whose Congress was elected by the party organizations throughout the country. It met every five years to elect the Central Committee (several hundred members), which, in turn, met twice a year to elect the Politburo (some 13 members). This body set economic, social affairs, and foreign policies, while the Secretariat (headed by a powerful general secretary, assisted by a large staff) ran the daily affairs of the country.

On the other hand, the government, which followed the party's directions, consisted of the Supreme Soviet of the USSR, a nominal Parliament elected every five years. It met twice a year to approve legislation and to select the Council of Ministers (consisting of the prime minister and a number of ministers) and the Presidium of the Supreme Soviet (consisting of a chairman and some deputies).[4]

The unanticipated economic and political changes, introduced primarily by Gorbachev in the late 1980s, surprised or fascinated many economists and politicians the world over. The dismantling of the Berlin Wall, a symbol of the cold war, and the withdrawal of Soviet troops from Eastern Europe led to dramatic changes of the economic and political systems of all these countries.

The main questions are: Why did all of these revolutionary and dramatic changes of our century occur in a short period of time and with not much resistance? Why were the peoples of the former Soviet republics and Eastern Europe ready and eager to embrace such drastic changes and reforms? As the author observed during his research trips to Russia and other republics, people complained and asked: Why have we been left far behind, economically and technologically, from other peoples of so many countries? They seemed to realize that their economic and political system was responsible for bureaucratic inertia, oppression, apathy, neglect, and inefficiency. The saying that "they pretend they pay us and we pretend we work" could be concluded from many conversations. Such neglect and lack of incentives in production were primarily the result of common ownership, a principle that Aristotle pointed out some 25 centuries ago, in criticizing Plato's ideal state of communism, that common ownership means common neglect.

Russia, which became a republic of the USSR in 1922, declared its independence from the Union on June 12, 1990. With a population close to 150 million and 77 percent of the land, it was the largest republic of the former USSR, more than twice the size of the United States. On December 8, 1991, the republics of Russia, Ukraine, and Byelorussia created a new Commonwealth of Independent States and declared that the USSR ceased to exist. Other republics joined the CIS later and in October 1993 all the former Soviet republics, except the three small Baltic countries, joined the CIS.

Although 83 percent of its population is Russian, Russia itself is a mosaic of ethnic groups. It has some 100 minorities, 31 of which are officially autonomous areas. One is Tatarstan (known in ancient times as the Khanate of Kazan) with a population of 3.5 million, 48 percent of which are Tatars, who press for independence from Russia. Mostly they are Christian Orthodox in faith.

Boris Yeltsin, the president of the Russian republic, proved to be an effective leader in opposing the failing coup of August 19–21, 1991, by hardline communists and speeding up reforms toward political democracy and a free market economy. Also, he managed to put down the communist/fascist uprising of October 3–4, 1993 in Moscow instigated by Parliament Speaker Ruslan Khasbulatov and Vice-President Alexander Rutskoi. In the elections of December 12, 1993, the reformists he supported got only 15 percent of the votes, compared to 23 percent for the ultra-nationalists, and 20 percent for the communists.

From another point of view, there is suspicion and at times border conflicts and ideological disputes between Russia, the world's largest inland country, and China, the world's most populous country. China's population of more than 1 billion looks at neighboring Russia with a vast land, large parts of which were ceded to Czar Alexander II by Manchu emperors about a century ago, as the Chinese claim. The Sino-Russian hostility, with roots in the Tatar-Mongol occupation of Russia for some 300 years, and this demographic uneasiness may force Russia to pursue a Russo-European accommodation and closer economic and even political ties with the EC.

ECONOMIC AND POLITICAL REFORMS

During the presidency of Mikhail Gorbachev (1985–91), and especially after the decision of the Communist Party Central Committee in June 1987 to introduce reforms and to decentralize the Soviet economy, gradual changes started taking place, but at a slow pace. More radical economic and political reforms were accepted by the national conference of the Communist Party, June 28–July 1, 1988. The 4,991 delegates of the party's first national conference in 47 years decided to increase efforts toward social and economic restructuring (*perestroika*) and political and sociocultural openness (*glasnost*).[5] Two major reforms introduced in the conference were to shift authority from local Communist Party bureaucrats to local government councils and establish a more powerful president, by indirect election. The tenure of all elected officials, including the chairman of the party or the president would be for five years with the limit of ten years at most. Gorbachev wanted to introduce a new human image of socialism and a democratic procedure.

It seemed that piecemeal reforms were not leading to the free market mechanism and the equilibrium of supply and demand. More drastic reforms that would lead to price decontrols, elimination of subsidies to inefficient enterprises, more freedom of business entry, easier investment credit to the private sector, currency convertibility, and encouragement of competition were needed.

Many economic and political changes of Boris Yeltsin were criticized as superficial and not effective. Even Yeltsin himself was considered as an un-polished and autocratic president who rules by decree, inviting charges of dictatorship. Nevertheless, he managed to maintain peaceful relations with the neighboring republics of the Commonwealth of Independent States and implement reforms toward privatization, although at a slower pace than expected. Moreover, the Russian people and their representatives in the Par-liament are accustomed to receive directions from above. They do not easily accept loyal opposition, whereas many think that the wholesale adoption of Western-style democracy is a utopia for Russia.

Regarding the efforts of the former Soviet republics to form a confeder-ation, there is the danger that in a political and economic confederation such as the CIS, each independent republic may want its own army, its own money, or its own customs service. In the final analysis they may turn against each other, as happened with the republics of Armenia and Azerbaijan. Even into the Russian Federation, 2 out of the 20 main subdivisions, the oil-rich Chechen-Ingush and Tatar republics, did not sign a federal agreement on March 31, 1992. Moreover, Russia wants the Crimean Peninsula back from Ukraine. (For efforts to create an economic and customs union among the European former Soviet republics, similar to the EC, see Chapter 10.)

Fiscal decentralization between the central government of Russia and its 91 regions (oblasts) is critical for the success of privatization and other economic reforms. Fiscal federalism, in the sense of tax revenue and expen-ditures allocation, is crucial for their distribution between national and sub-national governments. Through extensive decentralization, local authorities recently acquired significant power and responsibilities on budgetary matters and on selling or leasing public-sector assets to the private sector. State budget expenditures are distributed among the union (50.7 percent in 1989), the republics (32.8 percent), and local authorities (16.5 percent). To meet its budget deficit targets, the federal government must transfer more and more fiscal responsibilities to subnational governments. This leads to severe revenue expenditure mismatch of some poor oblasts, which oppose privatization of their enterprises from which they collect revenue. Nevertheless, some areas rich in natural resources, such as Yamal and Khanti-Mansisk (which produce about 80 percent of Russia's oil and gas) and Yakutia (which contains 99 percent of Russia's diamonds), are allowed to have greater fiscal autonomy.[6]

By using the remaining power levers, the *nomenklatura* (party members and government bureaucracies) quickly moved to capitalize its assets and influence. Former ministers, party bosses, university figures, and enterprise managers became heads of stock companies, commercial banks, and corporations and work for their own interests. This leads to a new class of entrepreneurs in the ex-planned economies with little resemblance to Western counterparts.

After price controls were lifted on January 2, 1992, and prices went up by more than three times, on the average, demand subsided and some products were returned to warehouses unsold. They included sour cream, boiled sausages, and other perishable goods. To ease the pains from drastic price increases, the Russian government reduced the value added taxes from 28 percent to about 15 percent, especially on food and other necessities. The value added taxes were introduced recently to replace the old turnover taxes that were levied at the wholesale level. Against these policies, severe criticism was made by the powerful Union of Industrialists and Entrepreneurs and the Liberal Democratic Party. They both formed the Civic Union, a movement that considers the new reformers as "utopians" and "neo-Bolsheviks" and the Commonwealth of Independent States as an ineffective amorphous creature. The representatives of this movement want slower transition, similar to what Gorbachev tried unsuccessfully. Others argue in favor of a "shock therapy," similar to that of Poland, although much time passed without implementing such drastic reforms.

Widespread unemployment, inflation, transfer of profits to Western banks, unpaid bills, crime, Mafia-style racketeering demanding money for protection, and corruption fuel criticism against the reformers, who are considered egg-headed theoretical economists deciding for everyone without much consideration of the practical results. These reformers try to implement Western economic models that may not fit Russia's uniqueness with numerous nationalities, a vast territory, a turbulent history, and not much knowledge of free enterprises and market competition, according to critics.

PRIVATIZATION AND WORKERS' OWNERSHIP

Problems of Management

Russia introduced a system of auctioning state property under which 25 percent of shares in individual enterprises is reserved for current employees. The crash reform program of transforming state-owned property to individuals, employees, and foreign investors includes factories, shops, and other enterprises.

Despite the Russian Parliament's adoption of a privatization law in July 1991, the transfer of enterprises from the public to the private sector remained slow. Moreover, managers of such enterprises formed their own joint stock companies, selling assets and leasing premises for their own profits. Under the privatization rules, a large number of committees were established all over Russia to implement privatization on a local level. On the other hand, foreign firms are not permitted to acquire shares in certain industries that deal with building materials or are under bankruptcy and suffer from lack of imported inputs.

After July 1, 1992, when Russia's President Yeltsin signed a related decree, privatization of state enterprises was accelerated. Such enterprises established joint worker-management committees, which proposed methods of privatization and the creation of joint-stock companies. In the process, managers and the government want to establish trust companies to take enterprises private and to acquire substantial stakes themselves, whereas doctors, teachers, and other professionals want a stake as well.

In spite of the intensive efforts of privatization, the Russian people have little faith and are suspicious regarding private property and free enterprises. After 75 years of state controls on all economic activities, people are not familiar with the merits of private ownership and the advantages of free markets.

There is criticism of privatization from many sides that the new factory managers behave like cooperative farm directors and miniczars, as in the old command economy. Also, it is argued that the new bureaucrats steal not only rubles through bribes as in the old system, but whole enterprises. They enjoy black sedans and summer villas, as did the previous communist elite they replaced. It seems that the whole process is a kind of renationalization not denationalization.

The privatization policy of Russia was helped by foreign firms in advisement and programming, mainly by Deloitte Touche, Credit Commercial de France SA, BBDO Marketing, and the law firms G. Henry Schroder Wagg and Co. of London and White and Case. Moreover, the International Finance Corporation, the private-sector arm of the World Bank, expanded its privatization program and provided how-to manuals for small-scale enterprises and would-be shop owners. Financing is also provided by the European Community through the European Bank for Reconstruction and Development.

A usual form of privatization or "corporatization" is to give workers up to 35 percent of voting or nonvoting shares in an enterprise for free or at a discount, while managers can buy 5 percent of voting shares at a discount. Also, distribution of vouchers to all citizens is another way of privatization, primarily of industries with more than 1,000 employees. The vouchers can be exchanged for shares, invested in mutual funds, or sold in the open market. Foreigners can buy shares at auctions. There are cases in which workers and managers can buy a controlling 51 percent stake in the enterprises in which they work, provided that they meet commitments to keep the enterprises operational. Proceeds are divided between central, regional, and local governments, so that government officials do not block sales.

Employees of enterprises in bad shape can get 20 percent of the shares if they fulfill their restructuring plans. Moreover, they can buy another 20 percent of the enterprises' shares at a discount.

On October 1, 1992, some 150 million Russians were given vouchers, worth about $60 for each citizen, to buy shares in state companies. Also, voucher holders, who control about one-third of such companies, can give vouchers to mutual funds, which can invest or sell the vouchers for them. Employers and managers control most of the shares and the government the rest. The diffusion of ownership to so many citizens makes the managers powerful. Probably the obligation of citizens to deposit the vouchers in a few mutual funds, as happened in Poland, can be more effective from the standpoint of oversight, although safeguards were provided (in contrast to Czechoslovakia's voucher program). It is expected that most state companies would be transferred to the private sector in about three years and reduce or eliminate thefts by the managers who were left in charge after the collapse of communist controls.

Paradoxically, a commercial bank controlled by Communist Party workers has been set up in St. Petersburg. The capital base of 3 million rubles came from the party's dues and budget. This action shows that the trend toward capitalism is so strong in the ex-planned economies of the former USSR and the East European countries that the communists turn themselves into capitalists.

Privatization Cases

To change the system of the monopoly of the state ownership and to stimulate production incentives, on March 6, 1990, the former Soviet parliament, with a vote of 350 in favor, 3 against, and 11 abstentions, cleared the way for the creation of worker-owned and private enterprises. The new legislation allows citizens to own property, to open businesses, and to create stock-owning societies. It permits property to be leased for life with the right of inheritance.

These measures, which resemble Lenin's New Economic Policy implemented in 1921–28, were not bold enough to transform the planning system into a Western-type mixed economy with mainly private ownership of the means of production. Moreover, to a large extent, local governments thwarted such measures as they wanted to keep control of the means of production. Nevertheless, the formation of new cooperatives with prosperous entrepreneurs and the spread of stock-holding workers and companies were growing through time, in spite of the ideological and bureaucratic inertia. Workers could buy or lease state enterprises, and were entitled to a share of after-tax profits.

The Moscow Low Voltage Equipment Factory, producing electrical equipment, was one of the first state enterprises to be transformed into a shareholding company. Some 1,600 employees and workers of the company put up 500 rubles each to hold 25 percent of the shares. The rest was sold to other individuals and investors, including local government committees, a bank, and an Italian company. Because of its efficient operation, the company, with permanent losses in the past, realized sizable profits and paid higher wages. The factory first became a worker-owned cooperative in 1988, when a related law was introduced in the former Soviet Union, and became a Western-style shareholding company. To improve quality and productivity, the workers were and still are responsible for repairing defects themselves or losing bonuses under a piecework system.

Some 45,000 workers of the Uralmash machine tool works in Sverdlovsk demanded, through their Workers Committee, not simply to have a voice in running the state-owned company, but to own it. They wanted to have property and to be masters of the factory, not hired labor, and thereby to increase productivity and wages.

After the failed putsch of August 1991, *Pravda*, long the voice of Communist Party ideology, came under the management of its staff and became the voice of civil liberties. In addition, the mayor of Moscow (Gavriil Popov) and other economists proposed plans of transferring restaurants, factories, and other stores to their workers for faster privatization and higher efficiency.

Privatization of state enterprises, particularly large firms, is slow in Russia, mainly because there is lack of managerial experience, lack of knowledge of free market operations, and lack of modern technology for competitive production. For decades people have been accustomed to receive orders from above (the planners) concerning what, how, and when to produce and to make changes. People cannot be ordered to capitalism by decree.

From that standpoint, Russia provides opportunities not only to foreign investors and entrepreneurs but also to business scholars and writers. Restructuring the country's industry and proceeding with the staggering job of transforming some 400 military plants to peaceful production is a challenge not only for Russia but for other countries as well, notably the United States. However, in the banking sector more than 2,000 private banks have been established during the first years of reforms in the early 1990s.

It seems that the EC and other Western countries can assist the Russian transition to a market economy not by giving money to the government, but by giving subsidies and other tax incentives to Western companies to do business in the former Soviet republics, thereby creating new markets and increasing employment in these republics and in the Western countries involved.

CLOSER RELATIONS WITH THE EC

The recent revolutionary changes in Russia and the other former Soviet republics created new conditions for the EC and the European continent. The dramatic economic and political reforms put Western leaders in a strange situation. Decades of ideological divisions and controls had not obliterated the concept of a European whole and a free European home, which was expressed at the December 1989 summit in Strasbourg, where the EC members favored an associated status of all former Eastern bloc countries. However, as Europe moves toward a self-reliant future it still needs the American presence for some time to come because it lacks a constructive pan-European ideology and leadership.

Until recently, the former Soviet republics and the Eastern bloc countries were seen as a threat to Western Europe, and their relations were all based on the context of U.S.-Soviet relations. However, the rapid changes in the East bloc countries for a free market system and decentralization in decision making point toward an economic interaction and an eventual partnership between them and the EC. As a result, the cold war polemics turned to mutual investment and development arguments.

The Russian system is facing a serious crisis that affects economics, ideology, leadership, and the feuding nationalities, with some neo-fascist characteristics. To avoid further deterioration, the West should support a peaceful transformation of the previous command system to a democratic market system.

In order to close the technological gap with other advanced countries, Russia and other former Soviet republics are interested in developing closer relations with the EC, as well as other industrial countries. Their program to transfer state enterprises to private owners will allow their economic-political system to be similar to that of the EC.

Russia is establishing commodity and stock exchange markets as well as mutual funds to facilitate new investment and joint ventures. The EC, the United States, Japan, and other nations provide aid to the former Soviet republics. Some $24 billion in aid was approved, through the European Bank for Reconstruction and Development (established in Paris in May 1990), to help reform their economies in a fashion similar to the U.S. Marshall Plan for Western Europe in the post-World War II years.

For political reasons, Victor Gerashchenko, the prime minister under Boris Yeltsin, called for corrections and took measures to change to a path of reforms by raising wages and providing subsidies to state-owned enterprises. This policy swells the budget deficit, which runs at $23 billion a year, aggravates inflation, which runs at about 400 percent a year, and delays privatization. However, privatization was criticized as a brutal and arbitrary measure similar to the farm collectivization of the 1920s when about 3 million people were annihilated and some 7 million were sent to Siberia.

Centuries of despotism and servility to czars and commissars made the Russian people skeptical about the democratic changes and the art of compromise. They remember what happened to those who reached for freedom under reformist czars, such as Peter the Great and Alexander II, who were among the first to perish. Fear, favor, xenophobia, stubbornness, and spinelessness became common characteristics of many people's behavior in the authoritarian tradition of Russia.

All these elements and the resistance to economic and political reforms by bureaucrats and the remaining industrial managers from the old regime make rapid changes problematic. It seems that the quick reforms of the "magic wand" of Jeffrey Sachs, the Harvard economist and adviser to the Russian government, are difficult to achieve. Nevertheless, Western governments and the International Monetary Fund increased their financial aid, but they pressed the Russian government and the central bank to control the money supply and the low-cost loans that inflate the economy.

FINANCIAL PROBLEMS

To keep the same monetary unit for all the republics and to make it convertible, it is suggested that a new "hard" ruble with full backing in a foreign reserve currency be issued and backed by gold reserves ($20 billion) and loans ($20 billion). A similar system was introduced during the Russian civil war when troops from Britain and other allied nations invaded Russia in the spring of 1918. With the proposal of John Maynard Keynes, who was a Treasury official at that time, the British established a National Emission Caisse that issued "British ruble" notes that were convertible into pounds at a fixed rate. This convertible ruble was to replace more than 2,000 separate "fiat" rubles used and backed by nothing. When most of the Allied troops withdrew from Russia in September 1919 the system was abandoned. Also, Alexander Hamilton in the United States in the late 1780s introduced a similar system, using gold and the property of the state as collaterals for government bonds.

The Moscow Narodny Bank Ltd., which was first established in London in 1915 as a cooperative bank, is currently acting as an investment bank and helps arrange joint ventures. It tries to attract Western companies to invest in Russia and to exploit its vast resources—mainly oil, gas, and forest products.

Some of the deals arranged by the Moscow Narodny Bank include a joint venture with a British company producing commercial vans, a hotel near Moscow's airport involving French and Belgian companies and banks, and a furniture factory in St. Petersburg financed by Finnish banks.

The Moscow Narodny Bank concluded deals with U.S. companies that involve an Estee Lauder cosmetics store in Moscow and the expansion of polyethylene plants whose products are sold in Western countries by Union

Carbide. With the breakdown of the centralized authority and the Byzantine system of the Soviet Union and the East European countries, expectations are that the activities of the bank will expand to other newly liberalized countries, such as the Czech and Slovak republics, Hungary, Romania, and Poland. The main shareholders of the bank are Gosbank (the central state bank) and Vneshekonombank (the Bank for Foreign Economic Affairs) of the former Soviet Union, although the authority of these controlling banks is gradually diminishing as important deals are transferred to ex-Soviet republics and individual enterprises.

Another financial institution, the Russian Companies Fund, was established recently to facilitate the transition of Russian companies from the public to the private sector and to help the emergence of new ones. The fund, which is promoted by Battery March Financial Management of Boston, is expected to raise $400 million to $1 billion for big investors in the near future. Depending on the speed of privatization and the convertibility of the ruble, more money can be raised by this and similar other funds.

The establishment of an expected stock market in Moscow would initially promote the sale of notes and bonds and eventually stocks. Some banks in St. Petersburg (Leningrad) are already selling notes, which can become tradeable, with 11 percent interest rate. Expectations are that the New York Stock Exchange would cooperate with its counterpart in Moscow for the sale of bonds and other financial instruments, as happened years back (1905) when the first Russian bonds were traded in New York.

For the reestablishment of a stock market (similar to the one that operated in St. Petersburg from 1703 to 1917), the New York Stock Exchange conducted seminars in Moscow in 1990 on regulating financial markets, raising capital, and stock speculation. Moreover, the first commodities exchange since the 1917 Bolshevik Revolution opened in Moscow in September 1990. A seat on the Moscow Exchange, which is like the Chicago Mercantile Exchange, costs about 100,000 rubles.

Some 40 nations agreed to allow the newly created European Bank for Reconstruction and Development to provide loans not only to the private sector, but also to the public sector of the ex-Soviet republics and other East European nations. Such loans to projects like roads, telecommunications, and other infrastructural facilities would help revive these economies. Other loans and credit lines are extended by the United States, mainly for food imports, medical products, and distribution facilities, as well as by the World Bank and the International Monetary Fund.

With a gross national product of more than $1 trillion, Russia, as the largest ex-Soviet republic, is entitled to about 6 percent of the total voting power and the right to appoint one of the 22 directors of each institution. On March 31, 1992, the IMF endorsed the Russian plan for economic reforms and to open the way for loans, full membership, and eventual integration of the Russian economy with the West. Also, the president of the United States announced that the seven main industrial countries would provide aid to the former Soviet republics amounting to $24 billion.

On April 4, 1993, U.S. President Bill Clinton met with Russian President Boris Yeltsin, in Vancouver, British Columbia, and offered $1.623 billion in aid and loans to Russia. Some $700 million or 43 percent of the package will go to grain and other food credits, $691 or 42 percent will go to direct grants, and the remaining $232 or 14 percent to other aid programs.

The package includes $194 million in food grants and $20 million in medical grants; $150 million in Overseas Private Investment Corporation insurance and guarantees, $82 million in Export-Import bank loans, and $2 million to establish American business centers in Russia; $130 million for dismantling weapons and $75 million for a Nuclear Warhead Storage Facility; $10 million for nuclear materials accountability control; $25 million for a program to bring about 3,000 Russians to the United Streets for training; and the rest of the money will be used to help the privatization of state-owned enterprises in Russia to encourage joint U.S.-Russian business ventures.

COOPERATION IN TRADE

During the post-World War II period, world trade has been growing year after year and at rates higher than the growth rates of output. The largest percentage (about 90 percent) of trade has been conducted among market economies and to a limited extent with the former USSR and other planned economies. This is another element promoting the expansion of the market vis-a-vis the planning system.

International trade leads to specialization and cheaper production, thereby generating economic benefits to the countries involved. Reduction in tariffs and other restrictions, which stimulate trade and increase prosperity, can be better achieved by countries with similar economic systems. From that standpoint, economic cooperation and integration of different nations lead to lower cost of production, cheaper prices, higher growth, and more trade.[7]

Foreign trade by planned economies and the former USSR had been exercised mainly through state agents and on a bilateral rather than multilateral basis. It had been largely an extension of the domestic trade system in which tariffs and exchange rates have played a limited role, if at all. In this form of barter-type monopolistic transactions, exports had been used to finance imports.

In their trade with the market economies, planners resorted to dumping operations—that is, selling abroad at lower prices, covering the difference with subsidies.

To improve telecommunications between the United States and the Soviet Union, AT&T proposed to use the Soviet Intersputnik satellite system for a closer connection of the two nations. Also, the Energetics Satellites Corporation of the United States signed a contract with Glavkosmos, the Soviet civilian space agency, to launch eight communication satellites worth $54 million.

The General Electric Company is negotiating multimillion-dollar contracts to supply jet engines to Aeroflot, the Soviet airline, to power planes it bought from Airbus Industrie, the European consortium based in France. Moreover, negotiations between the United States and Russia are conducted for the expansion of U.S. airline services to a number of Soviet cities and Aeroflot services to some American cities.

One can argue that what is needed for Russia is a new Marshall Plan in which not only the United States but also Western Europe, Japan, and possibly the World Bank and the International Monetary Fund can participate.

Some politicians propose to cut military spending to provide humanitarian and other aid to these countries for a safe transition to democracy and economic freedom. The end of the cold war leads to the reduction of spending for weapons and the possibility of shifting funds for such ventures. The splitting up of the former Comecon trade bloc and the inability of Russia and the East European countries to export to the West intensifies the problem.

Russia turned to large Western advertising agencies to place commercials and to exploit other opportunities. Aeroflot bought five planes from Airbus Industrie for $300 million, a transaction that paves the way for sales of American jets to Russia as well.

To increase sales of agricultural products to the Soviet Union, estimated at about $3.5 billion a year, the United States provides federal guarantees of commercial bank loans. Farmers and businesspeople want to increase farm and other product exports. They are in serious competition with Japan and the European Community, which provide such guaranteed loans, and they press for tariff concessions.

To facilitate trade with the Russians, the U.S. government waived the Jackson-Vanik amendment to the Trade Act of 1974, which bans not only tariff concessions but also credit guarantees to countries that prevent free emigration. Thus, the Export-Import Bank and the Credit Corporation can provide federal guaranteed loans to Russia for imports of American products. A second guarantee by the Russian Bank of Foreign Affairs is required so that payments in gold or hard currencies will be forthcoming. Moreover, IBM and the Upjohn Company are seeking similar credit guarantees for investment in computers and pharmaceutical plants in Russia.

OIL PRODUCTION AND TRADE

Although the former Soviet Union was the largest oil producer, it consumed a great deal and exported only about one-third of the 12 million barrels it produced per day. However, output gradually declined because of overexploitation of the oil fields in the 1980s, declining investment, and the use of inefficient equipment. It is expected, though, that the introduction of advanced technology by joint ventures and other foreign investment would increase production and reduce waste.

Crude oil reserves in the former Soviet Union were only about 60 billion barrels in 1988, an amount equal to that in Venezuela and Mexico and less than that in Saudi Arabia (255), Iraq, the United Arab Emirates, Kuwait, and Iran (about 100 billion barrels each), but more than that in the United States (26) and China (24).

Lower production of oil led to declining exports to about 3.3 million barrels a day, down from 4.1 million barrels daily in 1988. About half of the exported oil went to East European countries and the other half to the West. Annual oil exports yield about $20 billion or 40 percent of the total hard currency.

Drastic decreases in oil-industry investment (which used to absorb about 70 percent of new investment capital in the 1980s), in favor of other consumer products, was primarily responsible for the decline in production and exports in the former Soviet republics. Moreover, ethnic unrest, mainly in the oil republic of Azerbaijan, and the claims of some republics to their mineral resources were additional reasons for such a decline.

It should be noted, though, that Western high technology was not allowed into communist countries by the Cocom (Coordinating Committee on multilateral export controls). From that standpoint, in some areas, as this author observed, there are large numbers of small old-fashioned pumping equipment spread all over the place and mostly abandoned. However, Russian geology offers better opportunities for oil drilling than other countries, particularly for deep oil fields. Joint ventures with Western firms, such as those recently announced, would modernize the oil industry, especially in the Russian republic, which accounts for 85 percent of production in the former Soviet Union.

Texaco agreed with the Ministry of Geology of Russia to form joint ventures to study the feasibility and to handle oil production in the Arctic oil fields, south of the Barents Sea. It is estimated that there are reserves of more than 5 billion barrels in this area. For that reason, Texaco will install computer equipment to process geological data from the Arctic and other Russian regions.

The construction of the natural gas pipeline, which is built primarily by West European companies to link Siberia to Western Europe, is expected to reach many European nations. Although such a link would increase the influence of Moscow upon the economies of the other countries involved, low gas prices would relieve part of their energy and balance-of-trade burdens.

INVESTMENT AND JOINT VENTURES

European Investments

In order to attract foreign investment and modern technology, in April 1989 the former USSR allowed joint ventures with up to 99 percent foreign ownership. More than 400 such joint enterprises have been registered and more than 30 of them are in operation. Among the benefits offered are reductions in tariffs for imported production goods, a 20 percent tax reduction on exported profits, and freedom in hiring, firing, and personnel appointments.

To facilitate economic transactions and to exploit the opportunities created in the area, the Deutsche Bank arranged a credit line of $1.6 billion. The credit was extended to help Russia modernize its consumer goods industry and also to benefit the textile and shoe industries of Germany. About 30 percent of the total $16 billion loans to Moscow since 1984 was from Germany, 40 percent from Japan, and only 2 percent from American banks.

In addition to the credit package of $1.6 billion from Germany, Italy provided the former Soviet republics with $775 million export credits in 1988 and more credit and investment continue to flow into all the ex-Soviet republics from the West.

Although EC firms are more aggressive in pursuing joint ventures in Eastern Europe and the ex-Soviet republics, compared to American firms, U.S. companies, especially their subsidiaries in Europe, moved rapidly in establishing joint ventures in the area.

Investment ventures from Europe in Russia include Fiat SPA, Italy's largest auto company based in Turin, which has produced cars in Russia since 1970. It signed a joint venture to produce 300,000 cars at Velabuga near Moscow. The Russians will hold 70 percent of the venture. The initial investment is $1.4 billion, but it will increase to accommodate production of up to 900,000 cars. Moreover, Pirelli SPA is considering the establishment of a plant in Russia to produce about 10 million tires, while the Merloni SPA group would create a plant for electronic goods.

British Airways and Aeroflot, the world's largest airline with some 2,500 planes, plan the creation of a new international airline, named Air Russia, for flights all over the world. The airline, which will use Western jumbo jets, will provide a large market for British Airways, with about 220 planes, and hard currency for Russia. Aeroflot, which carries more than 134 million passengers a year, is expected to reorganize and innovate its operations under competitive conditions from American, European, Japanese, and other carriers, while British Airways, the newly privatized British carrier, will provide capital and new technology for Air Russia.

Pravda, the Russian newspaper founded by Vladimir Lenin in 1912, reached 13 million circulation in the 1970s, but fell to 2 million in 1992. Yannis Yannikos bought a 55 percent stake of *Pravda* for 1 million rubles and a pledge to cover its 60-million-ruble debt ($1 = 100 rubles). His family runs Akadimos, a publishing firm, and Steel Light Ltd, both in Greece.[8]

MTV Europe, the cable music video channel, agreed with Gostelradio, the Russian television company, to provide a weekly hour of programming to be included in "Glance," a youth-oriented program. It will present rock performers and advertising for European and American companies and is expected to be extended on a 24-hour basis. It is already operating in Eastern Europe.

Furthermore, Rupert Murdoch, who controls Fox Television in the United States and Sky Television in Britain, is eager to enter joint ventures with Russia on television production, books, and other publications. However, care should be taken to avoid duplications of similar public or private projects that spread rapidly into Eastern Europe and the former Soviet Union.

The Greek Public Enterprise of Gas signed an agreement with the Bank of Foreign Economic Relations of Russia for a loan to finance part of the construction of the gas pipeline by the Machinoebort Company of Russia for the flow of natural gas to Greece.

Western and other banks are moving in the area to facilitate the financing of investment and joint ventures. Thus, four west European banks and the Kansallis Banking Group of Finland formed a joint venture with three Russian banks to finance new investment. The new banking firm is known as the International Moscow Bank.

Other companies involved in Russian ventures include Honeywell, providing computerized controls in fertilizer plants; Combustion Engineering, dealing with renovating oil and petrochemical plants; and Eurocopter SA, a French-German joint venture, agreeing with three Russian Companies to build helicopters.

American Investments

There are more than 100 American ventures in the former USSR. Among the number of American companies that have entered Russia are Young and Rubicam, Ogilvy and Mather, and other advertising firms that are trying to help Mercedes-Benz, Allied Lyons, British Airways, ICI, and other companies establish themselves in the Russian market of some 150 million customers. They follow the example of Pepsico, which has sold its products since 1959 and currently manufactures them in Russia.

Italian and Japanese companies have joined in a consortium with Occidental

Petroleum Corporation to build a petrochemical plant in the former Soviet Union close to the Caspian Sea.

Pizza Hut, a unit of Pepsico Inc., opened two restaurants in Moscow (one near the Kremlin) that serve about 50,000 customers a week. About 60 to 80 percent of food supplies are coming from local suppliers. Pizza Hut, which also opened its first restaurant in Beijing recently, accepts Russian rubles as well as hard currencies readily exchanged. Expectations are for rapid expansion in other Russian cities as well.

McDonald's, which serves about 25 million people a day in 11,000 restaurants in 52 nations, serves about 30,000 people daily in spite of 45-minute waiting lines. It uses Russian supplies for raw materials and has built a large plant.

Other firms offer audio-video equipment and souvenirs in the hotel shops in Moscow and other cities.

American and Canadian firms are opening stores offering copying shops and international electronic transmission printing, with 51 percent Russian ownership and 49 percent for them, using Apple Computers. However, a serious problem arises from sales on rubles, which cannot be converted easily into hard currencies. On the other hand, there are complaints that Russian-Western ventures are still small and they do not involve needed high-stakes technology.

Bloomingdale's Department Store agreed to open stores in Moscow, while Union Carbide sent scientists to Russia to spread commercial applications of new technologies regarding catalysts and absorbents in oil operations.

Phoenix Group International will help set up factories in Russia to produce personal computers for schools and universities, supplying about 6 million computers in about three years.

The M.A.L. Sales Corporation agreed with Kimray, a Russian shoemaker, to convert a factory to produce leisure and work shoes. Some 50 million pairs of shoes are expected to be produced over the next decade for sale in Russia and the West. The M.A.L. company initially would provide the needed equipment and training. Later, it would share in the revenue, especially from the shoes sold in the West. Leather and other raw materials for shoes are ample in Russia and imports are not needed. This and other joint ventures came as a result of a seminar in April 1990, sponsored by the Harvard University Graduate School of Business and a related Russian government institute.

Otis Elevator Company, the world's largest elevator firm, agreed with Shcherbink Lift Plant of Russia to install and maintain elevator equipment near Moscow. The new company, in which the share of Otis is 55 percent, will be called Shcherbink Otis Lift. It will produce elevator equipment for small hotels and offices mainly for the Russian market.

In its long-term growth strategy, Polaroid Corporation has opened manufacturing operations and retail stores in Moscow and plans to move to other cities as well.

RJR Nabisco, the second-largest cigarette market in the United States, agreed to provide technical assistance to Russian tobacco factories. Also, it sells billions of cigarettes to Russia, as does its biggest rival, the Philip Morris Company. Cigarette shortages are due mainly to the breakdowns at many Russian tobacco factories and the shortfall of imports from Bulgaria, an important supplier of tobacco.

Phibro Energy, Inc. and Anglo-Suisse, Inc. agreed to participate in a joint venture with Varyeganneftegaz of Russia for oil and gas exploration in the western Siberian region. The ownership of the venture is 50 percent by Phibro and Anglo-Suisse and 50 percent for Varyeganneftegaz.

Cargill, Inc. opened offices in Moscow, as well as in Warsaw, to pursue investment possibilities in commodity merchandising, industrial products, agricultural products, processing, and transportation. Although Cargill has had trading relations with Russia and Poland for some 30 years, this is the first time it has established a physical presence in these countries.

Combustion Engineering Company led a consortium of Western firms to sign an agreement with Tobolsk Petrochemical Company of Russia to build and operate a petrochemical complex in Siberia worth $2 billion. The plant will process oil and gas for use in automobiles and medical items for Russian and foreign markets.

The state property committees seek advice from foreign consultants regarding legal matters, orientation, auditing, communication, and financing. Thus, Credit Commercial de France took charge of the disposal of GUM (Gosudarstveny Universalny Magasin), which runs 20 department stores in Moscow. Also, Goldman Sachs International is advising the Russian government and the managers of the state enterprises on matters of selling shares to foreign investors, who center mainly on medium-size plants and not much on vertically integrated large firms.

The Boeing Company agreed to establish a research center (in early 1993) in Moscow for aerospace technology, employing about 30 Russian engineers and some from Boeing.

To facilitate the establishment and improvement of new industries and joint ventures, U.S. law firms are rapidly moving into Russia and other CIS countries.[9] They include Davis, Graham and Stubbs; Cole, Corette and Abrutyn (both Washington, D.C. firms); Vinson and Elkins of Houston; Milbank, Tweed, Hadley and McCloy of New York; and Miller, Canfield, Paddock and Stone of Detroit. They provide services in a number of companies specializing in such sectors as energy, telecommunications, oil and drilling operations, gold mining, real estate, trade, stock exchanges, securities writings and other financial services, not only in Russia but Ukraine, Moldavia, Belarus and other CIS areas.

A correlation of gross domestic product on "investment" (INV) shows that investment is a significant variable in determining GDP for the former USSR (1972–88), according to United Nations statistics, GDP = −72.5 + 4.5INV (R = .68), and more so "exports" (EX), GDP = 257.5 + 4.7EX (R = .95). This means that each additional unit of exports is related to 4.7 units of GDP, and each unit of investment to 4.5 units of GDP, indicating a relatively high multiplier.

Other Former Soviet Republics

THE DISINTEGRATION OF THE USSR

Commonwealth of Independent States

After the Bolshevik Revolution, a number of neighboring republics formed the Union of Soviet Socialist Republics in 1922, which incorporated more republics later on, voluntarily or through annexation. Before its disintegration in 1991, the USSR included the Slavic part of the union—that is, Russia (the largest republic with 77 percent of the USSR), Ukraine (the second richest republic), Byelorussia (or Belarus), and Moldavia; the Caucasus (Azerbaijan, Armenia, and Georgia); Soviet Central Asia (Uzbekistan, Kazakhstan, Kyrgyzstan, Turkmenistan, and Tajikistan); and the Baltics (Lithuania, Latvia, and Estonia).

Table 10.1 shows the size of the European republics of the former USSR in terms of population, GNP per capita, and joint investment ventures. The first republics to become independent (on September 6, 1991) were the three Baltic states, which were occupied in 1940 by the Soviet army as a result of the secret Hitler-Stalin pact.

On December 8, 1991, the republics of Russia, Ukraine, and Byelorussia created a new Commonwealth of Independent States and declared that the USSR ceased to exist. Eleven remaining republics, except Georgia, joined the CIS later in the month. Table 10.2 shows some economic indicators of the Asian former USSR republics.

However, the CIS has not proved to be effective as yet and a number of the republics, especially Russia and those close to Western Europe, expressed their desires to join the EC. Moreover, six Muslim former Soviet republics

Table 10.1
Economic Indicators of the European Former USSR Republics, 1990

Republics	Population Millions	GNP Per Capita ($)	Joint Ventures (with foreign cos)
Ukraine	52.0	4,700	113
Byelorussia	10.2	5,960	33
Georgia	5.4	4,410	30
Moldavia	4.5	3,830	19
Armenia	3.4	4,710	5
Lithuania	3.7	5,880	-
Latvia	2.6	6,740	61
Estonia	1.5	6,240	116

Source: Europa World Book, National Geographic Maps; "The Soviet Union's Unequal Parts: Diverse and Restless," New York Times September 1, 1991, E2 and F6; and "Ta Dekapente Kommatia tou Sovietikou Pazl" (The Fifteen Pieces of the Soviet Pazl) To Vima, Athens, September 1, 1991, A16.

Table 10.2
Economic Indicators of the Asian Former USSR Republics, 1990

Republics	Population Millions	GNP Per Capita ($)	Joint Ventures (with foreign cos)
Uzbekistan	19.0	2,720	18
Kazakhstan	16.0	3,720	11
Azerbaijan	7.0	3,750	1
Tajikistan	5.0	2,340	-
Kyrgyzstan	4.1	3,030	-
Turkmenistan	3.4	3,370	-

Source: Europa World Book, National Geographic Maps; "The Soviet Union's Unequal Parts: Diverse and Restless, "The New York Times September 1, 1991, E2 and F6; and "Ta Dekapente Kommatia tou Sovietikou Pazl" (The Fifteen Pieces of the Soviet Pazl) To Vima, Athens, September 1, 1991, A16.

(Kazakhstan, Azerbaijan, Kyrgyzstan, Turkmenistan, Uzbekistan, and Taji-kistan), together with other Muslim countries (Iran, Pakistan, Turkey, and Afghanistan), formed the Economic Cooperation Organization (ECO) in November 1992, but with not much economic effectiveness to counter the EC. Also, the Black Sea Cooperation Organization (BSCO), which was formed by 10 Black Sea nations (Albania, Azerbaijan, Bulgaria, Georgia, Greece, Moldavia, Romania, Russia, Turkey, and Ukraine) on June 25, 1992, in Istanbul, is a weak bloc with limited importance. Otherwise, Greece is a full member and Turkey an associate member of the EC, whereas Bulgaria, Romania, and other Black Sea countries look for a closer cooperation and association with the EC. Expectations are that Russia, Ukraine, Belarus, Georgia, Armenia, and the three Baltic countries will pursue a policy of joining the EC in the coming years.

Nevertheless, three main Slavic countries (Russia, Ukraine, Belarus) agreed in July 1993 to create an economics and customs union and to coordinate economic policies. They are trying to establish a "single economic space," more effective than the CIS and similar to the EC. Other republics of the old Soviet Union may join the union, but on the terms they are setting out.

It seems that the future belongs to economic and political federations. This verifies what Pierre-Joseph Proudhon predicted in 1863, that in the twentieth century the era of federations will begin. This can be seen in the Soviet Union and other East European countries where there is a trend toward voluntary or democratic, not imposed, federations. The need for economic cooperation in a growing world economy is forcing reduction or elimination of trade and investment barriers and eventually the establishment of economic-political federations, which liquidate nationalism and promote socioeconomic convergence.

In addition to the old federations of the United States and Switzerland, similar federations of one form or another can be observed in Australia, Canada, Latin America and Central America (Argentina, Venezuela, Brazil, Mexico), Africa (Nigeria, South Africa), Asia (Malaysia, United Arab Emir-ates), and primarily in Europe (Germany, Austria, Belgium, the Czech and Slovak republics, Yugoslavia, the CIS), with the EC at the forefront.

The CIS tends to implement a political system of a loose federation similar to that of the United States and an economic system similar to that of the EC, with prospects of other East European countries joining such a system. However, such an East European or CIS federation should be based on a voluntary and democratic cooperation. Eventually, though, some or all of these states may join the EC.

The main problems the European republics of the former Soviet Union face are similar to those of Russia and the other CIS countries—that is, budget deficits, inflation, currency depreciation, and growing unemploy-ment.[1] Although some legal restrictions on management have been relaxed, most firms in these republics are still owned by the government and managers are controlled by government officials, who do not profit from the increase in the value of the firms. Therefore, their incentives for improvement are low, as are those of the managers. In other words, these firms are owned by everyone and nobody gets benefits from the increases in the value of the firms. In such cases, managers cut advertisement or capital expenditures and make profits from which they may receive bonuses. Price increases, which can be observed in all CIS countries, make producing firms profitable and consuming firms unprofitable.

The state-owned firms in the CIS are mostly monopolies with little incentive to develop an efficient system of production and distribution. They are largely sleeping monopolies, which are not interested in introducing new technology and improving quality. They are not under the pressure of competition to innovate and modernize their operations. Moreover, managers and government officials who supervise them have developed close relations and created strong barriers for new firms to enter the industry. They often try to retain monopoly power to get mutual benefits. In some cases, they resort to corruption, as the author observed during a trip to these countries, so that "one hand washes the other and both wash the face."

Comecon and CIS

In 1949 the Soviet Union and five East European countries (Bulgaria, Czechoslovakia, Hungary, Poland, and Romania) created the Council of Mutual Economic Assistance (Comecon), as a counterpart to the Organization for European Economic Cooperation (OEEC), now known as the Organization for Economic Cooperation and Development (OECD).

Albania and East Germany joined Comecon in 1949 and 1950, respectively; Yugoslavia became an observer. Mongolia joined in 1962, and Cuba in 1972. Cooperation with Albania was weak, if not nonexistent, and Yugoslavia had stronger ties with the EC than with Comecon. Afghanistan, Angola, Ethiopia, Laos, South Yemen, and Vietnam were contemplating joining Comecon. Nonsocialist countries such as Finland (1973), Iraq, and Mexico (1975) have become associate members, and negotiations between Comecon and some Latin American countries were conducted.

Initially, Comecon was not too effective, mainly because of lack of raw materials and labor. Its longevity and expansion made it more effective on matters of regional cooperation and economic development. However, transactions between the member nations remained mostly bilateral and, to a limited extent, multilateral. In contrast with the EC, where market integration was stressed, Comecon emphasized production integration and long-term economic development. Comecon was dissolved in 1990. To some extent, it was replaced by the Commonwealth of Independent States, which includes most of the former USSR.

In light of further trade and investment cooperation between the EC and the CIS nations, the question remains: Are the CIS countries expected to face problems similar to those experienced between the European Free Trade Association and the EC? It would seem that the trend toward more economic transactions between these two groups of countries does not represent a new movement toward integration, but a policy of gradually abandoning autarky in favor of a more open trade among neighboring nations. The aim is to avoid scarcities and eliminate trade obstacles among these countries.

From the viewpoint of overall trade of the CIS member countries, one should review trade with the West and trade among themselves. Although statistical evidence is insufficient and it is difficult to make predictions, it seems that East-West relations are expected to work in favor of trade creation (and may even lead to economic integration).[2]

The need for technological transformation is so great that some sacrifices among the CIS countries would be easily accepted. Thus, the economic relations of the CIS member countries and the EC members or associate members are expected to improve.

ECONOMIC REFORMS

Privatizations and the Market System

The drastic reforms and primarily the process of privatizations pursued in the ex-planned economies of the CIS present serious problems from a practical point of view. It is difficult to transfer factories, farms, and other property from a centrally controlled public sector to individuals or private companies. The consequences of privatization can be devilishly scary. Bureaucrats who control the process may sabotage it and managers may profit from it. Market prices for land, equipment, and many other items do not exist, and large amounts of money are not possessed by individuals to buy such things. To give away property to citizens, no one would have a large stake in big enterprises to control them. Privatizing large state farms may lead to small inefficient lots with miles of wire to fortify and protect them. Frequent disputes from possible violations by neighboring owners may appear.

To create mutual funds owned by large numbers of citizens may lead to collusive dealings and controls by the executives of such funds. Privatization, then, a simple and romantic idea, may turn out to be a nightmare in ex-planned economies. In Poland, for example, managers sold state enterprises with attractive terms to foreigners and they got sizable personal benefits. Even market economies, such as those of Britain and France, face serious problems in privatizing state enterprises, from the standpoint of price determination and time duration, although they have advanced stock markets and other related institutions.

The cataclysmic events in the republics of the former Soviet Union and the transition of their systems from command to demand-driven economies constitute the most significant economic changes in the world today. They demonstrate the superiority of the free market, the inferiority of communism, and the defects of central planning, which is characterized by lack of incentives, poor quality goods and services, delays, and bureaucratic inertia.

In some cases, direct state control is permitted to shrink to only 20 percent, so that state-owned enterprises would be accountable to others than the inefficient bureaucrats. In such cases, managers and entrepreneurs will be freer in their functions. The idea is not only to increase the productivity of the owners-workers, but also to lure savings from under mattresses and from being used for jewelry, art objects, and other unproductive consumer goods. The stocks issued are like debt instruments and pay fixed dividends, similar to bond interest, and aim at increasing investment, reducing inflation, and thereby being supportive of the market economy. However, there are problems of predetermined prices of the stocks by the authorities and the limited convertibility of the local currencies into dollars or other Western currencies. Similar problems occurred in the former Soviet Union with stocks issued during Lenin's New Economic Policy in the 1920s to stimulate investment and revitalize the stagnant economy.

A current serious problem is the privatization of state enterprises at the factory level. An effective way of transferring ownership and control to the private sector is to sell plants to their managers and key employees. Such a restructuring of state enterprises can take place by splitting them into viable and competitive firms under middle managers or interested employees with work experience and operational skills. The responsible government agencies can determine margins of realistic values of the assets to be sold and ask managers, employees, and other individuals, including foreign investors, to submit their proposals. These agencies or banks can provide working capital and facilitate the sale of plants by acting as bondholders.

By establishing management buyouts (MBOs) and market-oriented companies, work incentive would increase, apathy would be reduced, and widespread ownership would be fostered. Moreover, the distribution of raw materials and products would be improved, through decentralization, and business experience would be enhanced. Microeconomic managerial reforms or changes at the company level, through business training regarding production, distribution, and marketing, are needed to transform state firms into innovative and competitive economic units. Macroeconomic policies can support such restructuring. American and EC business schools and consultants, as well as joint ventures, can help the development of MBOs and the process of smooth transformation of state firms into free market companies.

In the postcommunist societies of the former Soviet republics, practical realism replaced idealism. The old ideological dichotomies of capitalism versus socialism or Left versus Right have changed and emphasis is placed on the democratic market systems. At the same time, the reassertion of nationalism with some dismal expectations for social unrest and regional conflicts are making their appearance obvious.[3]

The democratic challenge to authoritarian communism by intellectuals has been replaced, to a large extent, by free marketeering and aggressive profiteering. Many intellectuals are living with starvation salaries, drug abuse and crime have increased, prostitution and pimping have become widespread, and young girls are exported by panderers to other countries.

Nevertheless, some governments, even under the control of right-wing nationalists, realized that economic decisions cannot be left to the invisible hand of the market, as Adam Smith argued, but social welfare measures should be included in the new market and economic recovery policies. In other words, a demand-side Keynesian policy of investment spending together with a supply-side neoclassical policy of increase in production should be pursued by these newly established ex-Soviet states.

Introducing free enterprises to ex-Soviet republics is easier said than done. Usually there are two kinds of property rights—that of the owner (normally the state) and that of the user (a state-owned company, cooperative, or other public or private entities or individuals). In some cases, loan-equity deals (that is, lending money in return for a potential stake in enterprises) are made.

Some loan-equity deals eventually turn to debt-for-equity swaps leading to joint ventures and growing foreign investment. However, tight government controls, which remain from the years of communist rule, prohibit or delay such deals. More time is needed to develop a legal structure dealing with property rights and business establishments, accounting principles, and stock market operations.

In some excommunist republics, aggressive nationalism, quasi-feudalism, or new authoritarianism have been practiced instead of genuine free market democracy. Widespread apathy and disillusionment created new self-interest and bureaucratic elites, which led republics away from democracy and the market-driven system.

Fiscal Policy

To increase government expenditures in order to stimulate the economy and reduce unemployment may further fuel inflation. It works against the acceptable policy of reducing budget deficits and government intervention in the CIS economies. Moreover, financing growing government expenditures in a noninflationary manner is very difficult because tax revenues are declining. On the other hand, there is a well-accepted principle that "if you tax something, you get less of it. If you subsidize something, you get more of it."

It is expected that direct taxes or taxes on personal income and profits will acquire more importance than indirect taxes—that is, taxes on goods and services for all these former planned economies. Indeed the transfer of resources from the agricultural to the more money-using industrial and service sectors and higher urbanization will create a favorable climate for structural changes in taxation toward larger direct taxes.

Of the three main alternative means of financing government expenditures—taxation, issuance of government securities, and creation of money—it would seem that the first alternative is the most antiinflationary for the CIS member countries. The issuance of government bonds and other securities is not widespread in these economies, as it is in Western economies. Money creation, on the other hand, is clearly inflationary when it exceeds real economic growth, given that income velocity of money is expected to be constant in these economies.

Emphasizing reduction of government overspending for consumption and favoring investment would help revive productivity, combat inflation, and encourage exports. It would, most probably, have an antiinflation and antirecession function, helping to solve the dilemma of simultaneous inflation and unemployment that plagues the CIS countries. Such fiscal devices allow old enterprises to renew aging facilities and new enterprises to satisfy their desires for modern capital equipment and advanced technology.

The economic role of government, which expanded drastically during more than six decades under communism, is under intense criticism. Mandated spending programs, such as payments for price support and subsidies to inefficient enterprises, are difficult to control because they are related to unemployment and the decline in living standards. From that standpoint, it becomes difficult for the governments of these countries to exercise fiscal discipline, reduce budget deficits, and implement antiinflationary policies. On the other hand, Western aid to these countries may not help much.

The superficial notion that aid is some kind of gift may lead to all sorts of unwise spending. At the time of agreement, loan recipients may ignore or sidestep the fact that amortization and interest have to be paid. They may not seriously consider the cost involved and the fact that the productivity of borrowed capital must be higher than the cost. Such considerations become more and more important nowadays as many ex-USSR nations face growing difficulties in meeting debt-service payments. Even World Bank loans, which used to be given on much easier average terms, have been difficult to repay.

FORMER EUROPEAN SOVIET REPUBLICS

Ukraine

Ukraine, the Soviet breadbasket, was the second richest republic of the USSR. Kiev is its capital. It has a population of 52 million (about 75 percent Ukrainian, 20 percent Russian, and 1.3 percent Jewish). In faith, the Ukrainians are primarily Greek Orthodox and Roman Catholic. About 67 percent of its population is urban.

The first linkage of Russian city-states occurred in the tenth century around Kiev, which became the capital and the commercial center of the country. The adoption of the Eastern Orthodox religion and the schism from the Catholic Church in 1054, as well as the development of new commercial routes of Western Europe via Constantinople and Venice, made Kiev a less important trade and cultural center, especially after the Fourth Crusade (1204).

The Mongol occupation of Russia and the destruction of Kiev and other cities (from 1237 to 1452) cut ties with the West, forced people back to agriculture, and made them subservient to the autocratic Mongol rulers. As a result, the economic development of the region was held back. When independence was achieved in 1452, the capital was moved from Kiev to Moscow.

In 1648 the Cossacks of Don, a military people, rebelled against Polish rule and received help from the czars of Moscow, who later (1783) abolished their autonomy, while the Cossacks became czarist troops. Although Vladimir Lenin, the leader of the Bolshevik Revolution, recognized the right of self-determination, the Ukrainian Republic (which was formed on December 25, 1917), was, along with other states, officially incorporated into the USSR on December 30, 1922. In April 1986 the Chernobyl atomic energy plant spread radioactive contamination in neighboring areas and countries with lasting cancerous effects on the inhabitants. On December 1, 1991, it became an independent republic.

Ukraine has some 60 percent of the coal reserves and produces more than 40 percent of the agricultural output of the former USSR. Moreover, it is rich in iron mines, petroleum, uranium, coal, machine production, and chemicals.

Many state enterprises are converted by their managers into corporations owned by stockholders, a proportion of which is held by the managers them-selves.[4] Thus, the managers of Elecropribors, a Ukrainian state enterprise, would buy around 5 percent of the shares, the workers would acquire a part, and 30 percent of the shares would be kept by the government. In this case, the managers expect the workers to be passive stockholders in managerial decision making. As a result of the reforms, General Motors plans to establish new plants in Ukraine and Russia, in addition to those in East Germany and Poland. However, as long as nuclear weapons remain in the republic, foreign investment and aid will not increase much.

Byelorussia or Belarus

The Byelorussians, one of the ancient Slavic peoples, together with Ukrain-ians and Russians, created the Russian state during the ninth century with

Kiev its capital. After the Mongol occupation, the area came under Polish and Lithuanian rulers. Along with western Ukraine, Byelorussia was annexed by Russia in 1793, after the 1772–96 partitions of Poland. As a result of the Polish-Russian war of 1919, half of the western part of Byelorussia was taken by Poland, while the rest was reoccupied by the USSR in 1939 (Hitler-Stalin agreement). Recently it declared independence.

The population of the republic is 10.2 million, mostly Byelorussians (80 percent). There are also about 12 percent Russians, 4 percent Polish, and 2 percent Ukrainians. The main output of the republic is agricultural commodities (potatoes, fodder, cattle, sheep); forest, paper, and chemical products; machinery; and building materials. The urban population of Belarus is 66 percent of the total population.

Moldavia

In the ninth century, part of Moldavia belonged to the Slavic state of Kiev. After 1375 it was generally under the control of Poland. In the fifteenth century, Romanian princes controlled the area and in 1512 it fell under Turkish suzerainty. In the nineteenth century, Russian rulers subordinated it. In 1918 the western part of the region (Bessarabia) was ceded to Romania, but in 1940, following the cession of Bessarabia to the USSR by Romania, Moldavia became a republic of the Soviet Union. In 1941, during World War II, Moldavia was occupied by Romania but the Soviet army regained it in 1944.

Some 64 percent of its 4.3 million people are Moldavian, 14 percent Ukrainian, 13 percent Russian, and 4 percent Gagauz. Fruits, wine, grains, sunflower seeds, sugar beets, tobacco, and vegetables are the main products of the republic.

Armenia

Armenians are perhaps the most suffering people in history. From the seventh century B.C. onward, they have been living under almost continuous occupations by Persians, Romans, Byzantines, Arabs, and Turks. Under the Romans, Armenia, with an Indo-European distinct language, adopted Christianity in A.D. 301. After the Byzantine rule, the Ottoman Turks and Persia divided Armenia. In 1828 Russia conquered it. During the nineteenth century, the Armenians cooperated with Russia against the Ottoman Empire.

With the Treaty of Berlin (June 1878), Armenia was designated as an area of concern of the Allies (Britain, France, Italy, Russia). This served as a pretext for inflaming the Turks' hatred of Christian Armenians and organizing the slaughter of some 1.5 million people, primarily between 1915 and 1923. The Turkish Sultan Abdul Hamid II, "The Great Assassin," who had been associated with the Bulgarian massacres of 1876, resorted to the systematic genocide of the Armenians (similar to that of Jews by Hitler), not only in the mountains of Armenia bordering Russia, but also in the streets of Constantinople (1894–96, 1909) and through the long disastrous walk, "a death march," toward the Syrian borders in 1915–16.

Now there are only about 60,000 Armenians in Turkey, 3.4 million in the Armenian Republic, and about 3 million spread all over the world, mainly in the United States. On September 21, 1991, Armenia voted for its independence from the Soviet Union (which it had joined in 1922). Its main products are chemicals, cloth, and machinery.

Georgia

For some 3,000 years, a peculiar people have lived in the Caucasus. They are the Georgians, who are known for their long living and their Caucasian language. Total population of the republic is 5.5 million (69 percent Georgian, 9 percent Russian, 9 percent Armenian, 5 percent Azeri, and 3 percent Ossetian), mostly Christians. There was a Caucasian Empire from 1184 to 1213, when the Mongols conquered it. A number of invasions by Tamerlane (1386–1403) reduced it to ruins.

For protection from Persians and Turks, Georgia turned to Catherine II. Later it was annexed by Russia. In 1918 it became independent, but in 1921 it came under Soviet rule. Joseph Stalin, who ruled the Soviet Union from 1924 to 1953, was from Georgia and studied for the priesthood in Tbilisi, the capital.

Georgia produces primarily tea, grapes, citrus fruits, silk, tobacco, and bamboo; coal and manganese are mined. Its warm climate, the sea coast, and the impressive mountains are attractive to vacationing tourists.

Georgia is in conflict with Russia over the region of Abkhazia. Hundreds of people have been killed, mainly in Sukhumi, the regional capital on the Black Sea. The ongoing fighting between Abkhazians and Georgians, who are ancient foes, may lead to a full-scale Russian-Georgian war. Already there are accusations that Russian planes support the secessionist Abkhazians, although the Russian Defense Ministry denied such accusations. Eduard A. Shevardnadze, the Georgian leader and former secretary of state of the former Soviet Union urged Yeltsin to try to settle the conflict. In the meantime, Yeltsin transferred the Russian army headquarters from Tbilisi, the capital of Georgia, to Stavropol in Russia, and ordered the Cossacks, who were outlawed after the 1917 Bolshevik Revolution, to protect the Russian borders in the Caucasus.

The Baltic States: Lithuania, Latvia, and Estonia

The largest of the three Baltic states is Lithuania, with a population of 3.7 million (80 percent Lithuanians, 9 percent Russians, and 8 percent Polish).

Latvia has a population of 2.7 and Estonia 1.6 million, with large Russian minorities (34 percent and 30 percent, respectively). Lithuanians and Latvians belong to a Western-Slavic race that inhabited the Baltic shores from the fifth century B.C. Estonia was founded by Danes in 1219. In 1386 Lithuania and Latvia were united with Poland and defeated the Teutonic knights. Estonia was ruled by German states and by Sweden for many years. In the eighteenth century, all three Baltic states were occupied by the Russians. They became independent from 1920 to 1940. Then the Red Army occupied them (the secret Hitler-Stalin pact), making them members of the USSR. About a year later Hitler occupied them and in September 1944 Soviet forces reoccupied them. Many thousands of Baltic people were killed or deported by both Hitler and Stalin. On September 6, 1991, the Soviet Union recognized the independence of these three states.

The Baltic states produce primarily grain, flax, potatoes, and other farm and dairy products, as well as electronics, appliances, machine tools, amber, and textiles.

FORMER ASIAN SOVIET REPUBLICS

Azerbaijan

Initially Azerbaijan was part of the Persian Empire. Later it was occupied by Turkish tribes, which reached Bacu, its capital. In 1828 it was annexed by Russia. It declared independence in 1919 and was reoccupied by Russia in 1920. It became a Soviet republic in 1922. In August 1991 it declared independence from the former USSR.

Azerbaijan has a population of 7.1 million (76 percent Azeri Turkish, 8 percent Russian, and 8 percent Armenian). About half the population is Shiite Muslim. It also governs the Nagorno-Karabakh region with a mostly Christian Armenian population and the Nakhichevan Republic. Ethnic and territorial differences over Nagorno-Karabakh have flared up since 1988 between predominantly Muslim Azerbaijan and Christian Armenia with many deaths and extensive property destruction.

The republic is an important oil producer and refiner. The author, who visited the area in a research trip to the Soviet Union, observed that many oil wells are small and are abandoned or they operate with inefficient old-fashioned technology. Chemical and other heavy industry products, gold, cotton, tobacco, grapes, and livestock are the main products.

Kazakhstan

The Kazakhs are a mixture of Mongol and Turk peoples of the fifteenth century who came under Russian domination in 1731. Kazakhstan became a full member of the Soviet Union in 1936. The population of 16.5 million has over 100 ethnic groups, with Kazakhs 36 percent, Russians 41 percent, Ukrainians 6 percent, Tatars 2 percent, and many descendants of German farmers transplanted under Peter the Great. Serious anti-Russian riots occurred in 1916 and 1986.

The high plateaus of Kazakhstan are rich in the production of wheat, maize, rice, sugar, and other farm products; oil, coal, and natural gas; gold, uranium, lead, copper, zinc, and other metals. Nuclear weapons are tested there and Soviet space launches occurred in this republic, which was the second, after Russia, in the Union. In August 1991 an agreement was concluded with Russia to respect borders. The Caspian and Aral seas and Lake Balkhash provide fish that support a canning industry.

With the economic reforms and the privatization program of Nursultan Nazarbayev, the president of Kazakhstan, the republic is expected to increase productivity incentives. As a pragmatist, Nazarbayev thinks that people should be convinced of the merits of free enterprise and democracy and then to intensify reforms. He lifted all limits on cattle ownership, increased the number of independent farms, and helped establish a private cafe in every city and region, which proved to be successful examples of privatization in his conservative republic. A horizontal association among the former Soviet republics is needed to avoid economic instability and disaster, according to him.

The rich resources of Kazakhstan, which became independent with the collapse of the Soviet Union in 1991, attract Western investors to tap into the large treasure of oil, gas, minerals, and other products. Western multinationals from Germany and other EC countries, the United States, and Japan, are moving aggressively into the country to exploit some of the world's largest untapped reserves of oil, gas, chrome (which counts for 90 percent of that of the former Soviet Union), silver (60 percent), zinc and copper (40 percent), gold, uranium, and other significant deposits. Such multinationals include Chevron with a 40-year contract to exploit the Tengiz oilfield, BP, AT&T, Alcatel, and other large Western companies. It is estimated that Kazakhstan has about 25 billion barrels of oil reserves with expectations of 1.6 million barrels' production a day in the near future.[5]

Uzbekistan

The name of Uzbekistan came from a ruler of a Mongol-Turkish race (Han Uzbek), who conquered Central Asia (between the Volga River and the Aral Sea) during the Middle Ages. Until the Russians arrived in the mid–1800s, Uzbeks were the ruling class of the area. In 1917 the Russians of Taskent created the Autonomous Democracy of Turkistan, the borders of which were revised, and the Republic of Uzbekistan was established in 1924. It declared independence from the Soviet Union in August 1991.

The population of the republic is 19.9 million (69 percent Uzbek, 11 percent Russian, and 4 percent Tatars). The Uzbek Muslims, with strong nationalist movements, are the third largest nationality after Russians and Ukrainians. Bloody ethnic riots, such as those of 1989, are reported from time to time. Huge irrigation projects help cotton production but throat cancer and infant deaths are blamed on pesticides. Natural gas, gold, and cloth are additional important products of Uzbekistan.[6] Foreign investment in the area includes the Daewoo Group, the biggest conglomerate of South Korea, which agreed to set up three joint ventures in Uzbekistan to produce electronics, textiles, and automobiles. The 50–50 ventures with the Uzbek government would cost Daewoo close to $1 billion. One plant near Tashkent would produce about 200,000 subcompact cars a year.

Kyrgyzstan

Kyrgyzstan is a fertile land in the central mountainous area of the former USSR. It had a weak autonomy until the nineteenth century when the Russians occupied it. After 1917 a serious resistance occurred against the Soviets, but by 1924 it was incorporated in the USSR. In 1936 it became a full member of the union. The republic has a population of 4.4 million (52 percent Kyrgyz, 22 percent Russian, 13 percent Uzbek, 2.5 percent Ukrainian, and 1.6 percent Tatars). The Kyrgyz people came primarily from a Turkish nomadic tribe. It declared independence from the former USSR in August 1991.

Yaks, small but durable horses, and other livestock are bred in the Tien Shan Mountains. Gold, diamonds, machinery, cloth, and consumer goods are also among the main products of the republic.

Turkmenistan

Up to the mid-nineteenth century, when Russian troops occupied the area, Turkmenistan was inhabited by nomadic tribes. In 1881 and 1916 they resisted Russian occupation without much effectiveness. In 1924 the Republic of Turkmenistan, under the USSR, was established. It declared independence in 1991.

The population of the country is 3.6 million (68 percent Turkmeni, 13 percent Russians, 9 percent Uzbeks, and 3 percent Kazakhs). Turkmeni are mostly Sunni Muslims and speak a Turkic language, as Azeri, Uzbek, Kazakh, and Kyrgyz do as well. A good number of Turkmeni have also moved to Iraq, Iran, Turkey, Syria, and Afghanistan.

Turkmenistan is mostly a desert area (Kara-Kum). The main products are petroleum, coal, gold, diamonds, cotton, olives, sesame, dates, and figs. Also, Turkoman horses, Karakul sheep, and famous carpets are produced.

Tajikistan

Tajiks, who were once part of Alexander the Great's empire, are considered descendants of early Aryans and speak a Persian language. The population of Tajikistan is 5.1 million (62 percent Tajiks, 23 percent Uzbeks, 10 percent Russians, and 2 percent Tatars). Most of its people live in the valleys of the Pamir Mountains and have a high birth rate. The republic was controlled by Muslim rulers until its conquest by Russia in the late 1800s, and in 1929 it became a full Soviet republic.

Tajikistan produces oil, coal, gas, gold, and other minerals; cattle, sheep, fruits, wine, cotton, and other farm products. Also, energy is produced by hydroelectric power.

Notes

CHAPTER I

1. For a review of the reforms in East European countries, see Nicholas V. Gianaris, *Contemporary Economic Systems: A Regional and Country Approach* (Westport, CT: Praeger, 1993), chap. 10.

2. For the support for European integration, see "One Germany? First, One Europe," *New York Times*, November 25, 1989, A22.

3. Helmut Kohl, "European Integration," *Presidents and Prime Ministers*, 2, no. 1 (January–February 1993), 14.

4. "Poland-Hungary," *Presidents and Prime Ministers*, 2, no. 1 (January February 1993), 37.

5. Nicholas V. Gianaris, "Helping Eastern Europe Helps the West," *New York Times*, February 6, 1990, A28. For privatization and investment, see Dominick Salvatore, "Foreign Direct Investments and Privatization in Eastern Europe," *Review of Political Economy*, March 1992; and Jeffrey Sachs, *Capitalism in Europe After Communism* (Cambridge, MA: The M.I.T. Press, 1991), chaps. 2–4.

6. For such predictions, see Lester Thurow, *Head to Head: The Coming Economic Battle Among Japan, Europe, and America* (New York: W. Morrow, 1992), chap. 3.

CHAPTER 2

1. More information in Terrot Glover, *The Challenge of the Greeks and Other Essays* (New York: Macmillan, 1942), chaps. 1–3; and S. Todd Lowry, "Recent Literature on Ancient Greek Economic Thought," *Journal of Economic Literature*, 17 (March 1979), 65–86.

2. Frances Nicholson and Roger East, *From the Six to the Twelve: The Enlargement of the European Community* (London: St. James Press, 1987), chaps. 8–11; and Paul

Taylor, *The Limits of European Integration* (New York: Columbia University Press, 1983), chap. 2.

3. Further details in Anna Michalski and Helen Wallace, *The European Community: The Challenge of Enlargement* (London: Royal Institute for International Affairs, 1992), chap. 3.

4. Ibid., 127–129.

5. More information in Loukas Tsoukalis, *The New European Economy: The Politics and Economics of Integration* (New York: Oxford University Press, 1993).

6. For the performance of the EC nations, see Nicholas V. Gianaris, *The European Community and the United States: Economic Relations* (New York: Praeger, 1991), chap. 4; and Theodore Hitiris, *European Community Economics* (New York: St. Martin's Press, 1991).

CHAPTER 3

1. Aristotle, *Ethics*, IX, 8; and Nicholas V. Gianaris, *Contemporary Public Finance* (New York: Praeger, 1989), 20.

2. For the support of the private sector and free markets, see Adam Smith, *An Inquiry into the Nature and Causes of the Wealth of Nations*, E. Cannan, ed. (New York: Modern Library, 1937), 423.

3. Adolph Wagner, *Financzwissenschaft*, 3rd ed. (Leipzig, 1890); and Harry Oshima, "Shares of Government in Gross National Product for Various Countries," *American Economic Review*, June 1957.

4. More details can be found in Arthur Pigou, *The Economics of Welfare* (London: Macmillan, 1932); and Alan Peacock and Jack Wiseman, *The Growth of Public Expenditures in the United Kingdom* (New York: National Bureau of Economic Research, 1961).

5. Aristotle, *Politics*, 2.5, 1263a 38; and Ernest Barker, *The Political Thought of Plato and Aristotle* (New York: Dover, 1959), 391.

6. More details in Donald C. Downing, Jr., "EC Employment Law After Maastricht: Continental Social Europe?" *The International Lawyer*, 27, no. 1 (Spring 1993), 20–23; and EC Commission's report, COM (91)259, July 29, 1991, 131.

7. For the capital-labor comanagement or codetermination system, see W. R. Smyser, *The Economy of United Germany: Colossus at the Crossroads* (New York: St. Martin's Press, 1992), 79–83.

8. "Sprucing Up Savings," *Economist*, 310, no. 7594 (March 18, 1989), 60.

9. Donald Hancock, John Logue, and Bernt Schiller, eds., *Managing Modern Capitalism: Industrial Renewal and Workplace Democracy in the United States and Western Europe* (Westport, CT: Greenwood Press, 1991), Part II. For the support of ESOPs in Eastern Europe, see Lee Smith and Lewis Kaden, "East European Workers Will Need Incentives," *New York Times*, May 11, 1990, F13.

CHAPTER 4

1. Wolfgang Reinicke, *Building a New Europe* (Washington, DC: The Brookings Institution, 1992), 119–120. Member countries' statistics in "The European Community: A Survey," *Economist*, 328, no. 7818 (July 3–9, 1993), 1–20.

2. More on monetary aspects in Ash Amin and Michael Dietrich, eds., *Towards a New Europe* (Brookfield, VT: Edward Elgan, 1991), Part Four.

3. For the convergence of policies to speed the EC union, see John Pinder, *European Community: The Building of a Union* (New York: Oxford University Press, 1991); and Reinicke, *Building a New Europe*, chap. 5.

4. Norman Scott, "The Commercial Policy of the European Economic Community (EEC)," in Dominick Salvatore, ed., *National Trade Policies* (Westport, CT: Greenwood Press, 1992), 45–46.

5. Related comments in Spyros G. Makridakis and Associates, *Single Market Europe* (Oxford: Jossey-Bass, 1991), chap. 15.

6. Future expectations in Juliet Longe, ed., *The European Community and the Challenge of the Future* (New York: St. Martin's Press, 1989).

7. See statement of former French prime minister, now mayor of Paris, Jacques Chirac, in Carla Rapoport, "Them," *Fortune*, July 13, 1992, 18–22.

CHAPTER 5

1. For economic cost and development, see Jack Taylor, *The Economic Development of Poland, 1919–1950* (Ithaca, NY: Cornell University Press, 1952); and David Kemme and Keith Crane, "The Polish Economic Collapse: Contributing Factors and Economic Costs," *Journal of Comparative Economics*, 8 (March 1984).

2. Further analysis in Januasz G. Zielinski, *Economic Reforms in Polish Industry* (London: Oxford University Press, 1973), chap. 6.

3. Valtr Komarek, "Shock Therapy and Its Victims," *New York Times*, January 5, 1992, E13; and David Lipton and Jeffrey Sachs, "Creating a Market Economy in Eastern Europe: The Case of Poland," *Brookings Papers on Economic Activity*, Vol. 1 (Washington, DC: The Brookings Institution, 1990), 75–133 and 293–333.

4. More details in Wolfgang M. Reinicke, *Building a New Europe* (Washington, DC: The Brookings Institution, 1992), chap. 4.

5. Raphael Shen, *The Polish Economy: Legacies from the Past, Prospects for the Future* (New York: Praeger, 1992), 149–162; and "Don't Give Up Now," *Economist*, A Survey of Business in Eastern Europe, September 21, 1991, 18–19.

6. Anna Michalski and Helen Wallace, *The European Community: The Challenge of Enlargement* (London: Royal Institute for International Affairs, 1992), 117–118.

7. Brigitte Granville, "Convertibility and Exchange Rates in Poland, 1957–1990," *Soviet and Eastern Foreign Trade*, 27, no. 4 (Winter 1991–92), 71–97.

8. United Nations, *World Economic Survey 1991/1992* (New York: United Nations Publications, 1991), 266–267.

CHAPTER 6

1. Samuel Thomson, *Czechoslovakia in European History* (Princeton, NJ: Princeton University Press, 1953), 7–8; A. H. Hermann, *History of the Czechs* (New York: Penguin Books, 1975), 7–9; and Joseph A. Mikus, *Slovakia: A Political History: 1918–1950* (Milwaukee: Marquette University Press, 1963), 1–30; and Karel Kouba, "Systematic Changes in the Czechoslovak Economy and Its Opening in World Markets," *Soviet and Eastern European Foreign Trade*, 27, no. 2 (Summer 1991), 3–16.

2. Andrzej Rapaczynski and Roman Fryman, "Privatization in Eastern Europe: Is the State Withering Away?" *Finance and Development*, 30, no. 2 (June 1993), 10–13.

3. For the suggestion of giving some control to workers, see Olivier Blanchard et al., *Reform in Eastern Europe* (Cambridge, MA: The M.I.T. Press, 1992), 51–52.

4. Richard Stevenson, "Czech Capitalism Gets Stock Market," *New York Times*, June 22, 1993, D1.

5. John Kenneth Galbraith is critical of the rapid transition to unfettered capitalism in Central and East European countries. See his "The Rush to Capitalism," in David Kennett and Marc Lieberman, eds., *The Road to Capitalism: Economic Transformation in Eastern Europe and the Former Soviet Union* (New York: The Dryden Press, 1992), 92–98.

6. More in "A Survey of Business in Eastern Europe," *Economist*, September 21, 1991, 24–28; and Richard S. Stevenson, "In a Czech Plant, VW Shows How to Succeed in the East," *New York Times*, June 22, 1993, A1.

7. "Whirlpool Venture in Czechoslovakia," *New York Times*, November 26, 1991, D4.

CHAPTER 7

1. Foster W. Bovill, *Hungary and the Hungarians* (London: Methuen, 1908); Paul Ignotus, *Hungary* (New York: Praeger, 1972), chap. 1; C. A. MaCarntey, *Hungary, A Short History* (Chicago: Aldine, 1962); and Stephen R. Burant, ed., *Hungary: A Country Study* (Washington, DC: U.S. Government Printing Office, 1990).

2. Janos Kornai, *The Road to a Free Economy, Shifting from a Socialist System: The Examples of Hungary* (New York: W. W. Norton, 1990), chaps. 1–3. Also, Ivan T. Berend, *The Hungarian Economic Reforms, 1953–1988*, Soviet and East European Studies, 70 (New York: Cambridge University Press, 1990).

3. Further review in Xavier Richet, *The Hungarian Model: Markets and Planning in a Socialist Economy*, trans. by J. C. Whitehouse (New York: Cambridge University Press, 1989); and Irme Tarafas, "Hungary's Reforms: Past and Present," *Finance and Development*, 28, no. 1 (March 1991), 12–14.

4. In November 1991 Hungary set the legal foundation for the privatization of the banks. Wolfgang H. Reinicke, *Building a New Europe* (Washington, DC: The Brookings Institution, 1992), 48. Further comments on reforms in Frederic L. Pryor, *East European Economic Reforms: The Rebirth of the Market* (Stanford, CA: Stanford University Press, 1990).

5. More details in Tibor Palankai, *The European Community and Central European Integration: The Hungarian Case* (New York: Institute for East-West Security Studies, distributed by Westview Press, 1991); and Olivier Blanchard et al., *Reform in Eastern Europe* (Cambridge, MA: The M.I.T. Press, 1992), chap. 2.

6. Richard W. Stevenson, "East Europe's Low Wages Luring Manufacturers from West Europe," *New York Times*, May 11, 1993, D2.

7. More information in "Budapest Tries to Sell Hungarians on Capitalism," *New York Times*, May 6, 1993, A13.

CHAPTER 8

1. A historical review of the Balkan countries is in Nicholas V. Gianaris: *The Economies of the Balkan Countries: Albania, Bulgaria, Greece, Romania, Turkey, and Yugoslavia* (New York: Praeger, 1982), chaps. 1–3, and *Greece and Turkey: Economic and Geopolitical Perspectives* (New York: Praeger, 1988), chap. 2. Also see Robert D. Kaplan, *Balkan Ghosts: A Journey Through History* (New York: St. Martin's Press, 1993).

2. Clyde Farnsworth, "The Rise and Fall of Civilization According to Tax Collection," *New York Times*, October 3, 1993, E7. More details in Lefteris Stavrianos, *The Balkans Since 1453* (New York: Holt, Rinehart and Winston, 1958), 82–85; and F. Schevill, *The History of the Balkan Peninsula*, rev. ed. (New York: Harcourt, Brace, 1933), 10.

3. Athanasios Kanellopoulos (Euvoulos), "I Evropi kai o Horos tou Mellontos mas" (Europe and the Place of Our Future), *To Vima*, Athens, July 5, 1992, A14.

4. For the reduced interest in self-management in Bulgaria, see Derek C. Jones and Mieke Meurs, "Worker Participation and Worker Self-Management in Bulgaria," *Comparative Economic Studies*, 33, no. 4 (Winter 1991), 47–81.

5. For related statistics and reforms in Romania, see John Montias, *Development in Communist Romania* (Cambridge, MA: The M.I.T. Press, 1967); and H. Roberts, *Romania: Political Problems of an Agrarian State* (New Haven, CT: Yale University Press, 1951), 177. For recent investment data, see *Athens News*, July 14, 1993, 7.

6. Nicholas V. Gianaris, *Greece and Yugoslavia: An Economic Comparison* (New York: Praeger, 1984), chap. 2.

7. For the new problems of ethnicities and the principle of self-determination, see Daniel P. Moynihan, *Pandaemonium: Ethnicity in International Politics* (New York: Oxford University Press, 1993). More information in W. Gewehr, *The Rise of Nationalism in the Balkans, 1800–1930* (Hamden, CT: Anchor Books, 1967), chap. 2.

CHAPTER 9

1. For a historical review, see Michael Kort, *The Soviet Colossus: A History of the USSR* (New York: Scribner's, 1985); and Peter Lyosh-Chenko, *History of the National Economy of Russia* (New York: Macmillan, 1969).

2. Raymond Hutchings, *Soviet Economic Development* (New York: New York University Press, 1971), chaps. 4–6; and Paul Gregory and Robert Stuart, *Soviet Economic Structure and Performance* (New York: HarperCollins, 1990), chap. 3.

3. Gur Ofer, "Soviet Economic Growth: 1928–1985," *Journal of Economic Literature*, 25, no. 4 (December 1987), 1767–1833.

4. Heinz Kohler, *Comparative Economic Systems* (Glenview, IL: Scott, Foresman, 1989), 185–186; and Stephen Gardner, *Comparative Economic Systems* (New York: The Dryden Press, 1988), 252–256.

5. More information in Gail Sheehy, *The Man Who Changed the World* (New York: HarperCollins, 1990), chaps. 1–4; and A. Hewett, *Reforming the Soviet Economy* (Washington, DC: The Brookings Institution, 1988).

6. Jennie I. Litvack and Christine I. Wallich, "Intergovernmental Finance: Critical

to Russia's Transformation?" *Finance and Development*, 30, no. 2 (June 1993), 10–13; and Daniel Berkowitz and Beth Mitchneck, "Fiscal Decentralization in the Soviet Economy," *Comparative Economic Studies*, 34, no. 2 (Summer 1992), 1–18.

7. For Western support needed and the complaints that the drastic economic reforms are American-imposed, see John Mroz, "Russia and Eastern Europe: Will the West Let Them Fail?" *Foreign Affairs*, 72, no. 1 (1993), 44–57. Considerations of American business and politics by Russians in Richard M. Mills, *As Moscow Sees Us: American Politics and Society in the Soviet Mindset* (New York: Oxford University Press, 1990), 35–43. Also, David Lipton and Jeffrey D. Sachs, "Prospects for Russia's Economic Reforms," *Brookings Papers on Economic Activity*, vol. 2 (Washington, DC: The Brookings Institution, 1992), 213–263.

8. "Greek Bails Out 'Pravda' Newspaper," *St. Petersburg Times*, August 15, 1992, A10.

9. John M. Litwack, "Legality and Market Reform in the Soviet-Type Economies," in David Kennett and Marc Lieberman, eds., *The Road to Capitalism: Economic Transformation in Eastern Europe and the Former Soviet Union* (New York: The Dryden Press, 1992), chap. 13.

CHAPTER 10

1. For trade among the CIS, see Constantine Michalopoulos and David Tarr, "Energizing Trade of the States of the Former USSR," *Finance and Development*, March 1993, 22–25.

2. For the difficulties of calculations of national income, see Abram Bergson, "Must Soviet Factor Cost Be Adjusted?" *Comparative Economic Studies*, 33, no. 4 (Winter 1991), 121–125. Some valuable proposals in Merton J. Peck and Thomas J. Richard, eds., *What Is To Be Done? Proposals for the Soviet Transition to the Market* (New Haven, CT: Yale University Press, 1991).

3. Problems of disintegration of the former USSR in Nicholas V. Gianaris, *Contemporary Economic Systems: A Regional and Country Approach* (Westport, CT: Praeger, 1993), 118–120. Also, Lester C. Thurow, *Head to Head: The Coming Economic Battle Among Japan, Europe, and America* (New York: W. Morrow, 1992), 91–92.

4. For legal aspects of foreign investment, see Daniel Gogel and Mary Hartnett, "Foreign Investment in Ukraine: New Laws, Opportunities, and Issues," *The International Lawyer*, 27, no. 1 (Spring 1993), 189–209.

5. Mobil Oil Corporation and six other energy companies agreed with Kazakhstan to develop a large oil field in the Caspian Sea. Agis Salpukas, "Mobil Set For Venture in Caspian," *New York Times*, June 9, 1993, D3.

6. Valuable data in "Republics of the Former USSR: Vital Statistics," *Finance and Development*, September 1992, 25.

Bibliography

Amin, Ash, and Michael Dietrich, eds. *Towards a New Europe*. Brookfield, VT: Edward Elgan, 1991.

Aristotle. *Ethics*, IX, 8.

Barker, Ernest. *The Political Thought of Plato and Aristotle*. New York: Dover, 1959.

Berend, Ivan T. *The Hungarian Economic Reforms, 1953–1988*, Soviet and East European Studies, 70. New York: Cambridge University Press, 1990.

Bergson, Abram. "Must Soviet Factor Cost Be Adjusted?" *Comparative Economic Studies*, 33, no. 4 (Winter 1991): 121–125.

Berkowitz, Daniel, and Beth Mitchneck. "Fiscal Decentralization in the Soviet Economy." *Comparative Economic Studies*, 34, no. 2 (Summer 1992): 1–18.

Blanchard, Olivier, et al. *Reform in Eastern Europe*. Cambridge, MA: The M.I.T. Press, 1992.

Bovill, Foster W. *Hungary and the Hungarians*. London: Methuen, 1908.

Burant, Stephen R., ed. *Hungary: A Country Study*. Washington, DC: U.S. Government Printing Office, 1990.

Chirac, Jacques. In Carla Rapoport, "Them." *Fortune*, July 13, 1992: 18–22.

Downing, Donald C., Jr. "EC Employment Law After Maastricht: Continental Social Europe?" *The International Lawyer*, 27, no. 1 (Spring 1993): 20–23.

Farnsworth, Clyde. "The Rise and Fall of Civilization According to Tax Collection." *New York Times*, October 3, 1993: E7.

Galbraith, John Kenneth. "The Rush to Capitalism." In David Kennett and Marc Lieberman, eds., *The Road to Capitalism: Economic Transformation in Eastern Europe and the Former Soviet Union*. New York: The Dryden Press, 1992.

Gardner, Stephen. *Comparative Economic Systems*. New York: The Dryden Press, 1988.

Gewehr, W. *The Rise of Nationalism in the Balkans, 1800–1930*. Hamden, CT: Anchor Books, 1967.

Gianaris, Nicholas V. *Contemporary Economic Systems: A Regional and Country Approach*. Westport, CT: Praeger, 1993.

————. *Contemporary Public Finance*. New York: Praeger, 1989.

————. *The Economies of the Balkan Countries: Albania, Bulgaria, Greece, Romania, Turkey, and Yugoslavia*. New York: Praeger, 1982.

————. *The European Community and the United States: Economic Relations*. New York: Praeger, 1991.

————. *Greece and Turkey: Economic and Geopolitical Perspectives*. New York: Praeger, 1988.

————. *Greece and Yugoslavia: An Economic Comparison*. New York: Praeger, 1984.

————. "Helping Eastern Europe Helps the West." *New York Times*, February 8, 1990: A28.

Glover, Terrot. *The Challenge of the Greeks and Other Essays*. New York: Macmillan, 1942.

Gogel, Daniel, and Mary Hartnett. "Foreign Investment in Ukraine: New Laws, Opportunities, and Issues." *The International Lawyer*, 27, no. 1 (Spring 1993): 189–209.

Granville, Brigitte. "Convertibility and Exchange Rates in Poland, 1957–1990." *Soviet and Eastern Foreign Trade*, 27, no. 4 (Winter 1991–92): 71–97.

Gregory, Paul, and Robert Stuart. *Soviet Economic Structure and Performance*. New York: HarperCollins, 1990.

Hancock, Donald, John Logue, and Bernt Schiller, eds. *Managing Modern Capitalism: Industrial Renewal and Workplace Democracy in the United States and Western Europe*. Westport, CT: Greenwood Press, 1991.

Hermann, A. H. *History of the Czechs*. New York: Penguin Books, 1975.

Hewett, A. *Reforming the Soviet Economy*. Washington, DC: The Brookings Institution, 1988.

Hitiris, Theodore. *European Community Economics*. New York: St. Martin's Press, 1991.

Hutchings, Raymond. *Soviet Economic Development*. New York: New York University Press, 1971.

Ignotus, Paul. *Hungary*. New York: Praeger, 1972.

International Monetary Fund (IMF). *International Financial Statistics*, various issues.

Jones, Derek C., and Mieke Meurs. "Worker Participation and Worker Self-Management in Bulgaria." *Comparative Economic Studies*, 33, no. 4 (Winter 1991): 47–81.

Kanellopoulos, Athanasios (Euvoulos). "I Evropi kai o Horos tou Mellontos mas" (Europe and the Place of Our Future). *To Vima*, Athens, July 5, 1992, A14.

Kaplan, Robert D. *Balkan Ghosts: A Journey Through History*. St. Martin's Press, 1993.

Kemme, David, and Keith Crane. "The Polish Economic Collapse: Contributing Factors and Economic Costs." *Journal of Comparative Economics*, 8 (March 1984).

Kohl, Helmut. "European Integration." *Presidents and Prime Ministers*, 2, no. 1 (January–February 1993): 14.

Kohler, Heinz. *Comparative Economic Systems*. Glenview, IL: Scott, Foresman, 1989.

Komarek, Valtr. "Shock Therapy and Its Victims." *New York Times*, January 5, 1992: E13.

Kornai, Janos. *The Road to a Free Economy, Shifting from a Socialist System: The Examples of Hungary*. New York: W. W. Norton, 1990.

Kort, Michael. *The Soviet Colossus: A History of the USSR*. New York: Scribner's, 1985.

Kouba, Karel. "Systematic Changes in the Czechoslovak Economy and Its Opening in World Markets." *Soviet and Eastern European Foreign Trade*, 27, no. 2 (Summer 1991): 3–16.

Lipton, David, and Jeffrey Sachs. "Prospects for Russia's Economic Reforms." *Brookings Papers on Economic Activity*, Vol. 2. Washington, DC: The Brookings Institution, 1992.

———. "Creating a Market Economy in Eastern Europe: The Case of Poland." *Brookings Papers on Economic Activity*, Vol. 1. Washington, DC: The Brookings Institution, 1990, 75–133 and 293–333.

Litvack, Jennie I., Christine I. Wallich. "Intergovernmental Finance: Critical to Russia's Transformation?" *Finance and Development*, 30, no. 2 (June 1993): 10–13.

Litwack, John M. "Legality and Market Reform in the Soviet-Type Economies." In David Kennett and Marc Lieberman, eds., *The Road to Capitalism: Economic Transformation in Eastern Europe and the Former Soviet Union*. New York: The Dryden Press, 1992.

Longe, Juliet, ed. *The European Community and the Challenge of the Future*. New York: St. Martin's Press, 1989.

Lowry, Todd. "Recent Literature on Ancient Greek Economic Thought." *Journal of Economic Literature*, 17 (March 1979): 65–86.

Lyosh-Chenko, Peter. *History of the National Economy of Russia*. New York: Macmillan, 1969.

MaCarntey, C. A. *Hungary, A Short History*. Chicago: Aldine, 1962.

Makridakis, Spyros G. and Associates. *Single Market Europe*. Oxford: Jossey-Bass, 1991.

Michalopoulos, Constantine, and David Tarr. "Energizing Trade of the States of the Former USSR." *Finance and Development*, March 1993: 22–25.

Michalski, Anna, and Helen Wallace. *The European Community: The Challenge of Enlargement*. London: Royal Institute for International Affairs, 1992.

Mikus, Joseph A. *Slovakia: A Political History: 1918–1950*. Milwaukee: Marquette University Press, 1963.

Mills, Richard M. *As Moscow Sees Us: American Politics and Society in the Soviet Mindset*. New York: Oxford University Press, 1990.

Montias, John. *Development in Communist Romania*. Cambridge, MA: The M.I.T. Press, 1967.

Moynihan, Daniel P. *Pandaemonium: Ethnicity in International Politics*. New York: Oxford University Press, 1993.

Mroz, John. "Russia and Eastern Europe: Will the West Let Them Fail?" *Foreign Affairs*, 72, no. 1 (1993): 44–57.

Nicholson, Frances, and Roger East. *From the Six to the Twelve: The Enlargement of the European Community*. London: St. James Press, 1987.

Ofer, Gur. "Soviet Economic Growth: 1928–1985." *Journal of Economic Literature*, 25, no. 4 (December 1987): 1767–1833.

Organization for Economic Cooperation and Development (OECD). *National Accounts*. Paris: OECD, annual.

Oshima, Harry. "Shares of Government in Gross National Product for Various Countries." *American Economic Review*, June 1957.

Palankai, Tibor. *The European Community and Central European Integration: The*

Hungarian Case. New York: Institute for East-West Studies, distributed by Westview Press, 1991.

Peacock, Alan, and Jack Wiseman. *The Growth of Public Expenditures in the United Kingdom*. New York: National Bureau of Economic Research, 1961.

Peck, Merton J., and Thomas J. Richard, eds. *What Is To Be Done? Proposals for the Soviet Transition to the Market*. New Haven, CT: Yale University Press, 1991.

Pigou, Arthur. *The Economics of Welfare*. London: Macmillan, 1932.

Pinder, John. *European Community: The Building of a Union*. New York: Oxford University Press, 1991.

Pryor, Frederic L. *East European Economic Reforms: The Rebirth of the Market*. Stanford, CA: Stanford University Press, 1990.

Rapaczynski, Andrzej, and Roman Fryman. "Privatization in Eastern Europe: Is the State Withering Away?" *Finance and Development*, 30, no. 2 (June 1993): 10–13.

Reinicke, Wolfgang. *Building a New Europe*. Washington, DC: The Brookings Institution, 1992.

Richet, Xavier. *The Hungarian Model: Markets and Planning in a Socialist Economy*, trans. by J. C. Whitehouse. New York: Cambridge University Press, 1989.

Roberts, H. *Romania: Political Problems of an Agrarian State*. New Haven, CT: Yale University Press, 1951.

Sachs, Jeffrey. *Capitalism in Europe After Communism*. Cambridge, MA: The M.I.T. Press, 1991.

Salpukas, Agis. "Mobil Set for Venture in Caspian." *New York Times*, June 9, 1993: D3.

Salvatore, Dominick. "Foreign Direct Investments and Privatization in Eastern Europe." *Review of Political Economy*, March 1992.

Schevill, F. *The History of the Balkan Peninsula*, rev. ed. New York: Harcourt, Brace, 1933.

Scott, Norman. "The Commercial Policy of the European Economic Community (EEC)." In Dominick Salvatore, ed., *National Trade Policies*. Westport, CT: Greenwood Press, 1992.

Sheehy, Gail. *The Man Who Changed the World*. New York: HarperCollins, 1990.

Shen, Raphael. *The Polish Economy: Legacies from the Past, Prospects for the Future*. New York: Praeger, 1992.

Smith, Adam. *An Inquiry into the Nature and Causes of the Wealth of Nations*, E. Cannan, ed. New York: Modern Library, 1937.

Smith, Lee, and Lewis Kaden. "East European Workers Will Need Incentives." *New York Times*, May 11, 1990: 13F.

Smyser, W. R. *The Economy of United Germany: Colossus at the Crossroads*. New York: St. Martin's Press, 1992.

Stavrianos, Lefteris. *The Balkans Since 1453*. New York: Holt, Rinehart and Winston, 1958.

Stevenson, Richard. "Czech Capitalism Gets Stock Market." *New York Times*, June 22, 1993: D1.

———. "East Europe's Low Wages Luring Manufacturers from West Europe." *New York Times*, May 11, 1993: D2.

———. "In a Czech Plant, VW Shows How to Succeed in the East." *New York Times*, June 22, 1993: A1.

Tarafas, Irme. "Hungary's Reforms: Past and Present." *Finance and Development*, 28, no. 1 (March 1991): 12–14.

Taylor, Jack. *The Economic Development of Poland, 1919–1950*. Ithaca, NY: Cornell University Press, 1952.

Taylor, Paul. *The Limits of European Integration*. New York: Columbia University Press, 1983.

Thomson, Samuel. *Czechoslovakia in European History*. Princeton, NJ: Princeton University Press, 1953.

Thurow, Lester. *Head to Head: The Coming Economic Battle Among Japan, Europe, and America*. New York: W. Morrow, 1992.

Tsoukalis, Loukas. *The New European Economy: The Politics and Economics of Integration*. New York: Oxford University Press, 1993.

United Nations. *World Economic Survey 1991/1992*. New York: United Nations Publications, 1991.

———. *Yearbook of National Accounts Statistics*. New York: United Nations, various issues.

Wagner, Adolph. *Financzwissenschaft*, 3rd ed. Leipzig, 1890.

World Bank. *World Development Report*. New York: Oxford University Press, for the World Bank, annual.

Zielinski, Januasz G. *Economic Reforms in Polish Industry*. London: Oxford University Press, 1973.

Index

About the Author

NICHOLAS V. GIANARIS is Professor of Economics at Fordham University. Dr. Gianaris is author of many journal articles and a number of books, including *Contemporary Economic Systems: A Regional and Country Approach* (Praeger, 1993), *The European Community and the United States: Economic Relations* (Praeger, 1991), *Contemporary Public Finance* (Praeger, 1989), *Greece and Turkey: Economic and Geopolitical Perspectives* (Praeger, 1988), *Greece and Yugoslavia: An Economic Comparison* (Praeger, 1984), and *The Economies of the Balkan Countries: Albania, Bulgaria, Greece, Romania, Turkey, Yugoslavia* (Praeger, 1982).